# Curse of the
# Red Cross Ring

Earl B. Pilgrim

Flanker Press Ltd.
St. John's, Newfoundland
2000

Printed in Canada by Robinson-Blackmore Ltd. St. John's, Newfoundland, Canada

First printing September, 2000
Second printing October, 2000

Published in Canada by
Flanker Press Ltd.
PO Box 2522, Station C, St. John's
Newfoundland, Canada  A1C 6K1

Tel: (709) 739-4477
Fax: (709) 739-4420
Email: info@flankerpress.com
Website: www.flankerpress.com

Cover design and layout by City Design

**Canadian Cataloguing in Publication Data**

Pilgrim, Earl B. (Earl Baxter), 1939-

   Curse of the Red Cross Ring

   ISBN 1-894463-11-0

I. Title.

PS8581.1338C87 2000        C813'.54        C00-950204-1
PR9199.3.P493C87 2000

## About the Author

Earl Baxter Pilgrim was born in St. Anthony, Newfoundland, in 1939, son of Norman and Winnie (Roberts) Pilgrim. He received his early education in Roddickton, Newfoundland, later studying Forestry at the College of Trades and Technology in St. John's.

He began his adult career in 1960 as an Infantryman in the Canadian Army, serving with the Princess Patricia's Canadian Light Infantry. While there, he became involved in the sport of boxing, eventually becoming the Canadian Light Heavyweight Boxing Champion.

Following a stint in the Forces, he took a job as a Forest Ranger with the Newfoundland and Labrador Forestry Department. During this time, he came to recognize the plight of the big game population on Newfoundland's Great Northern Peninsula. After nine years as a forest warden, he became a wildlife protection officer with the Newfoundland Wildlife Service.

For seventeen years, he has devoted his efforts to the growth and conservation of the big game population on the Great Northern Peninsula. Under his surveillance, the moose and caribou populations have grown and prospered at an astonishing rate. As a game warden and a local storyteller, he has gained the respect of conservationist and poacher alike.

He has been presented with a number of awards: the Safari International, presented by the Provincial Wildlife Division; the Gunther Behr, presented by the Newfoundland and Labrador Wildlife Federation; and the Achievement "Beyond the Call of Duty" Award, presented by the White Bay Central Development Association.

Among his many achievements are his contributions as a conservationist for waterfowl. He has made a hobby of raising eider ducks, and it has been estimated that eighty percent of all nesting eiders in Newfoundland developed from his original twelve ducks.

He is married to the former Beatrice Compton of Englee. They have four children and make their home in Roddickton, Newfoundland.

Earl B. Pilgrim's previous books, *Will Anyone Search for Danny?*, *The Price Paid for Charley* and *Blood on the Hills* have become Canadian bestsellers.

*Curse of the Red Cross Ring* is his fourth book, a true story set in Beaumont (Long Island, Notre Dame Bay) and L'Anse au Pigeon on Quirpon (pronounced kar-poon) Island, Newfoundland. The names of some of the people in this book have been changed to protect their privacy.

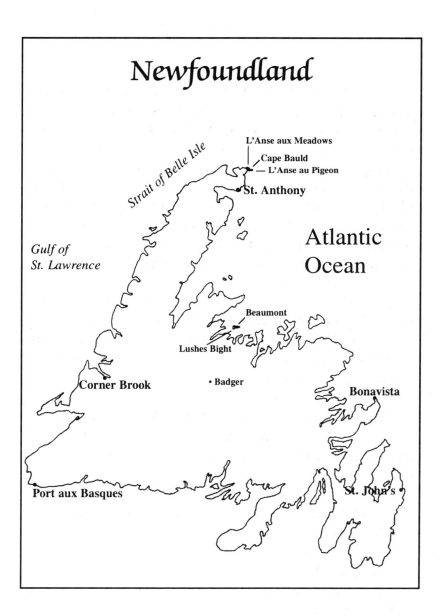

# Newfoundland

L'Anse aux Meadows

Cape Bauld

L'Anse au Pigeon

St. Anthony

Strait of Belle Isle

Gulf of
St. Lawrence

Atlantic
Ocean

Beaumont

Lushes Bight

Corner Brook

• Badger

Bonavista

Port aux Basques

St. John's

# Acknowledgements

I would like to thank the following people for their assistance and support in the research and writing of this book: George Adams; Bill Bartlett; Truman Billings; Victor Billings; Grace (Pilgrim) Brophy; Lindy Brophy; Barry Canning; Junior Canning; Vera Blackwood; Wesley Caravan; Pearce Cull; Annetta Cull; Iris Fillier; Darcy Fitzpatrick; Todd Flynn; Ford Hancock; Willis Hancock; Allan Hillier; Julie Hillier; Jerry Locke; Sonya Locke; Andy Johnson; Ray Norman; Bert Parsons; Gerald Hillier; Albert Locke; Ivan Manuels; Ramona Manuels; Peter Parsons Jr.; Baine Pilgrim; Nancy Pilgrim; Carl Pilgrim; Caesar Pilgrim; Barbara Pilgrim; Carla Pilgrim; Norman Pilgrim; Marsha Pilgrim; Pierce Pilgrim; Ross Randell; Frank Rideout; Nelson Roberts; George Robbins; Lucy Robbins; Leander Rowsell; Bob Tucker; Minnie Tucker; Gid Tucker; Norman Tucker; Roy Tucker; Lawrence Wilcox.

Special thanks to Barbara and Marsha Pilgrim for typing; Chantel Weir, computer specialist; Ross Decker for the encouragement to write; and my wife, Beatrice, for helping with research.

Special thanks to the Provincial Archives of Newfoundland and Labrador.

The publisher wishes to thank the following readers and editors: Jerry, Dione and Margo Cranford, Vera McDonald and Eileen Riche.

Earl B. Pilgrim

*This book is dedicated to Absalom "Happy" Tucker, who said he would be back and that someday this story would be told from the housetops.*

The sun looked boldly through its bloodshot eye as it peeked over the boiling ocean, and the breath of the toiling men mixed with the salty spray to give a pinkish hue as they hauled the huge cod trap. Giant swells slammed into the solid granite only a few hundred feet away. Soundings were made, and it was determined that the trap was full of codfish, about three hundred barrels—enough to load all the boats around the trap, and more.

"Look, Skipper," said one of the crew. "There's undertow coming right out to the doorways of the trap."

"Sure enough, I see it," Az said.

He then looked around at the men in the boats surrounding the bloated cod trap. If enough undertow were to start boiling, combined with the heavy sea that was rolling in, it could sweep away the whole cod trap, its moorings and contents.

"Listen, men," said Az, "you'd better start dipping the fish in right away, and make sure the cuts are wrapped tightly around the pins. Don't let the boat get too far away from the doorways. Hey," he yelled from the top of the engine house, "tie up that span line and don't let her go out any farther. Hold everything fast; I'll watch the swells."

"Okay," said Sod Mugford, who was holding onto the span line.

Then the skipper yelled at the top of his voice, "Tie everything on solid, and hold her fast. There's a huge breaker out there and it's coming straight at us."

Everyone saw it and froze for a moment, holding onto the part of the trap where they were. They held their breath as the great breaker rolled in under them, lifting everything as it passed. There was a fourteen-year-old boy with them, helping to haul the trap and keep the net in the boat. He wasn't fully prepared when the wave lifted the boats and their contents.

As the wave rolled in, the huge bag of fish was slow to rise with the wave, causing the boat to dip low in the water, as if it were going to roll over. With this sudden movement, the part of the trap that was on board started to get pulled out. The young boy saw it and started to panic; he grabbed it with his arms, and before he knew anything the trap twisted around the buttons of his rubber coat. It started to drag him out of the boat.

The men in the other boats saw what was happening and started yelling. The skipper, who was standing on the engine house, heard them yelling and saw them pointing.

Then he saw the young boy.

"My Great God," he whispered, and leaped from the engine house. The young boy was just going over the side of the boat, entangled in the cod trap, when the skipper grabbed him and tried in vain to pull him in. Then Az saw what had happened; the buttons on the boy's coat had hooked in the linnet. He reached down into the water and started to untangle the buttons while someone held onto the boy's legs.

"Get a knife! Get a knife and cut off the buttons," Az screamed.

Sod Mugford reached into the engine house and grabbed a knife. As quick as a flash, he cut the collar at the neck of the boy's oilskins and ripped the coat down the back. He then pulled the young boy back into the boat.

Before anyone could say a word, Sod heard another scream from the men around him. "The skipper's got his hand caught in the linnet!"

Az realized with mounting horror what had happened. He was wearing the Red Cross ring on his index finger, and while trying to unhook the buttons of the rubber coat, the ring had become caught in the linnet. He was helpless, and he knew he had only a few seconds before he would be pulled under.

Sod jumped to the skipper's aid. He grabbed the skipper's arm and gave a pull with all his strength. Az felt as though his fingers were being pulled from his hand, and the next thing he knew, he landed in the bottom of the boat with a terrible pain in his arm.

Az looked at his hand and saw blood coming from his fingers. He noticed that the ring was missing. "My ring is gone," he said. "Listen boys, my Red Cross ring is gone. Has anyone seen it?"

The men looked at him and shook their heads.

"Your ring is gone, all right, Skipper," said Sod. "I saw it come off your finger and pop right out into the trap. You should consider yourself lucky that your hand isn't gone, or that you never went under yourself."

Az couldn't believe it. He felt his finger—it was cut to the bone.

Sod watched the skipper put his handkerchief around his finger. Az was nearly in tears. "My ring, my Red Cross ring," he moaned, as he held his arm and looked out into the trap.

"Skipper," said Sod, "you shouldn't worry about that old ring. There's lots of them where that one came from."

Az gave Sod a sour look. "Listen, Sod, there are twenty-two fathoms of water down there where my ring went, and if you make one more remark like that I'll make you go down and pick it up."

Azariah Roberts climbed back onto the engine house and shook his head. "My ring," he said, "is gone forever."

# Part 1

# Death in Beaumont

# Chapter 1

In those days, before the turn of the twentieth century, a man became well known by the amount of fish he caught or the number of seals he killed. In other words, there were two things that made him famous in the British colony of Newfoundland—fish and seals. Captain Peter Brooks was in the fish category.

After a man acquired a reputation it became easier for him to pick a crew of good men. Kindness meant a captain gave a member of his crew a second chance; there were no third chances. Those who repeated a mistake were put ashore, no matter where they were. This sometimes created quite a fuss on board their wooden fishing schooners, and for this reason very few women were on board. After all, how could a skipper put a woman ashore? However, in the last decades of the 1800s, some fishing schooners had young women on board as cooks.

One early June in the 1890s, in the years before he had established his fishing premises at L'Anse au Pigeon, Captain Brooks was sailing north to Labrador to fish. The man who was hired as cook on his schooner fell ill, so he went into a small town called Englee.

Captain Brooks called for the midwife, who immediately took the cook off the schooner and put him to bed. He was too sick to proceed any farther, so the skipper tried to hire another man, but was unsuccessful. He had to depart Englee without one. He put to sea and proceeded to Labrador. After two days under sail, he was crossing the Strait of Belle Isle when he ran into a vicious northeaster. When he could battle the storm no longer, he turned around and ran with the wind. His ship had taken a terrible battering by the time it sailed into the small fishing village of Cooks Harbour.

Captain Brooks was no stranger here; he had fished at Cooks Harbour for part of one year and had gotten to know a lot of the people. After the schooner was safely anchored in the lun of Brandy Island, Captain Brooks went ashore to see a few of his old friends. One of them was William Crane.

William Crane was quite a fishermen who had built several large schooners, and whenever Captain Brooks visited him, there was a lot of talk.

After a two-hour conversation and several cups of tea, Captain Brooks told William of the misfortune of losing his cook, expressing his concern that the crew would have to shack for themselves for the whole summer.

He then asked William if there was a man in or around the town of Cooks Harbour who would be interested in a job as cook with him for the summer. "He'll get part of the voyage," he promised.

William knew of no man on that part of the coast. "Every man and boy, as I know, is getting ready for the summer fishing. In fact, there are several young men here who have been brought in from the south as sharemen."

"I expected that," said Captain Brooks. "Men are hard to get now."

As they ate their lunch, Captain Brooks commented on the cake that Mrs. Crane served him. "The cake is delicious. Mrs. Crane, I suppose you wouldn't mind coming as cook with us for the summer, would you? You're from Capstan Island, right?"

They all laughed. She looked at Captain Brooks and said, "Would you take a woman if there was one available?"

Brooks looked at her and said, "I don't see why not, if she was suitable. There are several women now going to Labrador as cooks, but the fact of the matter is all the women who are any good are already married or occupied."

Mrs. Crane spoke again. "I know of a young girl who would go to Labrador as a cook with you, Captain."

She got up from the table and went to the stove to fetch the teapot. William said nothing.

"You do?" said Brooks. He looked at her as she returned to the table and poured tea.

"Yes," she said, "I do."

"Who would that be, Mrs. Crane?"

"Emily Jane." She blushed.

She made the trip back to the stove with the teapot.

William looked up. His long beard bristled as he stared at his wife. He was about to say something, but decided against it.

"Bill has a daughter by his first wife, and I reared her up. She is a stout girl at fifteen. She would make a good cook for you; she is strong as an ox. Right, Bill?"

William turned to Captain Brooks. "My daughter is now at Cape Norman with the Campbells at the lighthouse. She's been serving with them for two years now. I had word a few days ago that she'll be returning home in a couple of days. The Campbells' two daughters are now old enough to work, so they don't need my daughter anymore."

He wiped his beard. "They told me that she's as good as three women, and Mr. Campbell said he'll want her back again in the fall."

"In the fall," said Mrs. Crane. "This is only June. We've nothing here for her to do."

William silenced his wife with a look.

He turned to Brooks and said, "Skipper, come outside. I have a new punt to show you, a new design."

The two men left the table and went outside. They walked into a large shed down near the shoreline. William lit his pipe and put his matches back in his pocket.

"There she is," he said with a grin, pointing to the trap punt. It was painted and ready to be launched. "I made her bigger in the midship-room. See that?"

Brooks's keen eyes saw the improvement. "She looks like a great boat, William. You must be proud of her."

"I am," he replied.

The two men talked for awhile, and William brought up the subject of his daughter. "I'm sorry my wife made those comments to you, but I have to tell you why."

He lit his pipe again and continued. "There have been problems between my daughter and her two stepsisters. I suppose my wife was hard on Emily Jane until she got to thirteen years old, when she started to fight back. It was then that I took her to Cape Norman to be with the Campbells. They accepted her as their own daughter, but now they have their own family growing up, and they only agreed to take her for two years. It's only right that she should return now. If she was a year or two older she might get married and have her own home. I don't know how long she would last with her stepmother."

William Crane showed pain in his eyes. He gave a sigh and said, "You could use a cook, but I don't know if she'll agree about going on the water, even if you did approve."

Captain Peter Brooks answered him. "William, I can see that you have a dilemma on your hands, and I wish I could help you, but a woman on board would give us a great problem. My schooner is geared for a crew of men. Where would she sleep? Where would she get privacy? How would the men react to a fifteen-year-old girl?"

The captain walked around the shed and came back to where the long-bearded man stood. William said nothing. The blue of his eyes was blurred with tears. He knew deep down in his soul that even if Captain Brooks agreed, it would be almost impossible for him to let his young daughter go to sea with a crew of rugged fishermen.

Captain Brooks looked at his friend, built with a strong frame around a soft heart.

"William," said Brooks, "if your daughter were in Lushes Bight I would put her to work in my store, or she could go to work in the firm. We have a lot of fish to make every year, and she could stay in the house with my wife, but getting her from Cooks Harbour to Lushes Bight is a problem. As for the cook's job, I was thinking we surely need her, and maybe we could arrange things to accommodate her. After we get to Labrador we'll be staying on land. There she can have her own room, but the problem is between here and Labrador."

William spoke. "Captain, I wouldn't want to cause you any trouble. I guess she'll have to do the best she can here with her stepmother. We might be able to work things out."

The captain moved closer to the new boat and put his arm on the gunwale. "I'm going on board the schooner in a few minutes. I guess the men have the water casks filled by now. I'll talk to them and see what they've got to say. I'll let you know."

He turned to William again and asked, "When could you have her ready to go on board the schooner?"

"Not until morning at first light. There is too much wind to send a boat to Cape Norman. I would have to walk up and walk back with her; this could take five or six hours."

"Okay," said Captain Brooks, "I'll let you know as soon as I can."

William Crane thanked him, and Brooks walked down to where his men were waiting for him.

"We got the two casks full, Skipper, and it's the best of water. We're ready to go on board."

"Great," said Captain Brooks. "Where's Az?"

"He was here just a minute ago," said one of the men.

Azariah Frederick Roberts was a young man of sixteen years. He had been with Captain Brooks now for three years;

5

this summer would be his fourth trip to Labrador, and he would get a man's share for the first time. His family came to Lushes Bight from Twillingate when Az was a small boy. He was a born fisherman and went in boat with his father at the age of seven.

Lushes Bight was the largest community on Long Island, located in western Notre Dame Bay. Not far away on the same island is the small town of Beaumont.

Az was talking to a man from Change Islands, a shareman for one of the crews. He heard Skipper Brooks and called, "I'm over here."

"Come here for a minute, Az," said the captain.

"Yes, sir," said Az. He quickly obeyed.

"Now, men," said the captain, "I have a proposition to put to you. As you know, we don't have a cook and we're shacking for ourselves; once we leave Newfoundland we won't get one."

The crew remained silent. "I have a chance for a cook," he said.

One of the men spoke up. "Well, that sounds pretty good, Skipper."

"Yes," said Brooks. Before anyone else could comment, he continued. "What makes it all the better is the fact that the cook I can get is a woman."

They looked directly into the captain's eyes. He answered their silent questions. "Yes, a woman, or I might say, a young girl."

They knew it wasn't safe to make a joke or a wisecrack.

"Sounds pretty good," one man said.

Captain Brooks then told them that he had spoken with an old friend who had a daughter who could go. When he finished, he asked them if they thought it would be possible for her to sleep in the bunk at the end of the forecastle. They agreed and were prepared to welcome her aboard.

"I wonder what the other five men will say?" asked the captain.

One man grinned and said, "I know for sure Art Windsor will be glad to get away from washing most of the dishes."

"Very well," said the captain, "we'll take her on."

Az spoke up. "One question, Skipper. What does she look like?"

The captain looked at Az. "Don't you worry about that, Az, me boy. We'll make you sleep in the hatch if she's too ugly for you to look at." They all laughed.

Captain Brooks met William Crane in the doorway of his house. He said, "I've explained the situation to my men about your daughter. Their answer is yes. They've agreed to have her as a cook on our schooner."

William was relieved.

The captain continued. "There are a few things I want to say. I'll be responsible for her at all times, in every way. I'll put her off here again when I return from Labrador."

William nodded. "I'll leave right away for Cape Norman and get her ready for pickup in the morning," he said.

"Say hello to the Campbells for me."

"I will," William replied.

It was 7:30 p.m. when William Crane arrived at the high towering lighthouse. He noticed it was very strongly built, to withstand the winds and weather that blew in from the North Atlantic. Everything was neatly painted, and walkways were built to make moving from building to building easier.

A misty rain was falling and the wind was beginning to ease up. William was greeted as he neared the house. He was met by Mr. Campbell.

"William, how are you?" said Campbell, holding out his hand.

"I'm fine," he replied as they shook hands.

The two men chatted for a few moments before William told him why he was there, and how he had a job for Emily Jane.

Mr. Campbell thought it was a great idea. "She couldn't go with a better man," he said. "I know Captain Peter Brooks very well, and under his protection you won't have anything to worry about."

William was relieved to hear such comments.

"I'm sure of that," he replied.

The door opened and Emily Jane came out, wearing a white apron and a long dress. She was a tall girl and stood very straight.

"Dad," she said, startled.

She put her arms around him and kissed him. "I'm glad to see you."

"I'm glad to see you too, my dear," he said.

They went into the house. William said hello to everyone, and Mrs. Campbell immediately put the dishes on the table.

"You'll be staying for the night, for sure," she said.

"Mrs. Campbell, I have to go right back. I'll have a cup of tea, but I'll have to get going before dark. I've come for Emily Jane."

The whole family fell silent. The Campbells knew that Emily Jane would have to return home sometime, but not this soon, and now they didn't want her to leave.

"There's no need of her leaving us so soon. She can stay with us for the summer, Mr. Crane," said Mrs. Campbell. She meant it.

William stirred his tea. "I have a job for Emily Jane. She has to go back home with me tonight."

Mrs. Campbell looked at Emily Jane and then at William. She knew the problem that the girl had at home, and she wasn't prepared to let her go back into that environment. "Maybe it's none of my business, but may I ask what the job is?"

"Mrs. Campbell, the job I have for her is cooking on the Labrador with Captain Peter Brooks. He is now at Cooks Harbour waiting for her."

Mrs. Campbell felt relieved in a way, but the thought of a fifteen-year-old girl going to Labrador with a crowd of men for the summer was unheard of. She didn't voice her concern. "That's great, Mr. Crane," she said, looking at Emily Jane. "I know Peter Brooks. He fished at Cooks Harbour one year with a large crew of men. Does he still have his store up south?"

"Yes," replied William. "He had a lunch with us this afternoon. The storm drove him into Cooks Harbour. He told me he has a new premises started now at L'Anse au Pigeon; that's over there near Cape Bauld."

"I know where it is," said Mr. Campbell. "It's on Quirpon Island."

"You're right," said William. "He has a fine crowd of men; there's nothing to worry about. They'll be staying on shore once they reach Labrador. It will take about two days, once the wind changes in their favour."

The girls and Mrs. Campbell gathered around Emily Jane. "Emily Jane," said Mrs. Campbell, looking directly at her, "do you want to go?"

Emily Jane lifted her head and looked around at her friends, and then at her father. "Yes," she said slowly. "I guess I'll have to go. Dad says it's okay, so it must be okay."

The Campbell daughters hugged her.

"Start getting your things together. I'll get you a lunch before you go, and I'll pack a lunch for you to eat on your way."

It seemed like only a few minutes passed before they were ready to leave. When all the thanks and goodbyes were said, Emily Jane turned with her father and walked away, heading for Cooks Harbour as darkness fell.

Mrs. Crane was told earlier by William that he was going to Cape Norman to fetch Emily Jane. He didn't tell her the reason, but she knew that he had agreed with Captain Brooks to ship Emily Jane with them in the morning. However, she decided to make sure that he wouldn't change his mind when he brought her back in the night.

It was well past midnight when William arrived at his home with his daughter. Emily Jane was about to say hello to her stepmother. It was the first time they had seen each other in two years.

Mrs. Crane was awake and in a very sour mood, ready to quarrel with anyone who came near her. "Now, Bill," she said loudly. "You got that strife breeder back here again. I tell you, Bill, don't let her go handy to my youngsters. You know what she did the day before she left."

Before Emily Jane left to go with the Campbells, a fight had begun between Mrs. Crane's two daughters and Emily Jane. The girls were much older, and when they started beating Emily Jane badly, she had looked around for something with which she could defend herself. She had grabbed a cobbler's knife belonging to her father and swung it at the handiest girl to her. She had cut Theresa across the nose—a little more to the side and she would have blinded her. William had immediately taken her to the Campbells'.

Mrs. Crane was still so angry it appeared she would attack Emily Jane. William had to step between them.

"Just a minute," he said to his wife, pushing her back. "Emily Jane isn't staying here tonight. I brought her here for you to say goodbye, but it's obvious you don't want that, do you?"

"Yes I do," she spat. "Goodbye!" She turned and walked into the bedroom.

William turned to Emily Jane. "We're going to Uncle Bill Allingham's." The two immediately left the house and walked over to the Allinghams' place. Emily Jane's father woke up Uncle Bill and told him his problem. His old friend agreed to take her in for the night.

"Emily Jane," her father said, "if it's a good morning, Captain Brooks will be ashore for you very early. I'll ask him if you can go to his home at Lushes Bight at the end of the voyage, instead of coming back here." Emily Jane kissed her father and went inside. William's shoulders slumped as he walked away.

At dawn the next morning, William Crane and his daughter walked down to the stage on the shoreline, a small bag full of clothes in his hand. It held the only possessions his daughter had. As he walked he thought, *I may never see Emily Jane again.*

He looked at her with tears in his eyes. Emily Jane was going away with a group of strangers, as it were. He thought of her mother, and how she resembled her. William felt a lump rise in his throat. *I feel as though I'm leading a lamb to the slaughter. Will I ever be able to forgive myself?*

*But I have no choice,* his mind and soul cried out. *I have other children of my own by my second wife and I love them also. What can I do?*

"Is that you, William?" a voice called. It was Peter Brooks, coming ashore. By now there was quite a commotion in the harbour. Schooners were hoisting their anchors.

"Yes, it's me," said William.

"Come onto the wharf."

William opened the stage door, and with Emily Jane he walked to the stagehead. Peter Brooks came to the head of the wharf and tied on his boat. He had five men with him. They all got out of the boat and looked at the fifteen-year-old girl. She was tall and wore a long heavy coat, bonnet and woollen mitts. She was dressed quite well, for the Campbells were fairly well-to-do people. They had given her good clothes and treated her well. In later years she spoke of how much she loved them.

"She looks like a very splendid girl, and someone who could do a good job for us," the captain said.

"Thank you, Captain," Emily Jane said.

He introduced the men to their new cook. "This is Dolf Windsor, Art Windsor, Edgar Colbourne, Edgar Rowbottom and young Az Roberts. We call him young Az because he was the youngest of the crew, but not anymore—you are."

Emily Jane smiled shyly and greeted each one.

"I want to speak to you alone, Captain," William said.

"Okay," said the captain. The two men walked into the stage.

"Captain, I wanted to say that my wife doesn't want Emily Jane back at our home anymore. She wasn't allowed to stay under our roof last night, so she had to go to Bill Allingham's. Would it be possible for her to go on to Lushes Bight with you in the fall if she proves favourable?"

"She sure can, Bill, and I can understand your problem. Again, I want to assure you that I will take care of her every minute, as though she was my own daughter. You can rest easy."

"I know you will," he said. The two men left the stage.

Emily Jane was still on the wharf, waiting for her father. She put her arms around him and kissed him as tears ran down her face. "I love you, Dad, and I'll always be thinking about you," she sobbed.

"Emily Jane," the old man stammered, "I want you to make me a promise."

"I will," she said.

"I want you to promise me that if we never meet again on earth, we'll meet again in heaven."

She put her arms around him again and with trembling lips said, "I will, Dad. I promise."

She kissed him again. "Goodbye, Dad."

"Goodbye, Emily Jane."

The young woman got aboard the small boat, and the crew pushed off.

As William Crane walked in off the wharf, he turned and looked again at his little girl. She waved to him, and he finally broke down and wept. It was the last time he ever saw her.

# Chapter 2

The voyage to Batteau, Labrador, took three days. A stormy southwest wind blew. There was a lot of ice around, but the southwest wind and the strong Labrador current kept the ice off. Hundreds of schooners dotted the coast, and there were reports of codfish in abundance. Emily Jane very quickly adapted to her new job and the environment.

She had been told the facts of life by Mrs. Campbell while staying with her for two years. She wasn't afraid of the men. They were all married except Az, who was still young like herself. They were taking the place of seasoned workers, so this made them more mature.

Captain Brooks was very religious and very strict. He would hold a service every Sunday in the morning and evening, and everyone paid attention, including Emily Jane, who was born an Anglican. Of course, young Az would wink at Emily Jane and make fun at the captain behind his back.

One Sunday afternoon they went for a walk around the beaches of Batteau. Emily Jane was surprised when Az told her that he could read and write. He had gone to school at Little Bay Islands, completed the Royal Reader and had reached grade eight. In fact, he spent his winters working in

Captain Brooks's store. He had been working with the captain ever since his father died when he was thirteen.

"Emily Jane, you're only fifteen."

She quickly butted in. "I'll soon be sixteen."

"Okay," he said, "you're only sixteen."

She then turned the tables. "You're only sixteen."

"I'll soon be seventeen," he said. They laughed.

"Emily Jane—" he began, but stopped.

"What were you going to say, Az?" she asked.

"I was going to say that, when you get to twenty-one, I want you to marry me."

She stopped and looked out at the ocean but didn't say anything.

They walked farther, and then she told him about her upbringing, how her mother had died when she was born.

She said, "When I came into this world, my mother went out. The only motherly love I ever knew was from Mrs. Campbell."

"My mother is still living," Az said. "She loves me. She didn't want me to become a fisherman; she is always afraid of the fish merchants—the Strongs, in particular. They're fish merchants in Little Bay Islands. If you go to Lushes Bight you'll hear a lot about them."

Az continued. "My mother is still at Lushes Bight. Everything I make, I give her. She is more religious than the skipper, and would go to church service every day in the week, if there was any."

The two laughed as they continued walking along the path. Az asked, "Do they have an Orange Lodge at Cooks Harbour?"

"No," she replied. "I never heard of that. What is it?"

"It's the Loyal Orange Society. It's made up of Protestants who get together once every month. It's about when King Billy fought the Catholics in Ireland. We call ourselves Orangemen."

Emily Jane turned to him. "Are you one of those Orangemen, Az?"

"Yes," he replied.

"Why are you one of them? Is there any fighting going on where you come from?"

"No," said Az, "but there might be."

"My," said Emily Jane, "I don't think I'll go up there this fall."

"But there's no one fighting up there. It's just a group of men getting together and doing different things." He looked at Emily Jane. "You could join the ladies' group when you go up."

"No, no," she said. "It sounds a bit strange to me."

Az laughed. "You're just like Mother. That's what she goes on with."

Az Roberts's mother was a very religious woman. It was said that she never hurt a fly in her life. She always condemned anyone who talked about violence of any kind. She used to hear the Orangemen talking about the Roman Catholic people, and she would say to them that they shouldn't be doing that. When Az wanted to join the Orange Order at a very young age, she wasn't very pleased.

"Az, my son," she would say, "don't join the Orange Lodge. You don't have to. All I ever saw was trouble. The Catholic people have never done anything to anyone in Lushes Bight or anywhere else on Long Island. They're our best friends. That stuff happened hundreds of years ago."

Az would say, "But, Mom, everybody else has joined up. Why can't I?"

One day, Az was so obsessed with joining that he asked his mother, "Mom, can you give me one reason why I shouldn't join the Orange Lodge?"

She knew that any reason she would point out, no matter what it was, he would ignore it. While they were talking, his older sister Sarah came into the kitchen and sat down at the table across from Az. She immediately sensed the tension.

"What's up, Mom?" she said.

15

Her mother didn't want to talk about it for fear of upsetting her son whom she loved dearly, but Az spoke up. "I want to join the Orange Lodge, but Mom isn't satisfied."

"Sarah, it's not that I'm not satisfied. It's because of our friends. We have close friends who are Roman Catholic, and I'm afraid they might think we don't like them if my son joins the Orange Lodge."

Sarah didn't say anything.

"Az," said his mother, "I think it's time I told you something. Before your father died, he told me that he didn't want you to become an Orangeman. That's all he said."

Az could hardly believe it. "Why? Why, Mom?"

"I don't know, my son," she said. "I don't know, but there's one thing I do know. If you do join, a curse may fall on you."

Sarah was wide-eyed. She knew her brother was determined to join the Orange Lodge.

"Az, do you hear Mom? She just said a curse might fall on you if you join!"

Her words went in one ear and out the other. "What's the use," he said. "I'll join anyway."

He showed up at the next meeting of the Lodge and joined.

As Emily Jane walked joyfully along the grassy slopes and rocky trail with Az, she breathed in the salty sea air and let out a contented sigh.

She looked at Az. "It seems strange to me to be holding a man's hand."

Az laughed. "That's how it's supposed to feel. But suppose I kissed you?"

She looked at him. To her, a kiss was only experienced when someone was either leaving home or arriving home. She had never seen or even heard of anyone kissing for any other reason, let alone being kissed herself!

"Let's sit down, Emily Jane," Az said as they came to a grassy knoll overlooking the harbour of Batteau. They talked about the little town, and about the Roberts families who lived there permanently. Az told her that he was related to them.

"Emily Jane, may I kiss you?" said Az.

She was shocked. She could hardly believe it, that this young man who she thought so much about, wanted to do such a thing to her. It was unbearable.

He sensed her reluctance. "Okay, okay," he said, "but before you get up and run, tell me something, Emily Jane. Tell me more about your upbringing."

Emily Jane calmed down. She then told Az of the problems she had at home and what she went through. She concluded by saying that she would never go back there again. She said, "I've found my home, Az, and that's with Captain Brooks."

"What about me, Emily Jane? Would you make a home with me?" he asked.

"Well," said Emily Jane, "maybe you should kiss me after all." Az then took her in his arms and kissed her.

As they neared the shack where they were staying, Emily Jane turned to Az and said, "I'll answer your question now, if you answer mine." She looked at him, then caught his hand. "Will you love me forever if I marry you?"

"Yes, I will," he said softly.

"Then I'll marry you when I am twenty-one. You keep this in mind, and mind your own business around the girls. Remember that you're spoken for."

He laughed and said, "I will. And you'd better remember that, too. You only have six years to wait."

"Five and a half," she said.

# Chapter 3

During the summers that Az Roberts spent fishing at Labrador while a young man, he would get up at four-thirty in the morning and be in bed at ten each night. Little time was spent courting. It was a busy place; there was lots of codfish. As the old-timers would say, "It was load and go."

Cod traps were full, and by August the salting sheds were usually filled a second time. All the fish was shipped to Little Bay Islands, to the firm of Strong. In late August or early September, everyone left for home unless the fish was scarce or late coming.

On the way home from Batteau in August, Captain Brooks called in at L'Anse au Pigeon. During the summer, he had been having a problem with his arm; he was an elderly man, and the voyage to Labrador appeared to be too much for him. The only one he talked to about his health was Az.

The sun was low on the horizon as they came into the harbour at L'Anse au Pigeon. "I'm tired of coming north, my son," Captain Brooks said. "From now on, this is as far as this schooner is going to go. We can get plenty of fish here."

"You're right, Skipper," said Az. "We should build a larger firm here and increase the manpower."

"You're right," said the captain.

The two men were standing near the wheel of the seventy-five-foot schooner. It was loaded to the gunwales with fish. The captain spoke. "Az, I want you to take charge of this firm here next year. I feel tired and a bit weary. There's lots of good men working for me. You can pick out a good crew, get bigger cod traps and whatever else you need, and come here. You should do all right."

Az wasn't surprised to hear the captain talking about giving up the Labrador. "I'm eighteen now, Skipper. Do you think I can take the responsibility of such a venture?"

The captain thought for a moment. "Only you can know that, Az."

"I guess you're right."

Captain Brooks changed the subject. "I wonder how they did with the fish here in the Pigeon this summer, Az?"

"We'll soon know. In about an hour's time, Captain, if the wind stays the same."

"I hope so. I'll be glad to get ashore. I guess Emily Jane will be glad to get ashore too."

"For sure," said Az.

"Az," said the captain, "I think you're in love with Emily Jane. She can make a good wife for you."

Az's face must have shown surprise. Before he could answer, the captain spoke again. "Remember what I said. She's seventeen now."

Nothing else was said as they got ready to go into L'Anse au Pigeon.

Captain Brooks finished his business and was ready to proceed home to Lushes Bight. The seven-man crew there was still fishing, well into their second voyage; a load of salted cod had already been shipped to the Strong mercantile firm at Little Bay Islands.

A young man named Happy Tucker was to go with them. He was glad to leave, because he hadn't seen his mother since

May. Happy met Emily Jane and was impressed with her; they began a friendship that would last forever.

Despite talking about quitting, Peter Brooks kept going to Labrador for two more years. He took Emily Jane with him as cook, but he didn't go into Cooks Harbour, because his friend William Crane had left the town and moved farther south in the Strait, to a small town called Pines Cove. It was a better place for firewood and they were nearer to the hunting grounds for caribou. He was also nearer to the town called Flower's Cove, where there were lots of food supplies.

By now, Az Roberts was courting Emily Jane, and he was becoming Captain Brooks's right-hand man. Although he was young, he was put in charge whenever Brooks was away.

In the summer of 1900, they were on their way back to Lushes Bight when Captain Brooks told his men this was his last year going to Labrador, for sure. He wouldn't be crossing the Strait anymore.

"We can do just as well here at L'Anse au Pigeon as we can on the Labrador," said Az. "The men here are getting more fish than we are. In fact, Skipper, they're doubling us every year."

"You're right," said the captain.

"But we have to make new plans," said Az.

"Oh yes," said the captain. "As soon as we get back home we'll decide what to do."

"That's a good idea," said Az.

The next year, Az Roberts was put in charge of L'Anse au Pigeon. He was twenty-one years of age. During the summer, his crew of men made a bumper voyage, but the premises were too small. They would have to be enlarged, and the crew would have to move from the tarpaper shacks to permanent, decent quarters.

Emily Jane was finding the cooking more difficult in the present surroundings. The crew all agreed, so when Az and his crew returned that fall, plans were made to enlarge the fishing capacity, and the captain decided to build a new, bigger schooner.

On December 13, 1901, Az Roberts and Emily Jane Crane were married at Lushes Bight. They celebrated their wedding in the Orange Lodge, of which Az was a member. They were married by Rev. H. Scott of the Methodist Church, and Az's best man was Peter Parsons, a renowned fishing captain out of Lushes Bight. Az continued to take Emily Jane to L'Anse au Pigeon, cooking for the fishing crew.

# Chapter 4

A bsalom "Happy" Tucker had gotten married a couple of years before Az. He already had two children by the time Az and Emily Jane were married. In 1906, Happy's wife Lucy (Rideout) of Twillingate, Newfoundland, was pregnant.

Happy was fishing in L'Anse au Pigeon, when late one evening in early July, someone saw a punt coming in the harbour. It was noted that the boat wasn't from the little town. There were two men on board, each with a pair of oars to pull the boat toward the wharf. Most of Az's crew were on the wharf putting away fish.

"They're rowing with a long stroke," said one of the men.

"I wonder who they are," said another. Everyone stopped working to look as the boat got closer. Someone recognized one of the men in the small punt.

"Why, that's Uncle Jim Morgan from home," said one of the men.

"Yes," said Az, "and that's young Artfield, his son."

Everyone was surprised. "I wonder where he came from? There must be a shipwreck somewhere."

As the punt got to the wharf, Artfield threw the line. One of the men caught it and pulled the punt to the front of the wharf.

"Artfield," said Az, "where did you come from, my son?"

"From home, Uncle Az," he replied.

"What? Rowed from Lushes Bight? That's over a hundred miles!"

"Yes, sir," he replied.

Az couldn't believe it. "Help them up, boys," he said.

"I'd say that the whole town is burned down or something else is wrong," said one of the men.

Jim Morgan was no ordinary man. Once, many years earlier, he had left Lushes Bight with his father in early May and rowed to Little Bay Islands to get food for his family. On returning they had been caught in young ice. The wind and tide pushed them onto the land near Stag Island. When the ice squeezed onto the land, the small rowboat had been crushed. They had to leave it and go for shore, but the ice couldn't bear their weight. Jim and his father fell through. Jim had tied a rope onto his father before they left the boat, and with it he pulled him out on several occasions. However, on nearing shore, his father fell in for the last time. Jim couldn't get him out, and the old man had died. For the next three days, Jim had sat near the shoreline of Stag Island with his dead father tied onto a pan of ice, until he was rescued by a passing schooner.

When Uncle Jim Morgan got up on the wharf, he could hardly stand, from being cramped up in the boat for so long. Someone caught him and steadied him.

"Where's Happy?" he said.

"He's in the stage, salting fish," said Az.

"I want to see him, Az."

"Come in the stage." The two men started walking toward the salting stage where Happy worked.

"What's up, Uncle Jim?" asked Az.

"Lucy's very sick; she can't have her baby. She went into labour two days before we left. We were four days coming down—that's six days ago. I'd say she's dead now. Granny Brenton sent me down to get Happy. She said that Lucy was hemorrhaging and wasn't expected to live."

They quickly went to Happy. The minute he saw Jim Morgan, Happy knew that something was wrong.

"Jim," he said, looking straight at him. "You have bad news for me?"

"I don't know if it's bad news or not, but you have to go back home now. Lucy isn't very good. She can't have the baby, and Granny Brenton said you have to come home immediately. She said for you to expect the worst."

Happy hung his head; he was a very quiet man. His eyes filled with tears as he put his arms around Jim Morgan.

"I'll get ready for home right away, Uncle Jim," he said.

Az said, "Yes, Happy, you get your things together. We'll get the schooner ready to take you home. It must be serious if Granny Brenton sent Jim and Artfield Morgan rowing to L'Anse au Pigeon in a seventeen-foot punt."

Happy headed for the bunkhouse to get his belongings.

Az turned to Jim Morgan. "We'll send two men with you two and Happy. That will be five. There should be no problems if you take the new schooner, the *Kokomo City*."

Az called Art Windsor, a very reliable man who knew the run from L'Anse au Pigeon to Notre Dame Bay like the back of his hand. He was to leave right away. Az told Art what his plans were, and he agreed to go.

He further instructed Art. "Stay only one night at home and head back as soon as you can."

"Sure will, Az," he said.

"We'll fish away here," said Az. "If Happy can't come back, tell Uncle Peter to send someone in his place. I need some supplies, so I'll write a note while you're getting ready. Make sure you take a cask of water."

"Okay," said Art. He headed off to the schooner.

Az told Emily Jane what was going on. She started to pack a box full of food for the trip. It was then that Jim and Artfield Morgan came into the cookhouse.

"Sit to the table, Uncle Jim," said Emily Jane.

Uncle Jim and Artfield sat down, and Emily Jane saw that their hands were calloused from rowing. Uncle Jim couldn't straighten his fingers.

"Why didn't they get a younger man to send with Artfield?" she said. "Uncle Jim, you must be completely beat!"

"I'll admit, I'm tired," he said. "I'll get some rest when I get on board the schooner." He then filled her in on the details about Lucy.

The schooner was prepared and the anchors hoisted. The lines from the shore were let go and the small boats towed her out of the little harbour. A light westerly wind was blowing. Soon the schooner was in full sail and heading along by Degrat and out along by the White Islands, on her way to Lushes Bight.

Forty-eight hours from the time she left L'Anse au Pigeon, the *Kokomo City* arrived at her home port of Lushes Bight. Rev. Scott and a dozen other people were at the wharf to meet the schooner. The people on the wharf were standing in silence as Captain Peter Brooks called Happy over to where Rev. Scott was standing alone.

"Your dear wife has passed away, Happy, but you are the father of a son. Your wife's last words were that she loved you and will meet you in a better world. As she closed her eyes for the last time, she said, 'If I have a boy, call him Truman; if it's a girl, call her Winnie.' Then she went to sleep."

Happy was broken-hearted, and he wept openly. "What will I do?" he cried.

The people gathered around him for comfort. "We have her in my house," said Captain Brooks. "We'll go there now."

Happy said nothing as the crowd marched along with him, everybody in tears.

Happy Tucker was a well-liked man. He held church service when the minister was away during the winter. He was a hard worker and a man who always cared for everyone. He

25

was known by everyone as Uncle Happy—even when he was barely twenty years old—and was respected by everyone.

In the living room, a casket was on a large round table. It sat there with the cover open, exposing the top half of Lucy's body. There was no undertaker or makeup artist; Lucy's hair was combed and set in the way she always wore it. She was young, just twenty-six years old.

Happy loved his wife. She worked every summer making fish in the sun on the flakes, employed by Captain Brooks for the Strong firm of Little Bay Islands. The Brooks family had made the funeral arrangement as beautiful as possible.

As he came into the house, Happy's two children met him. It was a scene that made everyone weep. Finally, he came into the living room where his dear wife lay. She was wrapped in a funeral veil of white; he could hardly believe his eyes.

"Lucy, my Lucy," he sobbed. The words came from the depths of his soul. His younger daughter was in his arms and his other daughter was clinging to him. Someone took the children from him. He leaned across his wife's body and wept aloud. Seeing her there like that, he knew she was gone forever. He knew that she would never reach out to love and comfort him, or welcome him home from Labrador.

She had been dead for three days and the funeral would be the next day. Mrs. Brooks came and put her arms around him and led him into the kitchen where Rev. Scott sat at the table.

"I'm sorry, Happy. It's impossible for us to express our grief to you about Lucy's passing. We can only pray for you."

"Thank you," said Happy. At that moment, Mrs. Maisie Paddock walked into the room, carrying the baby in her arms. Happy sat still as the tears continued to fall. Mrs. Paddock stood in front of him and wiped the tears away.

Happy's young daughter Bessie was in the arms of a woman standing near him. The child said, "Our baby, Daddy. Our baby brother."

Happy didn't know what to do. Memories haunted him; the sound of Lucy's voice echoed through his mind. *I'm hoping to have a son, Happy, and he's going to be just like you. I'm going to have a son, Happy, a son for you.*

Mrs. Paddock held out the baby to him. He reached out and took him. He could hardly believe it; sure enough, it was a son, the one Lucy said she would have. But now there was no Lucy. He was glad Lucy had told the people that she wanted him called Truman. It was a name they had talked about many times.

After Happy stopped crying, he said, "I'm going to christen him Truman."

Rev. Scott said, "I already christened the baby Truman Absalom Tucker at birth, because it looked like the child wouldn't live."

"Thank you, Reverend."

After the crowd started to leave, and Happy settled down, he started talking about the baby. Mrs. Brooks said that Mrs. Paddock wanted the baby; she was satisfied to rear him up or adopt him.

Happy then told her what Emily Jane and Az told him before he left L'Anse au Pigeon. Emily Jane had said, "Happy, if anything happens to your wife and the baby survives, you promise us that you'll let us have the child." He had agreed; if such a tragedy happened he would remember them.

Mrs. Brooks was pleased, because Emily Jane had lived with her and her husband, Captain Peter Brooks, for five years as a serving girl. "He'll have a good home," she said.

"I don't plan to put my other children out, Mrs. Brooks. I'll keep them as long as I can," he said.

"I'm sure you will, but in the meantime Maisie Paddock will take care of the baby."

"That would be wonderful," said Happy.

After he had a cup of tea, he went home to his empty house.

After the funeral, Happy tried to piece things together. Peter Brooks gave him a job working in the firm, and Mrs. Paddock looked after Truman while he worked. Mrs. Brooks and Sarah Brenton—Az Roberts's sister—looked after his two girls, Bessie and Susie.

When the *Kokomo City* went back, Happy had someone write a letter and sent it to Az and Emily Jane, telling them what went on and how he felt. "You can have Truman as I promised," it read. The letter ended with, "Emily Jane, pray for me. It's only God who can help me."

The next year Happy Tucker went to L'Anse au Pigeon. He kept his older children with him in the meantime, but he put Truman, now ten months old, with Mrs. Paddock for the summer. Happy had to make a living, and his place was with Az Roberts at L'Anse au Pigeon. He was the man who did all the maintenance around the premises and salted most of the fish they caught. Az thought there was no one else in the world like Happy, although they were completely different in many ways. Az Roberts was the type who liked a little fun. He would take a drink of rum or moonshine at times, but could handle it quite well. When working, there was never a stain of anything around, but when time afforded he would indulge.

Aunt Emily Jane was deadly opposed to any kind of drink; by now she was a religious woman. She had been saved in the Methodist Church, and was attending church regularly with Happy whenever they were at Lushes Bight. In the summer at L'Anse au Pigeon, Happy held services in the cookhouse. Az wouldn't attend. He would spend many Saturday nights at the lighthouse on Cape Bauld with his very close friend, Ned Fontaine.

When Truman was almost three years old, Happy was getting ready to go to L'Anse au Pigeon for the fishing season. This particular spring he couldn't leave Truman back at Lushes Bight. Truman cried and cried to go to L'Anse au Pigeon with him. Happy had talked it over with Az and Emily Jane, who had agreed to take him, but before the trip was made, Az had to get a few things straightened out. He made Happy sit down with Emily Jane and himself to discuss what the terms and conditions were.

Az knew that Happy was courting a girl, Mary Lambert, a fiery redhead. She was twenty and full of vigour; every drop of blood in her body was filled with energy. It was said that she was afraid of nothing that walked in shoe leather. It was Az who got the two of them together. Although Happy was thirty, Az figured it was important for him to marry a young woman in case he still wanted to have a crowd of youngsters.

As they sat down to talk about Truman's welfare, it was obvious to Happy that Emily Jane and Az wanted the child. "You cannot leave Truman here in Lushes Bight again this summer, Happy," said Emily Jane. "It will break his little heart. He wants to go to the Pigeon with me."

"Well, Happy," said Az, "the time has come now for you to make a decision. You know we have no children, and we may not have any; I'm not like you." He winked at Emily Jane.

Emily Jane quickly silenced that talk.

"Anyway," said Az, "we want to adopt Truman."

Happy sat there, silent. Az continued. "We know you're thinking about marrying Mary, but it will be difficult for her to take on a small child such as Truman. It's not that he's any trouble, but it might be inconvenient for both of you. As you know, when he's with us, it's almost as if he hasn't left you, because you spend most of your time with us anyway."

Happy nodded.

"If you agree," said Az, "he'll remain a Tucker and he'll never call me Dad. We want him for a son, but I could never replace you as his real father."

Happy realized he was talking to his two best friends, and two who could afford to give Truman everything he wanted.

"What will he call you if he can't call you Dad?"

"Let him call me whatever he wants," said Az.

"He'll be calling me Mom!" said Emily Jane. Az laughed.

"Okay," said Happy, "you can have him for a son."

# Chapter 5

By 1921, Azariah Roberts was an established skipper, deeply involved in the codfishery, and he was securing large voyages of salted cod at L'Anse au Pigeon. He and Emily now had two daughters, Winnifred and Grace. Az had built a new two-storey home in 1920, and that same year he had purchased the complete fishing premises from Captain Peter Brooks for the great sum of eighteen hundred dollars. This included the fishing equipment and land.

Az went to St. Anthony and acquired the services of a land surveyor, Ted McNeill, and had all of L'Anse au Pigeon surveyed. He also obtained a grant for the land at Degrat, near the Pigeon, for agriculture purposes. He set huge gardens and was self-sufficient in all varieties of vegetables. He also purchased the fishing schooner *Almeta* from the Strong firm of Little Bay Islands and built a cod oil factory in the town. By 1922, the operation involved twenty-three workers, so he decided to build houses for his employees to enable them to bring their women and children with them during the summer months.

In the fall of 1925, Az decided to stay all winter at the Pigeon. He had stocked his supplies and had cut and transported his firewood to his home, and he had bought dogs for transportation during the winter.

At Lushes Bight, he had been a strong member of the Orange Lodge on Long Island, taking part in all its activities, and had risen to the rank of Worshipful Master for two years. His ambition was to become a Red Cross man. His mother had already died, but he never forgot the warning she had given him many years earlier of what would happen if he joined the Orange Lodge.

One day at his home in Lushes Bight, he had been in a conversation with his sister Sarah about an unpleasant incident that had happened among some members of the Orange Lodge, involving alcohol. When Az tried to defend the members, his sister Sarah reminded him of what his mother had told him when he wanted to join the Lodge.

"I remember," Az said. "She said a curse would fall on me, but no misfortune has fallen on me. Sarah, I don't think Mom should have ever said that. It has haunted me all my life."

"Az," Sarah replied, "you're not dead yet, and I pray to God that nothing ever happens to you. It would break my heart."

Az loved his sister almost as much as he loved his mother, but he didn't want her to be going on with this nonsense.

"That's enough of that old foolishness, Sarah. They say if you predict enough stuff, some of it has to come true. I intend to be an Orangeman 'til I die."

Sarah said no more, and Az went on about his business.

Emily Jane was a happy woman at L'Anse au Pigeon, living a very different life from that as a young girl at Cooks Harbour. She had joined a fishing crew at an early age, and was treated with dignity and respect. She married a man who gave her everything, and she was free to come and go when and where she liked. Emily Jane could worship any way she pleased, and with whom she liked. She generally had serving girls or maids in the house, had plenty of money to spend and the best of clothes to wear, but she was a very modest woman. She was interested in only one thing—the Salvation Army. At Lushes Bight, she had been a staunch member of the Methodist church, but when the Salvation Army came along she became a soldier.

When Az and Emily Jane started living year-round at the Pigeon, Emily Jane immediately contacted the Salvation Army and promised that if they sent an officer she would see to it that a barracks would be built. It would be used as a church on Sunday and a school during the week. Emily Jane never had the opportunity of going to school, but she vowed that her children would get an education. Truman and Winnie had finished school, and Grace would finish soon.

In 1928, a young man by the name of Gideon Hancock, from Englee, Newfoundland, came to the Pigeon. He was twenty years old. Until the barracks could be started the following year, he would teach school in the cookhouse belonging to Az, and hold church there on Sunday. Emily Jane was excited.

Approximately one mile overland from L'Anse au Pigeon was the lighthouse of Cape Bauld. It was a large complex with a towering lighthouse painted white and red. Ocean traffic sailing to Labrador or going through the Strait of Belle Isle would see this huge spire if the weather was suitable, and in the days of sail would listen for the fog alarm, locally called "the foggle horn."

It isn't known for sure, but it is speculated that the lighthouse on Cape Bauld has saved thousands of lives. This great lighthouse was staffed by a French Canadian, what the old-timers would call a "Canadian," and his family, from Trois-Rivières, Quebec. His name was Edward "Ned" Fontaine, and as Az Roberts and Emily Jane got themselves established at the Pigeon they became the best of friends with the Fontaines. It was said by everyone in the L'Anse au

Pigeon area that Lightkeeper Ned Fontaine could make the foggle horn sing.

Ned and his wife Anastasia were the best of people. They were Catholics, but Ned, they said, was in the category of non-denominational. Religion wasn't his can of worms. One Sunday morning, Ned even went to the Salvation Army service at the cookhouse with Emily Jane. To tease her, Az would say that Ned must have been drunk and didn't know what he was doing. Although Emily Jane was a devoted Salvation Army soldier, and Az was an Orangeman, Ned Fontaine and Az Roberts became closer than any brothers could ever be.

Az had a trap berth right under the lighthouse, and every morning when Az came to haul his cod trap Ned would be attending the lamps in the lighthouse, towering high above the cliffs of Cape Bauld. Before Az caught hold of his trap, Ned would let out several loud blasts from the mighty horn that would be heard over ten miles away. It was said that Ned Fontaine kept the fish driven into Az Roberts's cod traps. Whatever the reason, the traps were always full of cod.

At least twice a month the two men got together on weekends for a sociable drink, either at Az's home in L'Anse au Pigeon or at the lighthouse on Cape Bauld. Every fall the two men would go to St. John's with their wives to get their winter supply of food. Emily Jane said that someday, if they kept drinking every time they went to St. John's, they would get in trouble.

It was an interesting time in the Pigeon. After Az had bought the entire fishing premises from Captain Peter Brooks, he could construct any kind of building anywhere. Unfortunately, there were very few trees on the island— L'Anse au Pigeon was located on an island approximately four miles long and two miles wide. There were a few scrubby trees on a hillside in a cove called L'Anse au Clue, on the southwest side, but Az would usually go to an area called Pistolet Bay and cut his firewood and logs.

The home of Azariah Roberts was just as busy as the cookhouse he had built for his seasonal workers. The table was eight feet long, and on Sundays this table would have to be set twice at every meal. Az never sat down to a meal with just his wife and two daughters, and that was the way he liked it. He loved a crowd, and his personality attracted them. He had storehouses filled with just about everything, and he was very generous. He had large vegetable gardens at Degrat, and he kept cattle. With his storehouses full, he didn't mind helping anyone. There was nothing thrown away or wasted. Empty cans were put away to be made into something else, and old clothes, when they were worn out, were made into rugs for the floors. Az owned all the houses in the town, and whoever lived in them kept them in good repair. He had no trouble with anyone living there.

Az Roberts had a lot of able men working for him during his years in the Pigeon, but one day he was approached by a young woman who was looking for a job. She came to his home and asked for Aunt Emily Jane. She was invited in and sat at the table across from Az and Emily Jane.

"I'm Gladys Pilgrim from Little Brehat," she said.

Az said, "You're Leonard Pilgrim's daughter. I can see Len in you."

"Yes, sir," she said with a grin. "I came here to see you for two reasons. First, I'm looking for a job. Secondly I'm trying to spread the Gospel, that is, for the Salvation Army. I am sixteen years old and can carry a hand barrow as good as any man under your roof."

Az looked at this handsome, well-built girl. He knew she meant business. He couldn't put her to cooking, since Emma Bridger and his daughter Winnie were doing that.

Emily Jane arched an eyebrow. "We need someone here with me in the house, Az."

"No," said Az. "I have a job for her. She can go to work right now."

"Where?" asked Emily Jane.

"Come with me, Gladys," he said. He got up and walked out the door, Gladys following. "I have a job for you in the stage, my dear, taking fish from the splitting table to the salting area. Do you know what that is?"

"Yes sir," she said. "I worked at that with my father."

"Great. You're now part of our crew."

"Thank you, sir," she said joyfully.

"By the way, Gladys, don't call me 'sir' anymore. Only Dr. Grenfell is 'sir.' Call me Az, or Skipper."

"I'll call you Skipper Az." They laughed.

Happy Tucker was now living in the Pigeon and was a member of the Salvation Army. Az had helped him build a small house near his own.

His oldest daughter, Bessie, was a beautiful young woman, and she fell in love with a young man, Sod Mugford, from Beaumont, Newfoundland. This man was known as a tyrant in Beaumont, a man who drank and fought almost every day of the week. He had a younger brother, Wesley, who was no better. When they got together, they could terrorize any town. However, Bessie fell in love with Sod, and before Happy could bat an eye, they were married. She moved to Beaumont with her husband.

Sod worked with Az Roberts at the Pigeon during the fishing season. It was said that Az and Aunt Emily Jane were the only two that he liked—Emily Jane because she liked everybody, and Az because he respected Sod for being a hard and willing worker.

The cold or the rain never bothered him. Sod Mugford could go for days, working full out, without any sleep. He never tired. On a few occasions he and Az would have a little drink together, but Az would watch him like a cat would watch a mouse.

Sod always went back to Beaumont each fall. Emily Jane didn't want Sod Mugford, with his moonshine can on the stove all winter long, in L'Anse au Pigeon. She pitied Bessie. However, when Sod was in the Pigeon he never got into any rackets because he knew Az wouldn't tolerate it.

Happy Tucker was heartbroken when his daughter married Sod Mugford, but he was the type of man who would always try to make the best out of a bad situation. He was prepared to put up with almost anything, but what he didn't like was Sod's drinking. He knew it was hell on earth for Bessie. Happy always said to Sod, "Your drinking will kill you someday, Sod, if you don't change your ways."

Sod wouldn't say much to his father-in-law. He liked it in the Pigeon, and he knew that if he gave Happy a rough time, Az wouldn't allow him back. With this in mind, he kept fairly quiet in the summertime, but when he arrived back in Beaumont in the fall, only God knows what he did.

From Beaumont, Sod usually went to the lumberwoods around Badger and Millertown for a couple of months. It appeared that Hugh Cole, the woods king of Badger, thought a lot of Sod, and gave him a job working in a forge, making sleds for horses to haul pulpwood. When he would return home from the lumberwoods in December, it would be hell on earth for Bessie, and a distressing time for the town of Beaumont.

# Chapter 6

William Cuff was an eighteen-year-old schoolteacher from Ochre Pit Cove. He was what the old folks would call a "smart feller." He was tall and skinny and full of life, a happy-go-lucky kid exploring the things around him. He had spent six weeks at the college in St. John's at what they called "summer school." This was preparing him to teach in the outports. On August 29, 1928, he landed at Beaumont. He carried two suitcases and a cardboard box. As he walked from the gangway, he was met by a man and a woman.

"Are you Mr. Cuff, the schoolteacher?" asked the man.

"Yes sir, I am." he replied.

"I'm Jim Burton, and this is my wife Virtue." They shook hands.

"Welcome to Beaumont," said Virtue.

"Thank you."

"Do you have any more luggage?" asked Jim.

"No, that's it," said Cuff.

"Hey, Edwin," Jim called, waving his hand. "Come here, I want you."

A young man, a little older than Cuff, quickly came over. "Yes, Dad. What is it?"

"I want you to meet Mr. Cuff, the new schoolteacher."

Edwin quickly reached out his hand and smiled politely. "How are you, Mr. Cuff? It's good to meet you." The two shook hands. Edwin wasn't a shy person. He was used to schoolteachers, because Jim and Virtue had boarded schoolteachers for years. "You'll like it here, Mr. Cuff."

"Call me Willie," he said to Edwin.

"Okay, Willie," said Edwin with a grin.

"Edwin, help us with the suitcases and the box. Bring it over to the boat," said Jim.

"Okay, Dad." Everyone stared at the Burtons as they put the young schoolteacher's things aboard their motorboat and went slowly up the harbour to the Burtons' fishing premises, almost a mile away.

Cuff was a good schoolteacher. He was teaching forty-seven pupils from primary to grade eight in the fall of 1928. He had no experience teaching, but he quickly established order and discipline in the classroom. Every moment of the day was occupied. He was tough, and the pupils knew it. He would make anyone who was out of line stay in after school, and on those who were extremely disobedient he learned to use the strap.

In those days it was common for the children to come home and say that this one or that one got a strapping. However, there was always one or two to whom the teacher had trouble giving a strapping. One of those was Wesley Mugford. He was fifteen and as saucy as they come. He was afraid of his mother, but not afraid of anything else that walked or crawled. Wes, as everyone called him, had said that Cuff would never give him a strapping. If he did, it would be over his dead body. Cuff was warned about this fellow, and was told that he shouldn't even allow Wes in school, due to the fact that he had gotten kicked out the year before. Of course, Wes didn't want to go to school, and had planned to get kicked out. The sooner the better.

The first day he was very quiet, not saying or doing anything, but on the second day he went back to his old tricks of throwing things around at the younger children. He did this all day. Whenever Cuff had his back turned, Wes would throw something and make one of the smaller children cry. Cuff said nothing. In the afternoon he caught Wes right in the act. He still said nothing. Wes knew that Cuff saw him, and thought that he was afraid to correct him. This went on all afternoon.

At 4:00 p.m., everyone left. Cuff sat down in his chair and stared at the ceiling. "Tomorrow," he said out loud, "Mr. Wesley, you and I are going to come face to face or I'll be hauling my frame out of here."

He got up from the desk and checked the old Giant wood stove. The fire had almost gone out. He went back to the desk and opened the bottom drawer. In it was a two-foot-long strap, part of the school's equipment. He had never struck anyone in his life. He took it out and examined it. He flicked it a few times.

"I'll put this on the desk. Maybe if Wes sees the strap he'll behave himself." He left it there, walked out and locked the door.

It was close to 5:00 p.m. when he got to the Burtons' house. Jim was in from fishing and had washed, ready for supper. Virtue and Edwin sat at the table just as Cuff walked in.

"What kind of a day did you have at school, Willie?" Jim asked.

Cuff squinted his eyes and shrugged his shoulders. "Pretty good, I guess, for the second day. It looks like it will be a busy year."

"I guess so," said Jim. "Teaching isn't for me," he added. Sensing that Cuff was a little frustrated, he said no more.

They sat down to have supper, when the door opened. A man of about twenty-five walked in. "How are you doing, Jim?" he asked. It was Bob Huxter, Jim Burton's next door neighbour.

"Pretty good, Bob," Jim said as he ate. "Have some supper."

"No, I ain't hungry. I'm mad."

Jim put down his fork and looked at him. "And what are you mad about?"

Bob stared at Cuff. "I don't know for sure whether I should be mad at Wes Mugford or at this here schoolteacher."

Right away Cuff knew what was going on. No one spoke for a moment, then he said, "Sir, do you have anyone at my school?"

"Yes, Mr. Cuff. I do." He looked very concerned. "My Lucy is going, and she's the one that Wes Mugford flicked the cardboard at this afternoon and hit in the eye. She's only seven, and when she got out he smacked her across the mouth. I talked to three or four more children, and they said you saw him and did nothing."

Jim Burton looked at Cuff, then at the man who was now standing in the middle of the kitchen. "Mr. Cuff, do you intend to do anything about it?" There was a pause, then he added, "Last year the same thing went on. The teacher had to kick him out after he did the same thing he did today."

Bob said, "I think you're afraid of him. I wish I was teaching for only one hour—I'd fix up with him. What he needs is a good lacing."

Cuff spoke for the first time. "You're right, sir, he needs a lacing."

"I'm not taking Lucy from school, even if I have to go to school with her."

"I don't guess you'll have to do that, sir."

Bob Huxter sat down. He had cooled a little.

Cuff turned to him and asked, "Have you talked to his father?"

"Talk to his father," Bob said. "Are you crazy? You would need a suit of armour on to go over there."

Cuff looked at him again. "You said a minute ago that I was afraid. I think you're afraid. And if you are, what are you afraid of?"

"Wes has a brother named Sod. He's capable of blowing your brains out if you happen to say anything to Wes."

"Is that so?" Cuff mused. "Why don't you all gang up on him and teach him a lesson?"

"Sod will get us one by one. But you're the teacher—you do it."

Bob walked out. There was a silence.

"What do you think of that, Willie?" asked Jim. "I don't know right offhand, but it looks to me like there's a problem in the town." No one commented.

Young Edwin left the table. He appeared to be very upset. Willie figured Edwin didn't like the comments made by Lucy's father.

Mrs. Burton leaned across the table. "This Sod Mugford," she said, "he's a real criminal, my son. He would cut your throat just as fast as he'd look at you. That's what's got young Wes like he is. No one knows what they're doing, and no one knows what they're capable of doing, but I know what I'd do if I was a man."

She lowered her voice to a whisper. "Edwin goes around with them. On times we've talked to him, but he thinks the sun shines out of Old Sod. You have a problem on your hands, William, but do your job. You have a lot of people on your side. Last year the teacher threw Wes out. You might have to do the same."

"Maybe," said Cuff. But then he thought, *Maybe Edwin's upset with me. He may be afraid I'm going to chastise Wes.*

"We'll see," he said. "We'll see."

The next day was sunny, and everybody was in school. Cuff read from the Bible, and everyone said the Lord's Prayer, except Wes. The morning began very quietly; everyone had seen the strap on the desk.

At 10:00 a.m., Wes got up from his desk, walked over to another student and told him something, then walked back again and sat down.

Cuff said nothing. He continued with the lecture.

A few minutes passed. Wes then threw a piece of cardboard at a small girl. She started to cry.

"Wesley Mugford," Cuff said sharply, "you'll be staying in during recess."

Wesley laughed. Without taking his eyes off the teacher, he picked up another piece of cardboard and threw it over his shoulder.

"Okay, children, we're going to have an early recess today. You can go out now." Very quickly, everyone began to file out.

Wesley got up to go, but as quick as a wink this tall eighteen-year-old schoolteacher was in front of him. "You sit down, Wesley. You're staying in."

Wesley was surprised at Cuff's quick move. He figured he'd better stay, so he sat back down in his seat. "Now, Mr. Mugford, I'm going to give you a strapping, five smacks on each hand."

"Oh, no you're not, Cuff." Wes had a wild look in his eyes. "Nobody ever strapped me, and you're not."

Wes jumped up and looked for a way out, but Cuff grabbed him. His hands were like steel and Wes found himself caught in a vise, staring eye to eye with the schoolteacher. Cuff picked him up and carried him to his desk where the strap lay.

"Now," he said, "you stand there." Pointing to a spot near the desk, he picked up the strap and looked Wesley straight in the eyes. It was the first time Wesley Mugford had ever seen such anger outside his own home.

"Hold out your hands," Cuff said in a voice that frightened Wes.

Slowly, Wes held them out. Willie Cuff brought the strap down on Wesley's hands.

*Right-left-right-left-right-left...*

Wes started to scream.

*...right-left-9-10.*

"Now, Mr. Mugford, you get out and don't come back 'til after Christmas." Wes went to the door. "Just a minute," said Cuff before he got to the door. "When you go home, tell your brother Sod that if he wants the same thing, I'll open school for him any night. Now get out."

Wes opened the door, and to his surprise the porch was full of students. They had heard every word. They let Wes pass through.

Wes Mugford went to Sod's house and walked in. There were very poor furnishings inside. Sod's wife Bessie was dressing their one-year-old girl, Ramona, and he was sitting at the table. Sod wore about two weeks of beard that looked greasy. He was heavily built, with big hands, and he was a very strong man.

Sod and Bessie had three children—Ramona was the youngest, Polly was four, and Rita the oldest at six years.

Uncle Happy said many times that the biggest mistake he had ever made was letting Bessie marry Sod Mugford. Sod was a drunkard, a wild man. He was rarely home at night, and when he was, he was usually drinking. The moonshine can was seldom off the stove, and the beer keg was never empty. Their house was always full of gangs of drinkers every night. It was the hangout for the town punks, of which Sod was the king.

Uncle Happy brought food almost every week for his daughter and for her children, and he often prayed that God would free her from her misery. The only comfort Bessie would get was when Sod went north in the spring to L'Anse au Pigeon with Az Roberts and Trum Tucker. When she saw the schooners returning in the fall, she would shudder.

"What's this? Out of school early, Wes?" asked Sod. Wes said nothing as Sod took a draw from his cigarette and started coughing. "What's wrong with you, Wes? What happened?"

"The teacher got onto me."

Sod put out his cigarette and sat upright. "Got onto you? What do you mean, got onto you? How?" he roared. His temper raged; he started cursing. Sod noticed that Wes was keeping his hands in his pockets. "Let me see your hands," he yelled. As Wes held them out, Sod could see that they were red and swollen.

"He kicked me and punched me in the stomach and knocked the wind out of me, then gave me a strapping," said Wes. He was inwardly pleased as he saw how angry Sod was becoming. "He also called Mom everything, saying she was the scum of Long Island. And that's not all. He told me to tell you to go over; he wants to beat the gob off you. He said you was a pig."

Sod became very quiet. He lit another cigarette, then he said very slowly, "Wesley, my boy, get the britch-loader ready. I'm going over to the school to shoot the bugger."

"You're not game," said Wes, smirking.

"Oh yes I'm game, you just wait and see."

Bessie couldn't believe what she was hearing. She looked at Sod and knew he was serious.

Sod buttoned up his shirt and started putting on his boots.

Wes looked around the room with a devilish grin on his face. "Where's she at, Sod? Where's the britch-loader? And the cartridges? I'll get them for you."

"In the room on the shelf," Sod said. "Take six cartridges."

There was a silence.

Bessie put the little girl down on the couch and walked over to Sod. She was frightened. "Do you know what you're saying, Sod?"

By now Wes was standing in the kitchen with the shotgun.

"You stay out of this, Bess," Sod screamed. "This is none of your business."

"Oh, yes it is," she said. "You're planning to kill a man, Sod. You're planning to shoot the schoolteacher."

"He's not getting away with it. I'm going to kill the bastard. Just look at the state poor Wes is in."

"'Poor Wes,' that's all I hear. What about poor me or the poor youngsters? Can't you see what will happen to us?"

Sod grabbed her and threw her to one side as if she were a rag doll. "Get out of my way," he yelled.

"What's wrong, boys?" said a voice.

Bessie turned toward the doorway and saw Edwin Burton standing there, grinning from ear to ear. He seemed to be enjoying the goings-on.

"Edwin, for God's sake, try and stop Sod will you?" Bessie was desperate.

"Wes," said Edwin, "what are you doing with the britch-loader, going birding?"

"No," said Sod. "We're going to shoot that schoolteacher over at the school. You should see what he's after doing with poor Wes."

Edwin laughed. "Put the britch-loader away, Sod. Do you realize what will happen if you venture toward the school with that gun? Every man and woman for miles around will tear you apart piece by piece, and besides that, you'll be hanged."

Wes spoke up. "Don't listen to him, Sod, don't listen to him. He's just trying to talk you out of it. Come on."

Edwin Burton was sensible enough to know what could happen. Every family had children in school. "Before you even get over there you'll be shot on the road," he said.

Bessie looked relieved, but Sod Mugford wasn't easily talked out of anything. Wes was about to put a shell in the gun when Bessie jumped him. There was a scuffle. She hit Wes in the mouth with her fist and knocked him down.

"You take that, Wes Mugford," she said as she grabbed the shotgun from him.

Sod stepped in. "Okay, okay, Bess. I won't go to the school and shoot him today, but the bugger's going to catch it just the same."

Bessie let out a sigh of relief, then started crying.

"My, oh my," she said as she walked over and picked up Ramona. "I always thought I had married the devil, and now I'm sure of it."

Sod looked at her and said, "Do you know that the devil's a murderer? If I'm the devil, I'll be just like him." The three men laughed.

"You'll all come to a devil's end, all three of you," she said, "and I pray to God that your souls will rot in a devil's hell." They just laughed.

"Come outside, Sod, I want to talk to you," Edwin said. The three of them went outside and shut the door.

All was quiet in school after the ruckus caused by Wes Mugford, and now everyone had a lot of respect for Cuff. He had taken on Wesley and Sod Mugford and had won. This is what everyone said, but there were people who told him to be aware, to keep his distance.

Eventually, everyone learned about the goings-on at Sod Mugford's house that morning with the shotgun. Bessie had told certain people; the word got around and people started talking. Some of the men even suggested that the magistrate be called to investigate the incident. They knew that Sod Mugford was never through with something until he had completed it, no matter what it was. It was guaranteed that he'd get even.

# Chapter 7

Walter Brenton had lived in Lushes Bight all his life. He was a fisherman and had spent many summers going to Labrador with Captain Peter Brooks. After his family had reached a working age he gave up going north, acquired his own fishing gear and started fishing from Lushes Bight. He did fairly well.

Walter had two daughters. The oldest was Lillian and the other was Blanche. They were beautiful girls. However, Lillian was the more glamorous of the two. She had a slender body, and her long wavy hair and blue eyes made her very attractive to all the young men. She was an active girl and was known to be a very hard worker, helping her father cure his fish and working with her mother around the house.

Blanche was a totally different girl. She was sort of boyish but very lovable. She was short with big shoulders and big hands, and very strong. The two girls were very contented living with their parents, working side by side on the fish flakes and around the house. They were very obedient to their parents. Of course, Skipper Walter expected it.

During the summer of 1928, Edwin Burton had started going out with Lillian. He fell in love with her instantly. They went out together a few times, and they became very serious. Edwin started coming to her house, and she would go on walks with him. Lillian was very careful not to be alone with him, especially late at night. For modesty's sake, she was very careful.

Walter wasn't very happy that his daughter was seeing Edwin Burton, who was known to be buddies with Sod and Wes Mugford. He would say to his daughter, "Be careful, Lillian. This young Edwin's too close to the moonshine can for me. He spends too much time at Sod Mugford's house to be sensible, so whatever you do, be careful."

"I'll be careful, Dad," she assured him. "He's just a friend."

Wesley Mugford had been trying to get Blanche Brenton's attention, although she was two years older than he was. He was crazy about her. He had walked her home a couple of times, but when Walter found out about it he immediately put a stop to it, saying that he wasn't going to have any criminals around, especially Wes Mugford.

He had told his daughter Blanche, "My dear, look at poor Bessie over there with Sod, living in hell on earth, half starving, with half enough to wear, and God only knows what will happen to her."

She had taken her father's words to heart. The only reason Walter hadn't stopped Lillian from going out with Edwin was because Jim Burton was a good friend. This was how he felt, and he had let his daughters know it.

After the incident between Cuff and Wes, he became nervous. Walter Brenton knew that the Mugfords would get even.

"You haven't seen the end of it yet," Walter told his family. "I'm a bit scared, Lillian, that Edwin will side with Sod and Wes. According to Bessie, they're planning something, and Edwin's in it with them."

"Dad," she said, "you don't think that, do you?"

"I'm uneasy, my dear. Maybe it's better for you to give him up for your own good."

After the young schoolteacher arrived, Lillian had seen him one day in the local store. She had introduced herself to him and shaken hands with him. Maybe this was her way out. She could leave Edwin and get a date with Willie Cuff.

"Dad," she said, "if you want me to stop seeing Edwin, then I will."

Walter Brenton was delighted.

Cuff was not a church-goer, but one Sunday evening he walked into the Methodist church and sat in the third seat. The minister rose and welcomed him. Everyone looked around and smiled. Sitting across from him and a few seats farther up was Lillian. He was glad to have met her that day, and when he left the store his heart had been pounding. He had never seen such a beautiful girl before. He'd repeated her name over and over. He couldn't get her face out of his mind. "I must see her again," he had said.

Lillian Brenton was dressed in a dark blue dress with a lace collar. She looked around and smiled. Mrs. Burton, Cuff's boarding lady, was at the organ and she played beautifully. Cuff glanced again in Lillian's direction. She looked prettier than ever. He had heard that she had given up going out with Edwin, and for this reason Edwin was now spending a lot of time at Sod Mugford's house, even staying all night. He had heard Jim Burton say that he wouldn't be surprised if Edwin moved in with Sod. His father had tried to talk sense into him on many occasions, but it was no use.

It was a fine church meeting that ended at 10:30 p.m. As Cuff walked through the door he saw Lillian standing near the church bridge. She was smiling at him.

"Good evening, Miss Brenton," he said very politely.

"Good evening, Mr. Cuff," she said, moving toward him.

"My, you look lovely."

"Thank you," she said. It was too dark now to see if she was blushing, because the door was closed.

"Would you mind if I walked you home, Miss Brenton?"

"It would be a pleasure, Mr. Cuff."

"Call me Willie," he said.

"And you can call me Lillian."

"Okay, Lillian. Thank you," he said as he held out his arm. She found him to be very charming, and as she caught his arm she felt a warmth go through her as she had never felt before.

The people standing around saw the two of them disappear into the darkness as they slowly walked along the narrow road toward her home.

After the morning session at school, Cuff came home at twelve-thirty. He sat at the table and was greeted by Virtue Burton. Jim wasn't around; he was out hauling his trawls. When Cuff finished eating, he sat drinking tea.

"Did you have a good morning at school?" Mrs. Burton politely asked.

"Very busy, but good," he replied.

"I guess you'll always find it that way, especially with a crowd of children," she replied.

"Yes, for sure," he said.

"Did you enjoy the meeting last night?" she asked.

"Yes, I certainly did. I could have stayed there longer."

"I'm glad you joined us. You're welcome any time."

"Thank you," he said.

Mrs. Burton lifted the kettle back from the centre of the stove. "I heard you walked Lillian Brenton home last night. Isn't she a lovely girl? She deserves a good man. I'm glad you walked her home."

Cuff squirmed as he searched for the right words. "Yes, Mrs. Burton, I'm glad I walked her home too. She seems to be a very pleasant girl, and very intelligent."

"Have you met her father, Walter Brenton? He's a good man and loves his family."

"No, I haven't met him, but I think I've seen him."

She then leaned over and whispered, "You know, William, Edwin used to take her out, but I heard that Walter was against it because he knew that Edwin was too friendly with Wes and Sod Mugford. I couldn't blame him for separating his daughter from Edwin. We tried to tell him that the Mugfords were trouble, and we were right. I'm glad that you walked her home. I hope you continue to do so."

"I just walked her home, Mrs. Burton. I don't know, I may never see her again."

Mrs. Burton grinned and said, "You'll see her again, William. I can see it in your eyes."

Willie Cuff laughed.

As the school day ended and Cuff walked into his boarding house, he came face to face with Edwin Burton.

"How are you, Edwin?" he asked.

Jim Burton was sitting at the table. It was obvious that Jim, his wife and Edwin had been in a heated conversation. Cuff hurried to his bedroom and shut the door.

"I tell you, Edwin, you'll get in deep trouble," said Jim. "What do you think Jack Caravan will do for you?"

"He'll get me a job."

"Where?" asked Jim.

"In the woods, cutting pulpwood at Roberts Arm," said Edwin.

"Yes, I can see you now in the woods with the crosscut and axe. You're not a lumberjack."

"Jack's doing all right," said Edwin.

"Now listen, Edwin. Jack Caravan's a different man than you. He's big and tough—he can cut wood, and he knows everyone up there."

"Well, that's just it," replied Edwin. "He knows everybody. He can get me in the camp."

"When do you plan to go, Edwin?" asked Mrs. Burton.

"Tomorrow morning, Mom."

"I hate to see you go, Edwin. Is there anyone else going from here besides Jack?"

"Yes," replied Edwin. "Wesley Mugford."

"Well, God help us," said Jim. "'Tis all bad enough for Jack Caravan to drag you away, but to take Wes Mugford with you! There's no one knows what trouble you'll get into. All you need now is the devil himself, Old Sod."

Edwin was angry. "Listen, Dad. Sod Mugford never did anything to you in his life."

"Just a moment," said Jim. "Yes, he did."

"What did he do?"

Jim looked at Edwin, then replied, "Look at yourself, son. You're twenty years old. Sod Mugford has turned you into an old man. When you were twelve he was teaching you to swear, he was giving you the baccy when you were fourteen, and when you were fifteen he was giving you moonshine to drink. And now he's sending you away with Jack Caravan to work in the logging camps."

Edwin said nothing.

"What do you want, my son?" asked Jim.

"I want to borrow ten dollars."

"Okay, I'll give it to you tomorrow morning when the boat leaves."

"Okay," said Edwin, and went out the door.

"Edwin," Jim called after him.

The door opened and Edwin looked inside. "Yes, Dad, what is it?"

"How long will you be gone?"

"Until Christmas." Edwin left and shut the door.

"I don't know what will happen to Edwin," said Mrs. Burton. "I wonder if Sod's going?" she said with a worried look.

"I would say he is," said Jim.

Sod Mugford had been up there working before, but not cutting wood. He was working in a forge, making sledges and shoeing horses. He was a hard worker and a powerful man. When he went to work on a job there was no trouble with him, and people around logging camps thought a lot of him. The same went for the fishing boat. Azariah Roberts had said that without the booze Sod would have been a perfect man, due to his ability to work.

As they were talking, the next door neighbour, Bob Huxter, came in. "How are you today, Jim?" he asked.

"I'm not very pleased, Bob. We were just into it with Edwin. He's leaving tomorrow morning with Jack Caravan to go up into the woods, he said. He's going in around Roberts Arm somewhere."

"I know where they're going," Bob said. "They're not going to Roberts Arm. They're going into the Millertown area. I just heard that Sod and Wes are going. Sod got a job up there somewhere, repairing sledges with Hugh Cole up on the Mary Ann Lake. One of the boys was telling me about it."

"Is that so?" Jim mused. "I figured there was more to it than that. Jack Caravan came back yesterday, and he hasn't left Sod's presence since he came. I suppose I should stop him. Edwin wanted ten dollars, but he won't get a cent from me. They'll only booze it away."

"Listen, Jim. You might as well make up your mind. You can't stop Edwin. He's sure to go, money or not. Maybe it's the best thing for him, to get out and see what it's like to make a living for himself."

Jim drummed his fingers on the table and said, "Maybe you're right."

# Chapter 8

Happy Tucker had built a small three-room house in L'Anse au Pigeon. Az Roberts and his crew of men had helped him during the blowy days. They built it on Az's land near his barn. He had a large wind charger that gave electricity to his fishing premises and kept his wet-cell batteries charged up. He ran wires to Happy's house and gave him electricity.

Happy and his wife Mary were very grateful. They had made up their minds that they would stay at L'Anse au Pigeon the winter of 1928-29, especially now since they would be building a Salvation Army barracks in the town.

In the first week of October, Happy received a telegram from Bessie. It read, "Sod gone work. Millertown. Coming with you for winter. Arriving next week. Signed Bessie."

Bessie's welfare was a constant concern to Happy. He knew that Sod's drinking caused horror for his daughter and her children. However, if she moved to the Pigeon, their troubles might end. Although he knew there would be a problem finding a place for her to live, he was prepared to look after her. He would have to talk to Az.

He took the telegram to Winnie, Az's daughter, and she read it to the crowd.

Aunt Emily Jane was glad. "At least Old Sod isn't coming. That's one good thing about it, 'cause I don't want to see another moonshine can here in L'Anse au Pigeon." Az said nothing. He liked a little 'shine every now and then with hot water, or sometimes straight.

Az had quite a lot of lumber on hand. "I think we could build a small house for Bessie," he said. "If everyone joined in, we could have it finished in a week. We could have two small bedrooms, a kitchen and a pantry."

Happy said, "You could build it next to me, right over that big flat rock."

"Yes," Az agreed. "All we need are the nails and felt. I have some windows and an outside door."

"I don't think it will take us very long to put the four walls up. I'd say that it would only take us about a day," said Happy.

"For sure," said Az. "Happy, you wire Bessie and tell her to bring her stove, feather beds fitted, washing tub and dishes, and tell her to bring some floor canvas for the kitchen." He stopped. He knew she might not have any money. "Tell her to go to Peter Brooks and tell him to ship me a roll of floor canvas and a Waterloo stove. She can use that, and we'll be needing the stove in the spring."

"Okay," said Happy. He knew Az would help her. It was too bad about Sod's drinking and fighting. If he would only get saved, thought Happy. What a relief it would be to Bessie.

"Happy, you go and round up the crowd and tell them to come to the cookhouse in about an hour."

"Okay," he said, and away he went.

It took less than a week to build a two-bedroom house for Bessie Mugford. There were many problems facing them, and the biggest was finding firewood for the winter. On Quirpon Island there was very little wood growing; the trees were just shrubs. What did grow there was hugging the ground. Az had to send a boat and a crew to Pistolet Bay for a load of wood to keep Bessie going for the winter. Az also knew that when

Sod came back to L'Anse au Pigeon next spring and saw the new house, he wouldn't leave as long as there was lots of fish caught in L'Anse au Pigeon. But there was one thing Emily Jane impressed upon Az, and that was to make sure it was clear to Happy and Bessie when she arrived that he was only letting her live in the house temporarily, and that it was owned by Az and his firm.

It was the first week in November when Bessie arrived with her three children. Happy was so excited to see his grandchildren.

Everybody helped put Bessie's things in place. They had two bedsteads and a couch, and for the first time Bessie now had a brand new stove and plenty of wood to burn. Az supplied the food for her and her children. She was under the umbrella of Az Roberts, and she knew that as long as he had a store full of everything, he would never let her go hungry.

Willie Cuff was doing quite well with his teaching job. Everything was going fine. He breathed a sigh of relief when Sod and Wes Mugford left town and went to the lumber camps.

He was also relieved when Edwin went away. There were two reasons. First, there was no tension around the boarding house. Secondly, Cuff had no worries about anyone saying something to him about his going out with Lillian. Cuff loved her, there was no doubt about it, and she was in love with him. They saw each other whenever his work permitted it. She would visit him at Jim's house, or he would go to her house in Lushes Bight. Though Cuff was as busy as a bee, it was a very exciting time for him. His love for Lillian made it all seem like heaven.

When the news came to him that Bessie Mugford was going down to live on the French Shore with her father, Cuff was even more relieved. Some said she was leaving Sod. Others said she was running away from him, that she couldn't take any more, and that she was taking her youngsters and going for good. Cuff told Lillian he wasn't happy to see anyone leave town, but to be rid of Sod and Wes would be a relief. He assured Lillian that he wasn't frightened of what they might do, but the truth was he had been uneasy and even a little scared whenever he saw them.

Hugh Cole was a woods manager for the AND Company, in charge of the Badger area for over forty years. He was known as the mayor of Badger. When he met Sod Mugford, he hired him to go around to the camps doing sledge repairs, working out of the forge in Badger.

Sod Mugford was glad when he was advised by the foreman that Bessie and the children had gone down to L'Anse au Pigeon with her father for the winter. He knew that Az Roberts would never let them be hungry or go cold; they would be better off there than at home. Besides, he wouldn't have to go home as often.

One night, Sod came to the logging camps where Wes and Edwin were cutting pulp. He was sent there to help repair the horse-sledge and make new ones. Sod worked mostly with iron. It was a great reunion, although they had only been separated for six weeks.

"Have you heard any news from home?" asked Wes.

"Oh yes, there's lots of news from home," Sod replied.

"What is it?" asked Edwin.

"I had a word from Bess a couple of weeks ago. She's left home and gone down to L'Anse au Pigeon with Az Roberts for the winter." They laughed.

"Old Az will take care of her," said Wes.

"Well, no, she won't be living with Az and Aunt Emily Jane. She's going to live with her father next door to Az. It's the same as being in the house with him. For sure they'll be eating out of the one flour barrel," said Sod.

"So, you got it made now for the rest of the winter, Sod. You don't even have to go home if you don't want to. Did you hear anything else?" asked Wes.

Sod started to grin. "Yes," he said, "there's lots of old news flying around. Someone said that Cuff's getting married to Lillian Brenton pretty soon, and Edwin is invited to the wedding!"

Sod looked at Edwin with a mocking grin. Edwin blushed but said nothing. He knew Sod was rubbing it in, how Cuff had taken his girl from him.

Wes started to swear. He looked at Edwin. "If it was me, he wouldn't get away with it, if it was the last thing I'd do."

Edwin looked at Wes. "You have no room to talk, Wes. Look at what he did to you. He gave you a lacing and challenged Sod, so don't give me that. You fellows haven't done anything."

"Just a minute, Edwin. I know how you feel about Lillian, but as for me and Wes, we're going to get even with Mr. Cuff." Sod was getting angry. He took out a cigarette.

"How do you plan to get even with Cuff, Sod?" Edwin asked.

"Poison the bastard," Sod said as he lit the cigarette between his teeth.

Edwin was silent. The blood drained from his face.

Wes spoke up. "How do you plan to do that, Sod?"

Before Sod could answer, Jack Caravan came into the bunkhouse and walked over to them.

"Sod," he said, "how are you doing?" He and Sod shook hands.

"Not bad, old buddy. How have you been?"

"Pretty good, only the wood's bad. Any news from home?"

Sod told Jack about Bessie and the children.

"Tell him about the wedding, Sod," said Wes. He winked at Jack. Jack knew that they had been tormenting Edwin.

"I suppose we'll all go home to the wedding when it takes place," Jack said, laughing.

"I'll 'wedding' Cuff when I land my feet back home again," said Sod.

"I wouldn't put up with it," said Jack. "I've got to go, boys."

He got up and left.

"Now, what were you talking about, Sod?" asked Edwin very anxiously.

"Well, Edwin my son, every day I handles enough poison to kill every soul in Beaumont ten times over, and if we could get some of that stuff down inside Cuff's gullet he would go belly up pretty quick."

Wes took a long draw on a cigarette. "How would you get that into him, Sod? Tie him up and pour it down his throat?"

"No, no, me hearties," he said. "I got the plan all made up."

"Well, how?" asked Edwin.

"It's like this, Edwin. You have to play the biggest part. I was talking to a buddy of mine the other day out at Badger. He used to be overseas in the fourteen-eighteen war. He was telling me what some fellows done. They put some flux in rum, mixed it fifty-fifty and gave it to a couple of Germans. It killed them instantly. So, if we mixed some in moonshine and gave it to Cuff, he would be gone pretty quick."

Wes was excited. "Let's head for home right away," he said.

Edwin spoke up. "Cuff doesn't drink. He told us so when he came."

Sod held up his hand. "Edwin, that's your job, to get him drinking at Christmas when we go home."

Edwin and Wes started to grin.

"That's a month's time, Sod," said Edwin.

"Yes," said Sod. "But let me tell you one thing, boys. Keep this to yourselves. Don't tell one soul."

They promised they wouldn't.

"What time are you leaving for home, Sod?" asked Edwin.

"I'm leaving Badger on the twentieth of December. That's when you fellows will have to be in Badger, so we'll leave together." They agreed.

"Let's get Jack to help us," said Edwin.

"Okay," said Sod. Satisfied with the plans, he got up and went to his own bunkhouse.

It was a cold evening at L'Anse au Pigeon. The sun had gone down behind the middle hill with a she-moon—a new moon lying on its back—hanging low in the western sky. Az Roberts sat at the kitchen table with his daughter, Winnie. They were doing an audit of his summer's fishing activity and sale of goods to the town. Sitting near the stove was Gideon Hancock, the young Salvation Army officer. He was playing a concertina, and Emily Jane was singing along with the tune.

Az was disturbed, because he wanted to get the paperwork done. The sound of the fifty-two-button concertina and his wife's singing *Will you go, will you go, oh say will you go to the Eden above* drove his blood pressure up. He knew how to stop the singing. He winked at Winnie and said, "Just a minute, Gid. Come here."

Gideon stopped the music. "Did you say something, Skipper?" He knew that the skipper didn't appreciate too much of his religious activity, especially so early in the evening. However, Aunt Emily Jane insisted on his playing all the time if he would do it.

"Yes," said Az. "Come over to the table." Gideon Hancock put down the small instrument and pulled a chair up to the table. Az lit his pipe, then said, "I'm thinking about starting a chapter of the Orange Lodge here in the Pigeon pretty soon, Gid. I figured there's enough of us here now with the men from Quirpon. We could have a good crowd."

Gideon grinned. He knew what was coming next.

Emily Jane, who was knitting and gently rocking in her chair, looked at her husband with an arched eyebrow. She stopped rocking.

Emily Jane was a tall woman. She wore glasses and was always well dressed. Whenever she rose in the morning she would put a brooch on her dress, or whatever she was wearing, which had the crest of the Salvation Army. Behind her back, Az would say that she was a religious fanatic.

"Say that again, Fred, my dear." His full name was Azariah Frederick Roberts, and in private she always called him Fred. "Did I hear something about the Orange Lodge?"

"Yes, Mrs. Roberts," said Gideon.

"What was it I heard?" she asked.

"Oh, never mind, Mom," said Winnie. "Pop was only joking."

"No, I wasn't joking," said Az.

"What did you say, anyway?" Emily Jane asked.

"I said I was going to start an Orange Lodge here in the Pigeon," said Az.

She put down her knitting and tucked her white apron in around her legs on both sides. "You know what you promised me after that trip to St. John's, Az." The gentleness of "Fred, my dear" was gone.

While they were on a business trip in St. John's a few years before, accompanied by their close friends, Ned Fontaine and his wife Anastasia, the two men went out for a night on the town—at least this is what they had told their wives.

Az had other plans. He had everything arranged in advance to go to the Orange Lodge at St. John's and take the degree of the Red Cross, a high order in the Orange Lodge. The only one who knew anything about it was his buddy Ned Fontaine, who was a Roman Catholic.

At five o'clock the next morning, the two lads came back to the hotel, drunk as lords. Az had charged Ned not to tell Emily Jane about it, because he knew how much it would upset her. But when they opened the door to let them in, Ned said, "Ladies, make way for the Red Cross man, Azariah Roberts."

Az said later that if he'd had a gun he would have shot Ned. But the cat was out of the bag and Emily Jane was very upset. She cried for two days. She told him that if she had somewhere to go, she would leave him. She said, "Az, what you've done is something I'll never forgive you for. You broke your promise to me."

He had said, "I got a gold ring, Emily Jane, solid gold."

"Where is it, Az?"

"I have it in my pocket. It's too small. The only finger I can get it on is my little finger."

She looked at him. "Az," she said, "that Red Cross ring will be a curse to you. You just wait and see."

Ned Fontaine spoke up for his friend. "Aunt Emily Jane, leave him alone. That will never hurt him, even if he had half a dozen Red Cross rings!" He laughed.

Mrs. Fontaine said to her husband, "'Tis a wonder you didn't join the Red Cross crowd yourself. You're foolish enough."

Old Ned laughed. "As soon as I get back home, I'm going to St. Anthony and joining the Orange Lodge right away." He grinned and looked at Emily Jane. "Or the Salvation Army."

Anastasia Fontaine said, "You're too big a drunk for that, Ned." He doubled over, laughing.

"Listen, Emily Jane," said Az, "you're right. I realize now that I did break my promise to you. I'm sorry for that. I'll never go to the Orange Lodge again."

"I'll hold you to your promise."

The ring was too small for Az's finger, so when he returned home, he went to his forge. With a hacksaw, he cut the ring and pried it open enough to fit his middle finger. Then he filled the open space with lead.

For the past two years, every time he looked at the Red Cross ring he was reminded of what he had promised Emily Jane.

With his hands under the table, Az twisted the ring around on his finger as her warning rang in his ears. *That Red Cross ring will be a curse to you. You just wait and see.*

"Okay, Emily Jane," he said. "Okay."

"Remember, Fred, you're not dead yet. The Man above knows it all."

Az was sorry he had brought it up. "Oh, forget it," he said. "Gid, go back to that squeezebox again and play 'til she goes to sleep."

Gideon laughed as he picked up the concertina and started to play and sing, *We invite you all to come along we'll have a glorious time, we're going to a country where the moon-light never shines.*

Az looked at Winnie and sighed. "Winn," he said, "give me the report on the cod oil." Winnie laughed as they continued their business.

# Chapter 9

It was a few days before Christmas when Sod Mugford, Edwin Burton and Jack Caravan returned to Beaumont. They had quite a lot of money to spend.

Cuff had just come home from the school when he saw Edwin coming in the yard. His mind immediately raced to Lillian. What would Edwin do or say to him? He hadn't had time to think of any defense.

Edwin stepped inside.

"Edwin!" yelled Mrs. Burton. She was surprised to see him. She ran to him and they hugged and kissed with great affection.

When the excitement of meeting his mother was over, he noticed Cuff for the first time. "Willie," he said. "Good to see you. How have you been?" He held out his hand and gave Cuff a hearty handshake.

"I'm fine. And how are you?"

"I'm great. I've worked hard pushing the crosscut." He laughed.

*Well,* thought Cuff, *there are no hard feelings here. Maybe the trip away from home straightened Edwin out.* He was very friendly and pleasant. For sure he had heard about his and

Lillian's wedding plans. Maybe Edwin had found another girl. He hoped so.

At that moment Jim came in. He and his wife were overjoyed to see Edwin. Jim was a very happy man, in fact. He had no son of his own, but longed for one, so he thought about adoption. When Edwin came along, and was available, Jim was delighted when his wife agreed. Edwin had always been a very obedient child and was a model son until he started getting involved with Sod Mugford. One thing led to another, until he had come home drunk, and Jim could smell tobacco on him. And before long, Edwin started to answer him back, to the point of becoming saucy, and the next thing, they were shouting in full-scale arguments. But Jim Burton still loved him.

After the excitement settled down and supper was cleared away, Edwin got into a conversation with Cuff, telling him about the woods work and life in the logging camps. He told him about poor Wes, how he looked forward to coming home for Christmas. The day before they were supposed to leave for Beaumont, Wes had cut himself and had to go to Grand Falls to the hospital. He would have to stay there over the holidays.

"It's too bad he couldn't make it home for Christmas," Edwin said. He then asked Cuff if there was anything going on around town, such as a time or a dance or perhaps a house party.

"I think there's a time scheduled for Christmas Eve at the Orange Lodge. Later, on Boxing Day, there's a soup supper and a square dance at the Lodge."

"That's great," said Edwin. "You and I have to buddy up at Christmas and go."

Cuff was shocked to hear it. "We sure will," he said, anxious to become Edwin's friend.

"I know you're going out with Lillian," Edwin said, "but I don't mind that. She's free to have whoever she wants. There are lots of girls around. Maybe I could get a date with her younger sister, Blanche. To tell you the truth, I thought more about Blanche Brenton than I did Lillian." Edwin was careful to say the things that Cuff wanted to hear.

*Well, well,* thought Cuff. *This is quite a surprise. It's a wonder how people can change.*

"Sure," said Cuff. "Maybe Lillian could arrange that."

"We'll see," said Edwin. "I'm not the fellow I used to be. I haven't been hanging around Sod or Wes since I left here." He smiled and nodded in all the right places, and Cuff believed every word of it. "Maybe we should take a dodge around shore the once," Edwin said.

"Sure," said Cuff. "What time should we go?"

Edwin took out a new pocketwatch. "Oh, around eight o'clock."

"Okay," said Cuff. "I have some school work to do first, but I'll be ready by eight." He left and went to his room.

When Cuff shut the door, Edwin ground his teeth. "The plan is working, Sod," he said to himself. "I think he might fall for it, as you said. Give him lots of rope and he'll hang himself."

Edwin grinned and added, "Or poison himself."

Jack Caravan was not the bravest man in the world. He knew that if he got into trouble of any kind, his father would go completely berserk. He was afraid of him. His father used to say, "Jack, if you ever get in any trouble around here, don't come home, because you'll never set foot in this house again. And if I ever know you to poke your nose under Sod Mugford's roof, stay there." Jack wouldn't say anything, but he couldn't understand how his old man could go to church on Sunday and hate Sod Mugford so much on Monday.

He asked his mother the same question. She said, "'Tis not the fact that he hates Sod, Jack. It's because of poor Bessie and her youngsters. Look how Sod treats them. The only comfort she gets is when she goes down to L'Anse au Pigeon summertime with Az Roberts. And that's because Sod is afraid of Az."

"Don't go talking about Az Roberts, Mom," said Jack. "That's all I've heard the whole time I was growin' up, Az Roberts this, Az Roberts that. The old man thinks he's some kind of a god."

"Don't let your father hear you say that, whatever you do. Your father is the Worshipful Master in the Lodge, and Az is a Red Cross man. So, for goodness sake, don't get a racket going."

Jack snorted. "One thing about it, Mom. If I was Sod, I would never go handy to Bessie and her youngsters again. They could stay at L'Anse au Pigeon, for all I care."

Sod Mugford went to his father's house when he returned home. It was getting dark. He was in a very bad mood. He had a three-weeks beard, and first looking at him one would say that he had been dragged up from the bottom of the ocean. As he walked into his father's house, he knew he wouldn't receive a warm welcome.

Sam Mugford was sitting at the table, about to have supper. A loaf of bread was on the table near him, and a large sheath knife was pushed through it.

The old man looked up when Sod walked in.

"Oh," he said, kind of surprised. "You is back." Sod didn't speak. "I thought you was goin' to stay for the winter."

"No, I'm back," said Sod.

"How long is you goin' to stay, Sod?"

"Not very long, maybe a couple days."

The old man picked up the loaf of bread and pulled the knife out. He held it up in the lamplight, cocked one eye, then said, "This Green River cuts like a lance." He looked at Sod. As quick as a wink, with one stroke he cut off a slice of bread and flicked it at him. Sod caught it. "You can stay here one night, Sod, seeing the sun is gone below. But tomorrow you is in your own house."

"Okay," said Sod as he walked to the table and picked up the molasses jar.

The old man started to eat.

"So, Sod, yer Bessie's gone down with Az Roberts and took 'er youngsters with her. I guess you's happy now. Look. She said to me before she left to tell you if you came back that you isn't to poke your ugly nose down in L'Anse au Pigeon. If you do, she'll have Az give you a lacin'. Said Az can do it, see."

Sod grinned. "Where's the old woman?"

"I wish she was gone down with Az Roberts too. I'd be a lot better off." Sod wisely kept his comments to himself. He had to stay here for the night.

Then the old man added, "She spends her time playing cards from house to house. There's nothing else I can do to her, only kick her out." Again Sod had to keep the old man on side, so he didn't comment. His father stopped eating for a moment, then asked, "Where's Wes at, Sod? How come he's not home?"

Sod answered his father without looking at him. "He chopped his foot and had to go to Grand Falls hospital. He might be there for a month."

The old man didn't show any emotion. "How stupid is he? Didn't he have anything else to cut?"

"He could have cut his throat."

The old man waved his knife. "Or yours. Maybe he should come home and do a little job on that schoolteacher, the one who laced him with the leather belt." He plunged the knife into the loaf of bread again. "I reared a bunch of men who is gutless. They even let a skinny rat like Cuff beat them up and make a laughin' stock of every Mugford in Beaumont. By rights, Sod, I should make you sleep out in the dog's house."

"You just wait, old man, 'til we're finished with him. I got his medicine in a mustard bottle, all ready for him. Just wait and see."

His father shook his head. "I've heard that before, Sod. Seeing is believing."

Sod thought about the rumours going around about Cuff and the Mugfords. "Wait and see," he said. "You just wait and see."

Seventy years later, Mr. Bert Parsons sat in an easy chair near the table at the seniors home in Springdale, Newfoundland. He was close to ninety years old, but his memory was extraordinarily sharp.

"I know more about that nasty affair than anybody," he stated.

"I was going to the Orange Lodge to attend a meeting. It was dark. I heard Sod and Edwin was home from the woods. We always said that if Sod and Wes came back, there would be nothing too bad that they wouldn't do with young Cuff. As I was walking along, I saw Sod coming. It was a pretty good evening. When he got close to me, I recognized him.

"'How are you, Sod?' I said. 'I heard you was home.' He just grunted. 'There's a Lodge meeting tonight. You should go,' I said. Sod was a member of the Orange Lodge, you see.

"'I wouldn't be caught dead there,' he replied.

"'What are you up to, over on this side of the harbour?' I asked. He was making me mad.

"He started to walk away, then turned around and said, 'I got a score to settle, Bert, and when I gets it done I'll be leaving. But none of it is any of your business.' He then turned and walked away, mumbling and swearing as he went.

"I can't say if he mentioned Cuff's name or not, but I said to him, 'You be careful, Sod, because Cuff has a lot of friends here now. If you harm one hair on his head, the people here will break your neck.'

"Sod looked back and said, 'He may break his own neck before it's all over.' He went past the Orange Lodge and the old school, and I saw him stop at Jim Burton's. He appeared to be waiting for young Edwin."

Edwin Burton looked at the timepiece on the shelf over the table. It was 7:00 p.m. He knew he was supposed to meet Sod at seven somewhere between his and Sod's house. He had become so distracted with the Christmas tree his mother had decorated, he had forgotten all about the hatred he had for Cuff. He even forgot the raging jealousy he had for Lillian. For a few minutes he had been trying to guess what was in the packages under the tree.

"I have to go," he said suddenly, and sprang to his feet.

"Don't forget, Edwin, that you and Mr. Cuff are supposed to go visiting at eight. He'll be waiting for you." Mrs. Burton seemed so happy.

"I won't forget, Mother," he assured her, and rushed out the door. As he stepped outside, he saw Sod standing in the light shining from Cuff's bedroom window.

Inside, Willie Cuff was sitting at a small table, working on some school reports. He had a few more details to take care of. Tomorrow would be Christmas Eve, and they were going to have a Christmas tree party at the school. However, he could hardly concentrate on his work after meeting Edwin.

"I wonder what could have made him change his attitude toward me, especially now that I'm going out with Lillian?" He smiled at the thought of her name.

Edwin noticed that Sod was staring at Cuff's window, and he noted the scowl on Sod's ugly face.

"Look at that in there," said Sod.

"Don't talk so loud, Sod. Someone might hear you," whispered Edwin.

"I wish I had a .22 rifle. I'd lodge a bullet in the back of his head pretty quick. He wouldn't get the chance to drink the flux. I say flux is too good for him."

Edwin looked through the window. "You're right, Sod, you're right, but we can't shoot him. We'd never get away with it. Come on." Edwin had to drag him away from the house. Sod gave one last sneer at the window before he turned and left with Edwin.

As they walked down the road and around the bottom of the harbour, Sod started to cool down some. "I had four bottles of moonshine brought in from outside this evening, and I'm going to polish off a bottle right now."

Edwin stopped. He said, "No, you're not, Sod."

Sod almost jumped out of his boots. He narrowed his eyes at Edwin. "You young squirt! Who do you think you're talking to?"

There is no doubt that, if Sod had been drinking, he would have had Edwin by the throat. Edwin put his hand on Sod's shoulder. "Sod," he said, "we have been planning for a long time to make away with Cuff. We have all the details in place, and part of our plan is that you wouldn't go drinking before it happened. You got a long tongue when you're drinking. You said so yourself."

"Take your hand off my shoulder, Edwin Burton."

"Listen, Sod. If you have as much as one hot toddy, I'm calling the whole thing off. Do you hear me?"

"Okay, Edwin," Sod growled, "but don't be saucy with me, all right?"

"I'm not being saucy with you, Sod. I'm just trying to keep you in line with our plans, so listen."

Sod was more obsessed with killing Cuff than either Edwin or Wes, although Cuff hadn't done anything to him personally. He figured that, due to the fact that Cuff had strapped Wes, he had done it to him too. After rehearsing it a thousand times with Wes and Edwin that fall in the lumber camps, he was now ready to kill Cuff all by himself in broad daylight, anywhere, and in front of anybody. With four bottles of moonshine under his pillow to keep him company, he was prepared to sit in his house until Cuff came to him.

"I got the fire lit. It should be warmed up by now," Sod said. He was cold and looking forward to getting indoors.

"Okay," said Edwin.

It didn't take them very long to go around the bottom of the harbour to Sod's bungalow.

Bessie had taken most of the homemade furniture with her when she moved down to L'Anse au Pigeon. There were no tables or chairs left. There were two stools along the wall, so he went into the bedroom, dragged out a dresser and put it in the middle of the kitchen near the stove.

"I wish I had old Bess holt now by the hair of the head. She would get a fast ride from the Pigeon to Beaumont, I can guarantee you that, Edwin," said Sod, shaking his fist. "Imagine," he shouted, "she down there with Az Roberts. The likes was never heard before."

Edwin wouldn't comment on that for fear of upsetting him.

Sod looked at Edwin. "When this job's over," he said, "after we gets the flux in the body of Cuff, I'm going straight back to Badger for the winter. In fact, I'll never return to this mangy place again."

"Me, too," said Edwin.

They were silent for a moment.

Edwin started talking. "Sod," he said in a low voice, "I did as you told me. I shook hands with Cuff. In fact, I almost hugged him. I could tell he took me serious. He agreed to go out around with me sometime around eight o'clock. Imagine, going out with me."

"Yes," added Sod with a grin, "his murderer."

The word "murder" still frightened Edwin a little, though they had talked about it so often within the last two months that the shock was beginning to soften.

"Sod, I'm going to bring Cuff over here to meet you now."

Sod jumped. "Oh, no yer not, Edwin," he yelled.

"Why not? Didn't we say this is how it would go?"

"No, we didn't," said Sod. "We said *you* would get friendly with Cuff."

"Why not bring him here?" asked Edwin.

"Not on your life. He'll never poke his nose in here."

"All right," said Edwin. "But how do we get him to drink? Mom says he's never taken a drink in his life."

"That's the best part. He don't know what moonshine tastes like. He won't know the difference if we can get him to drink it. I'll have it all ready. I'll have the bottle of flux in my left pocket, and moonshine in an identical bottle in my right pocket. Jack will be there. He'll edge him on. Jack will have some water for a chaser. Once we get a good gulp down in him, he's a goner. The people will think he's drunk on moonshine. As soon as he passes out, I'll throw some 'shine over his mouth. He'll stink like a billy goat. I can tell you this much. You'll have no more worries about losing Lillian Brenton to Cuff."

Sod could see that Edwin was nervous. "You got no worries, Edwin. No one will ever find out. Flux leaves no marks."

"I know, I know," said Edwin. "We've gone over that a thousand times up in the camp. What worries me is I'll have to tell Mom and Dad so many lies. I'm not sure if I'll be able to lie good enough to convince them."

Sod swore. "What? Are you getting faint-hearted? I knew you was a weasel. Just wait 'til Wes comes back." He glared at Edwin.

"Just a minute, Sod, just a minute. I'm not afraid, and I'm going to go through with our plans. The only thing is, I want to be sure for afterwards, so we don't get caught."

Sod stood and paced the floor. "I should get my old mother to do it instead of you. It seems like she's the only one here in Beaumont that got either bit of guts in her. She wouldn't mind putting a bullet square between his two eyes."

"Sit down," said Edwin. "I am not getting faint-hearted. I want to do it, and the sooner the better."

Sod sat down, reassured. "Edwin, that's more like it. You see, I'm only doing it for you. Don't you see how you would spend the rest of your life? Imagine seeing Lillian and Cuff next door with a crowd of youngsters, laughing at you every day. 'Tis all bad enough, so get rid of him while you got the chance. I'll take the blame. Don't worry."

Edwin gave Sod the same broad smile he had given Willie Cuff earlier. "Good enough. We'll go full steam ahead."

"Good," said Sod. "Get him used to the taste of moonshine by Boxing Day. Now, you'd better go. He'll be waiting for you." He laughed, then said, "And kiss him if you got to."

"If I have to, I will. Just stick to your part of the plan." Edwin stepped outside to go meet with Willie Cuff.

# Chapter 10

Cuff and Edwin spent the next few days going from house to house. Everyone was surprised to see them together.

Cuff was very pleasantly surprised and relieved to have Edwin's friendship. It was more than he had really hoped for. He thought more than once that night how Edwin had changed in such a few short months. It was a blessing to everyone, especially to his mother and father. And what a relief it would be to Lillian. They had talked about it every time they were together.

Cuff and Lillian had feared the day when the Mugfords and Edwin would return. They had decided they would stop going back and forth to Lushes Bight and Beaumont alone, especially at night, for fear of being attacked by them. But now Cuff's fears were gone. Edwin was his friend. He was convinced of it.

They were walking back to the house at about 11:00 p.m. They had just left the Orange Lodge, of which Edwin was a member. They had only dropped in for half an hour.

They arrived at the boarding house, and Mrs. Burton had a lunch prepared for them on the table. She was so happy. She was convinced that Edwin had changed. He had even brought home some money, and a gift for her and Jim.

Cuff and the Burton family went to bed with contented minds.

As Edwin lay in bed and thought about his conversation with Sod, he realized that he was a very dangerous man, and he was sure that Sod would kill him if he didn't do as instructed. He thought about Lillian, and couldn't bear the thought of Cuff going out with her. His mind raced. He felt rage rise up in him. But murder? Maybe it would be better if he took Cuff over to Sod's house and let him beat up the schoolteacher right and proper. Perhaps Sod would stop at that. The other option was murder, and for sure, they would all hang.

*Just a little flux in moonshine, just a little flux in moonshine.* These words sounded and resounded back and forth through Edwin's mind as he drifted off to sleep.

Walter Brenton lived in Lushes Bight, just a hop, skip and a jump, as they say, from Beaumont. It was a fifteen- to twenty-minute walk. Almost everyone went back and forth night and day. The dogs and cats went back and forth, the sheep and goats went back and forth, and lovers went back and forth. This included young Cuff and Lillian. Walter Brenton kept a pretty close watch on his two daughters; he wouldn't let them walk the trail alone after dark, and he wouldn't go to bed until they came home.

Walter was sitting near the stove in his kitchen binding a dogs harness, when Stewart Brenton, his cousin, walked in. Walter had a large darning needle and cod twine.

"What are you doing, Uncle Walt?" Stew asked.

"Bindin' this dog's harness, see? It belongs to Jumbo. He got it all busted up. He won't bust this one up when I'm finished."

Stewart looked at what he was doing. "He must be a strong brute, Uncle Walt. I wish I had three or four like him." The two men talked about the dogs and the firewood. The conversation shifted to Az Roberts and about the team of dogs he had when he lived in Lushes Bight. Stew's mother was Sarah Roberts Brenton, and Az was his uncle.

Finally, their conversation turned to current events. "I wonder why Old Sod didn't go down to L'Anse au Pigeon instead of coming back to Beaumont for Christmas?" Stewart said. "I suppose Bessie doesn't want to see him down there for Christmas. I'd say he knows it, too."

Walter put down the harness and needle and took out his pipe. He tapped it on the stove fender, leaving a small pile of ash. "So, Sod and his gang have arrived back, is that right?"

"Yes, I've seen them. Just before dark, they walked down along here. Wes wasn't with them. There were three of them: Sod, Edwin Burton, and Jack Caravan."

Walter lit his pipe. "Watch out, now," he said. "They'll lick down some 'shine. Sod will be drunk now for a month, and this Edwin, I bet, is just as bad."

Stewart knew what was going on between Cuff and Lillian, and had learned that they were afraid of the three of them coming home for Christmas. He knew they were capable of anything.

"You just listen to what I say, Stew." Walter took a long drag from his pipe. "This is one Christmas that we won't enjoy here at Lushes Bight and Beaumont."

"Do you think so, Uncle Walt? Why?"

"'Cause, my son, Sod Mugford and his gang have come home to create a problem for someone. You just wait and see."

"What for, Uncle Walt? Do you think they'll attack the schoolteacher, Cuff?"

Walter spoke up. "Attack the schoolteacher? Yes, my son. Cuff had better stay indoors if he knows what's good for him."

"Jack has nothing against Cuff, has he?" said Stew.

"No, but he's in with Sod, and anybody that's in with Sod Mugford is game for anything."

"Uncle Walt, I don't think it's that bad. Cuff won't be going near them. You don't have to worry," Stewart said.

Walter put away his pipe and picked up his dog harness.

Stew got ready to leave. He said, "This is one Christmas I wish I was down with Uncle Az and Aunt Emily Jane."

Walter looked at him and grinned. "What's wrong with you, Stew? Are you going after Bessie? If Sod knew that, it wouldn't be Cuff he'd be after. It would be you." He started to laugh.

"Uncle Walter, you're terrible."

As Stew walked through the doorway, Walter yelled, "See you later at the Lodge."

Later that day, Walter said to his wife, "Mildred, Stewart agrees with me that Sod Mugford's up to no good and might be after William. Perhaps we shouldn't let the girls go to the Christmas party at the Lodge in Beaumont."

"Listen, Walter," Mildred said. "Don't you pay any heed to Stew. He just has a dislike for young Wes and Sod."

"Stew isn't always wrong,"

"Walter," she said, "the girls are looking forward to going to the Lodge party. Maybe we should all go."

"We'll see," he said.

Walter's fears were unfounded. The Lodge Christmas party at Beaumont went off without incident.

# Chapter 11

Beaumont was a glorious little town. Situated at the bottom of Cutwell Arm, the land in Beaumont was hilly but fertile. Everyone there was a hard worker, and all of them worked in the fishing industry. Most were employed at the inshore fishery at Beaumont, while others went to the French Shore, and farther north, to the coast of Labrador. Historians say that Beaumont was once the home of the Beothuk Indians. Artifacts have been found all over the land around the harbour, and there is no doubt that the first settlers encountered these people. If you drive through the little town today, you can easily visualize them paddling along the beaches in their birch bark canoes.

On Christmas Day, December 25, 1928, everyone in the little town was moving from house to house, visiting one another, having lunches and exchanging gifts. Everyone was enjoying the holiday, especially the old-timers.

Sod Mugford sat in his house, and he was in a very sour mood. He was still angry with Edwin Burton for chastising him about drinking. He had seen Edwin and the schoolteacher walking along the road together the night before, going up to the Orange Lodge to the time and Christmas party. He couldn't understand how Edwin could stomach such "scruff," as he called the schoolteacher. There were four bottles of moonshine sitting on the floor in the corner of the room. Sod wasn't sure he could wait for tomorrow night, to get some flux into Cuff's belly and watch him die.

"My, oh my, what a fool I am. I should go in and drink every lick of it," he said out loud. "Imagine, four bottles full." He couldn't resist it any longer. "I got to have a snort," he said as he went for the bedroom. But just as he did, he heard someone coming. He sat down again. The door opened, and his mother walked in.

"Sod," she said loudly. "What's you doin' here all alone sittin' at the washstand?"

Sod didn't answer. He hated his mother; she was nothing but a troublemaker. In fact, Bessie hated her too. They fought one time for half an hour, and if some men hadn't stepped in, Bessie would have torn her to pieces. The older woman wouldn't give in. Bessie's stepbrother Bob Tucker said that Hazel Mugford was the devil let loose. She was a tyrant, and would fight at the drop of a hat, but she was no match for Bessie.

She stood in the middle of the kitchen, looking down at Sod. He was sitting on a wooden stool, smoking a cigarette that was poorly rolled up. She inspected the interior of the house and grimaced.

"What are you lookin' for, old woman?" Sod snapped.

"'Tis none of your business. This place is a real pigsty. I can still smell old Bess here." She snarled as her beady eyes searched the kitchen.

Sod straightened up. "Look, old woman," he said. "You look too much like a witch to be under this roof, and if you don't leave I'll beat your brains out."

"Just a minute, Sod," she said with a half-grin. He knew she had some news to tell him, and it was sure to be unpleasant. For sure, she wouldn't come here to bring him good tidings.

"Do you know what's going around Long Island, Sod? Walter Brenton's friend from Lushes Bight was down here to the time at the Lodge last night. He was telling the crowd that he wouldn't be letting his girls travel alone between Lushes Bight and Beaumont after dark, for fear of them being attacked by Sod Mugford and his gang. But he said that if he was a younger man he'd measure the length of Sod Mugford and Edwin Burton, or any Mugford who lived in Beaumont, for that matter." Sod just stared at her. He knew she was goading him. "This is Christmas Day, Sod. Why isn't you drunk?"

Hazel knew that if her son had been drinking, he would be on the warpath by now. But, for some reason, he hadn't touched a stain. *I wonder why? Something must be wrong. What have they got up their sleeves? Yes, they're planning something. Maybe they're going to make away with somebody.*

She wouldn't push her luck any further. She knew Sod was capable of punching her in the mouth—he had struck her many times before.

"I'm leaving, Sod," she said.

Sod remained silent as the door clicked shut.

There was a lot of talk going through the town about Sod Mugford, Edwin Burton and the schoolteacher Cuff. What people couldn't figure out was the apparent close friendship between Edwin and Cuff. "I don't understand it," said one man. "Edwin Burton could never change that much." They were very suspicious about what was happening, because several people saw Edwin sneaking over to Sod's house several times. Also, they were seen with their heads together, talking on at least two occasions at night on the road.

"Sod and Edwin are planning something," said another man. "I bet they'll rob or even beat up young Cuff before Christmas is over. I wouldn't want to meet with them, especially after dark." Despite all the talk in the town, nobody spoke a word of advice or warning to the young schoolteacher, because they were all fearful of Sod.

On Christmas Night, there was a concert at the United Church. The United Church was formed from the amalgamation of several churches, including the fire-and-brimstone Methodists. Even Cuff took part in a play. The church was full. Walter Brenton was there with his family; Lillian and Blanche sat together, a seat ahead of their father.

Virtue Burton supplied the music for the concert, which lasted for two hours. When it was over, the minister reminded everyone that the following night, Boxing Night, there would be an old-fashioned time at the Orange Lodge, starting at 7:00 p.m., and all would be welcome. The proceeds would be going to the Ladies' Aid Society. Because of his natural reluctance for dancing, the minister didn't add the fact that there would be a square dance after the soup supper.

When everyone had gone and the instruments were being packed away, Lillian came to William. "It was a wonderful concert," she said, smiling. "There should be one every week."

"Thank you," he said. "Where are you going now, Lillian?"

Last night he had seen her only briefly. Her father and mother had come with them to search for the Christmas tree, and they had all walked back together. Her father said he came with them because he was afraid to send his two daughters alone, for fear of the dogs. And tonight was the same.

"We're going back home to Lushes Bight, Willie," she said.

"Why?" he asked.

"Dad says there's a lot of strange dog teams around, and he's afraid we might get attacked by some of them."

Cuff figured it could be possible. "Stay down overnight," he said.

"Dad wouldn't let me, but don't worry. I'll see you later over Christmas, after he cools down."

"Will you be here for the dance tomorrow night?" he asked.

"No," she said, "we're going to be busy."

Cuff was disappointed. "Okay," he said, "I'll see you later." Lillian joined her family and left.

Cuff helped the others put the rest of the equipment away and left the church. He felt a little angry. He couldn't see how or why Lillian had to go home with her parents. Maybe her father didn't trust him anymore. For some reason he was keeping a very tight rope on his two daughters. Cuff grumbled to himself as he walked.

"Hey, Cuff," a voice called from behind him. "What are you doing now?"

Cuff looked back and saw Edwin walking toward him. "Nothing," he said.

Edwin had to put the second part of his plan into place. He would have to face Sod in the morning, and he knew he was anxious. Sod had four bottles of moonshine, and if he started drinking, it would be the end of everything. Edwin decided to make his move. "Let's you and I take a dodge down to Jack Caravan's place and see what he's at," said Edwin.

"I've never been in his house," said Cuff. He had heard about Jack and knew he was no angel. However, after just seeing his darling Lillian leave for home with her parents, he was now free to go anywhere. "Well, okay," he said.

In about fifteen minutes they reached Jack's house. Jack's father and mother were just leaving. They both greeted Cuff, surprised to see the schoolteacher at their home.

"We're going over to Lushes Bight. We'll be back later tonight, Jack," said his mother.

"Okay," he said. "We'll make sure the doors are shut before we leave, Mom."

"Good," she added. "There are lots of dogs roaming around tonight, so make sure you do."

After Mr. and Mrs. Caravan left, the three men sat at the table, figuring where they should go for a bit of fun. "If this wasn't Christmas night, we could go jannying," said Jack.

"We sure would," said Edwin. He kicked Jack under the table and winked at him.

Jack knew what Edwin meant; they had rehearsed their plan in the camp many times. He stood up. "Edwin, 'tis Christmas, and I don't know about you, but I'm going to have a drink of stuff."

"I don't know," said Edwin. "Your father might come back."

"No, they're gone, and they won't be back 'til late."

Jack went into his bedroom and brought out a mustard bottle full of moonshine. He placed it on the table and went to the Waterloo stove. The kettle was singing. He picked it up.

"I'm going to have a hot toddy," said Jack, and brought it to the table. "What about you, Edwin?"

"Yes, a small one," Edwin said. "Put the kettle back on the stove 'til you're ready, Jack."

"Right."

Jack unscrewed the stopper from the bottle and poured a small drop of the moonshine in his and Edwin's mugs. He brought over the sugar basin and put a heaping spoonful into each mug. "That should do," he said. "The sugar takes the alcohol out of it; you put sugar in it and you won't get tipsy."

Cuff watched very closely. He had never tasted strong drink in his life, neither had he smoked a cigarette. Jack went to the stove and picked up the boiling kettle. As he walked to the table, the steam billowed upward. He slowly poured the hot water into the mugs; the aroma of the moonshine was in the air. "Do you smell that stuff, boys? That's good 'shine."

Jack put the kettle back onto the stove, and the steam immediately shot upward. Edwin started stirring the sugar through the liquid, the steam rising out of the mugs.

"This is great stuff," said Jack. "Mom takes it all the time like this. It's good for the flu and the asthma."

Edwin spoke up. "Almost every clergyman who came to Beaumont has drunk this for medicine." He watched Cuff as he soaked up every word.

"Cold water is the best, so they say," said Jack. This was how they planned to trick Cuff into drinking the mixture of flux and moonshine, when the opportunity arose.

Edwin and Jack started sipping on their drink.

"What does that stuff taste like?" asked Cuff.

Edwin could hardly believe himself. Cuff was wondering what moonshine tasted like! Could it be that he wanted a drink?

Edwin held out his mug. "Have a taste," he said.

Jack held up his hand and grinned. "Cuff, it could be poison! Don't drink after him. I'll make you a small one."

Jack went to the pantry and got a mug and put it on the table. He was careful at what he was doing. He poured a small shot into the mug and added the right amount of hot water. He also added the right amount of sugar and put the mug in front of Cuff. "Now, take your time and sip it; be careful not to scald your tongue."

Cuff took a sip, and then another, until all the liquid in the cup was gone. "This stuff isn't too bad," he said.

"Anything is bad if you get too much of it," said Jack.

"I guess you're right," said Cuff.

Edwin spoke under his breath. "Even poison—even flux." He smiled widely and said to Cuff and Jack, "We'll have one more small one."

Jack cut him off. "No, some other time." He didn't want to push his luck; tomorrow night was coming, and with it another chance.

It was Boxing Day, and what a beautiful day it was—no wind. Cuff was out of bed and ready to go to Lushes Bight. He had a note waiting for him when he arrived home last night. It was from Lillian. She wanted him to come to her home on Boxing Day for lunch. He was excited, but he was feeling kind of guilty for having had his first drink. He thought for a moment, then said to himself, "I suppose it wasn't a drink as such; it was a hot toddy, and I suppose every clergyman in the country has had one this Christmas."

Anyway, Cuff was now off to Lushes Bight to see Lillian on this glorious morning. Why worry about anything? He was now out of school for two weeks, so let it go. He would have a great time. *Wes Mugford's in the hospital at Grand Falls, and Sod has crawled into his hovel. He doesn't even come out through his door, and Edwin's become my friend.*

"Yes," he said out loud as he walked along the well-worn snow road, "Edwin has surely changed; he's one fellow I can trust."

*But how could Edwin give up Lillian so easily? I wonder if he's straightforward with me? I wonder if he's pretending?*

He shook his head, putting it all out of his mind, and walked on.

It was sunny but cold as Edwin Burton headed for Sod Mugford's house. The snow crunched under his feet as he hurried along. He knew Sod would be excited. Edwin was carrying good news for him. He went quickly around the harbour bottom and up to Sod's house. There was smoke coming out of the stovepipe and the door was barred from the inside, so he knew that Sod was at home. He knocked, but there was no answer. He was afraid to knock too hard—he didn't want to have Sod screaming on this beautiful quiet morning. He tapped again, and in an even voice said, "Sod, are you at home? It's me, Edwin. I've got something to tell you."

There was no answer. He looked toward Sod's parents' house and saw the old woman looking over at him. She was shaking her fist. Edwin was afraid of her. She was saying, "Youse get home, Edwin Burton, youse get home!"

Edwin had always been afraid of the old woman, ever since he was a boy. He watched her one time, when she threw a garden prong at Wes. It was only by a miracle that she didn't kill him.

He saw her leave the window and move in the direction of the door. "If you're in there, Sod, come right now, or I'm leaving. Your mother's on the warpath," he yelled. He was sure he could be heard across the harbour. He saw the old woman come around the corner of the house. She had a stick in her hand. At that moment the door opened and Sod appeared in the doorway. He saw Edwin, and at the same time he caught a glimpse of his mother coming toward the house.

"Come in, Edwin," he growled.

Edwin stepped past him into the porch and Sod stepped outside. He had no boots on his feet, only wool socks. The old woman stopped; she knew it was dangerous to go any closer.

Sod let out a yell that almost everyone in Beaumont surely heard. "Old woman," he screamed, "what are you doin'? If you take one more step towards this house it will be your last."

Hazel didn't come any farther. She looked at Sod and said, "What's that Edwin Burton doing over here? I bet he's up to something no good!"

Sod was furious. He was tired, hungry, cranky and hadn't had anything to eat since his supper the previous evening. It didn't take him very long to tell his mother what he thought of her.

After he finished calling her everything he could think of, she spoke up. "Sod," she said with a soft voice, "you and that Edwin are up to something." She had a smirk on her face that irritated him. "I'd say you're going to break in somewhere tonight, or burn one of the churches. Maybe you're going to burn down the school."

She paused for a moment. "Yes, Sod, burn the school, and make sure that Cuff is in it."

He laughed. He knew his mother would like to see that young schoolteacher laid out, especially after what he had done to poor old Wes. Sod then turned and walked inside.

The old lady stood there and just snarled at the house. "They're up to something. Why isn't Sod drunk this Christmas? He has the 'shine, so I wonder why he isn't drinkin' it? What have they got in there?" She vowed that, when they left the house, she would return and find out what was in there. As she turned to walk away she saw the black tracks left in the snow by Sod's socks. "What kind of a state is that house in?" she said aloud. "It's worse than a pig's pen." She then turned and walked back to her house.

Inside Sod's house, Edwin asked, "What's wrong with your mother? I thought you were going to beat her face off."

"I should have," Sod answered. "She hasn't stopped since I landed home. Last night she accused me of chopping Wes, just to make sure he wouldn't be home for Christmas."

He sat down, his hair sticking straight up. He lit a cigarette. "What's on your mind, Edwin?" he asked, not looking Edwin's way.

"I have some good news for you, but your mother—" He paused. "Last night, I had Cuff over to Jack's house, and we cracked the moonshine to him."

Sod could hardly believe his ears. He hadn't had any special meal during Christmas, nobody had invited him to a dinner or to their house, and he hadn't had a single Christmas gift or a card given to him. His mother and father lived next door and they hadn't even looked his way, only to cause trouble, but to hear Edwin say that he had gotten the schoolteacher to drink moonshine was worth all the dinners and gifts that he could wish for this Christmas.

He grinned with delight. "You're not telling me the truth, Edwin." He sat up straight and took the cigarette from his mouth.

"Oh, yes I am," said Edwin.

"Well, well. I had underestimated you, Edwin. I thought you'd never be able to do it."

"He had a couple of hot toddies—maybe three or four. I never counted them anyway. His legs were some wobbly when he went home."

This was an exaggeration. Edwin knew he couldn't lie to Sod, because if Cuff had gotten drunk last night Sod would have heard about it before now. "We got two hot toddies in him, not too strong, but just enough to encourage him to go at it again, maybe tonight."

"That's good, that's good!" said Sod. "I'm glad you didn't turn him off."

"We didn't," said Edwin. "He enjoyed it."

"Good. Tonight we may get our plan to work. Did he tell you where he was going?"

"I know where he's going," said Edwin. "He's going to the soup supper and the dance, he told me. He wants me to go with him. He's going to try and persuade Blanche and Lillian to come from Lushes Bight with him this evening for the dance."

Sod started to grin. "Don't worry; they won't be coming, because Stew Brenton told someone up here the other night that Walter Brenton would never let them two come up here by themselves while I'm here in Beaumont. He's afraid I'm going to attack them or cut their throats, the poor fool. Don't worry, Cuff will be alone."

"You're right, Old Sod," said Edwin. "You know everything. You should have been a clergyman."

Sod laughed. "For a day or two, Edwin, I thought I was going to have to shoot that schoolteacher. I didn't think you were going to do what we planned."

"I didn't think it was going to work until Jack got involved," Edwin said. "It's like Jack said up in the camp—there was a big part he could do in making it work."

"You're right. Now, we got a job to do and we might as well get at it right now." He got up from the wooden stool and walked into the bedroom. He brought out his large packsack. Inside was a package wrapped in a dark dirty towel, almost as stiff as cardboard. He put it on the floor, untied it, and slowly unrolled it. "This is Cuff's medicine," he said. "One good gulp of this and it's bye-bye for the United Church schoolteacher in Beaumont!" He laughed.

Sod now had the bottle unwrapped and was holding it up. He couldn't see it clearly, so he went to the window and called

Edwin over. They held it up to the light. "Just look at it, Edwin. It's as clear as crystal, just as clear as water."

On the container there was a skull and crossbones, and right under that there was written POISON in big letters. Sod was possessed; the thought of poisoning Cuff appeared to have driven him over the edge, and the look in his eyes frightened Edwin.

Sod went into the same bedroom and brought out a bottle of moonshine. "Just look at this," he said. He held the bottle up to the sunlight. It was the same as the flux—as clear as crystal also. "Now Edwin, remember one thing. There is a red stopper on this bottle that the flux is in. The mustard bottle with a blue stopper on it will have the moonshine in it. When we get in contact with Cuff and he gets a few drinks in him, I'll mix the two. I'll throw out half the moonshine and add the flux, about fifty-fifty. Then I'll give 'er a few shakes and hand it to him. Once he passes out, he won't come to anymore."

Edwin felt a knot in his stomach. He knew this was planning murder, but when he thought about Lillian, *his* Lillian, maybe with Cuff right now, laughing at him, rage filled him and pushed the knot from his stomach. "Yes," he said, "we'll get someone to carry him home, and that will be the end of it."

Sod poured moonshine into the mustard bottle while holding it up to the sunlight in the windows. He screwed the blue stopper on, and picked up the other bottle. Holding one in each hand, he rehearsed it again with Edwin. "Tell me, Edwin, what you see?" said Sod with an evil grin.

"I see poison in the bottle with the red stopper—flux—and I see moonshine in the one with the blue stopper," said Edwin.

What Edwin didn't see were the two beady eyes peeking through the curtain at them from the house a hundred feet away. Hazel had an old pair of binoculars, and she was watching Sod and Edwin and the two mustard bottles. She could pick out the red and blue stoppers. "I don't like the look on Sod's face," she said out loud. "The gleam in his eyes is like the devil's himself."

"What's you sayin', Haze?" asked the old man.

"Nothing," she said, "nothing. But I'm going to get even with Mr. Sod, you just wait and see. I'm not going to put up with him around here all this winter."

She walked to the stove. "Just you wait and see!"

# Chapter 12

Cuff spent most of the day around Lushes Bight. He had lunch at the Brenton home. Walter Brenton and his family welcomed him with open arms, and Cuff enjoyed being with them. He went visiting in the afternoon with Lillian and Blanche. They went to see Lillian's grandparents and some of her uncles and aunts. It was an enjoyable day.

"We're not going to Beaumont tonight," Lillian told him. "Dad's nervous; he doesn't want us walking home late at night. He said you could stay down here all night if you wanted to. You could stay at our house." There was pleading in her voice.

"I can't," Willie said. "I have to be at the time. It's in honour of the Home League, and for me not to be there would be impolite. People expect me to be there." He paused. "I thought you would be there; I was counting on it."

Lillian felt bad. "I can't go against Father," she said. "He's been right so many times."

Cuff wasn't pleased, but he didn't show his feelings. It was almost 5:00 p.m. when he said goodbye. Lillian walked with him to the edge of town, out of sight of the last house. The sun was setting, casting a golden glow over the frozen landscape. "Lillian, I love you and I've had a glorious day. Thanks for everything." He put his arms around her and kissed her. As she walked back toward her home, he waved to her and shouted, "I love you Lillian. Goodbye!"

Lillian heard him. She turned to see him waving and smiling. She waved back.

William Cuff turned away and walked into eternity.

Sod had the kettle boiling for tea. However, by the time he was finished showing the flux and moonshine to Edwin, the smell of the 'shine got to him. He couldn't resist putting the bottle to his mouth and taking a long drink. Edwin saw the bubbles rising as Sod kept the bottle tilted. He took three big gulps before taking the bottle away from his mouth. He rolled his eyes and smacked his lips as the stuff brought tears to his eyes.

"'Tis like water, Edwin, 'tis like water. Look, my first drink this Christmas!" He would have taken another, only for the fact that Edwin reminded him that there would be plenty of time for drinking after tonight.

Sod was now in a good mood. He went to the pantry and came out with a slice of buttered bread and a cup full of molasses. He sat down on the wooden bench and made a mug of tea. "This is my breakfast," he said. "I'm as hungry now as any dog in Beaumont. In fact, I could eat any dog in Beaumont now, skin and all."

Edwin laughed as Sod continued. "We're going over around shore now, Edwin my boy, over to the shop. I'm going to buy some bully beef and salt beef."

Edwin was quiet as Sod ate his breakfast.

"What's wrong with you, Edwin?" asked Sod.

"Oh, nothing."

"Oh yes, there's something wrong with you, Edwin, so out with it."

Edwin had to tell him what was bothering him. "Sod, I'm a bit scared about the stuff out there in the porch."

"Scared! Did you say scared?" Sod was shouting and stamping his foot.

"Just a minute! Let me explain. I'm not scared of what we're going to do with Cuff. I'm scared of getting that stuff mixed up. It might be a job seeing the different colours of the stoppers. A feller could drink the wrong stuff and get poisoned himself."

Sod quieted down. "Maybe you're right, Edwin, but they're all the bottles we got."

Edwin knew now that Sod was concerned himself. "I know what we'll do, Sod. Let's get a piece of sticking plaster and stick it on the flux bottle and mark FLUX on it. That way we'll know. We'll mix the dose in the other bottle to give Cuff. No one knows about it except us."

"You're some smart, Edwin," said Sod with a grin. "We got some sticking plaster here. Bess always had lots around that she used for going over the seams in the floor." Edwin laughed. Sod went out and got the flux bottle and brought it in. Edwin tore off two inches of the sticking plaster and stuck it on the side of the bottle. He then took a pencil and wrote FLUX on the plaster.

Sod said, "What's that you wrote on there?"

"Flux, Sod."

"You're sure, Edwin?"

"Yes, I'm sure," said Edwin. He knew Sod couldn't read, so he spelled it out for him. "F-L-U-X."

"Okay," said Sod, looking at it again carefully. He went out into the porch again and placed it on the window bench. "Sit up there," he said to the bottle, "and don't move." He came back into the kitchen. "Let's go," he said to Edwin. "Let's get over to the store."

Edwin noticed that Sod was feeling the effects of the moonshine. When he was drinking, he had a tendency to be loud. "Sod, you'd better not go yelling."

To spite Edwin, Sod let out a roar and started laughing. He knew Edwin was nervous. "Everything's all right, Edwin. I'm not drunk." The two of them stepped outside, shut the door and left to walk around the bottom of the harbour.

Hazel Mugford was watching Sod's house and wondering what her son and Edwin were up to. She was mixing bread when she heard them say something about being "scared." She wondered what was up.

"Get back from the window, Haze," said Sam. "You know what he's like; he could throw a boot or something if he sees you glowering over at him."

The old woman didn't like being bossed around by anyone. "You mind your own business!" she cawed. She wasn't too happy. There was dough hanging from her hands, she had flour all over the front of her dress, and her hair was wild. The old man was about to tell her about the state she was in when the old woman whispered, "They're coming out, Zam."

She made squeaking sounds. "Yes, they're coming out and they're going somewhere. Don't make a sound." There was complete silence as she watched them go around the house and onto the snowy road that led around the harbour. The old woman pulled on her boots.

"Where's you goin', Haze?" asked the old man.

"I'm goin' to see what's in them two bottles down there in Sod's porch," she said with deadly determination.

The old man knew that it would be impossible to stop her. "If you gets caught I won't pick up for you. You can take your own medicine."

The old lady didn't speak as she went straight to the door. She dashed to Sod's house and went directly to the two bottles that were side by side on the window bench. She picked up one and shook it. She unscrewed the stopper, and the smell of moonshine was strong in her nostrils. "Moonshine," she said out loud. She put the stopper back on.

Hazel took the stopper off the second bottle and looked at it. "It looks like water," she said. "That's funny."

She spotted the label on the bottle and held it up to the sunlight, bringing it closer to her eyes. Hazel couldn't read, but she could spell out the letters. F-L-U-X. She put the stopper back on, and put the bottle back in its place. "I wonder what that is?" she said out loud. She then took the bottle and turned it around so that the markings were facing toward the outside. "I'll get Zam to come down and have a look at the letters," she said, and with that she bolted outside and ran for her house.

When she went in, the old man wasn't pleased. "You're lucky Sod didn't catch you in that porch snooping around. If he finds out, he'll break your neck."

"You never mind," she said. "Something pretty strange is going on down there."

"What do you mean?" he asked.

"Look, there's two bottles. One's full of moonshine, and the other's full of something else. I saw the letters, but I can't remember them." She looked directly at the old man. "If you hadn't screamed at me I would have remembered, but now 'tis gone."

The old man was fired up. "You got a mind like a crow and a brain like a beach bird." He paused and then said, "The whole lot of you is dumb. I should have married Beller. At least she knows her letters."

"I knows what it is now," she lied, "but I'm not going to tell you." She knew that the old man wanted to know what it was more than she did.

"I'll look for meself," he said. He pulled on an old pair of logan bottoms and made a mad dash for Sod's house.

"Just a minute," she yelled. "Don't open the door. Just look at the bottle through the window."

He went to the porch window and looked at the bottles. "Flux," he said. "Now I knows what they're up to." Sam came back in the house. "I knows what it is now, and I knows what they're up to," he said to his wife. "They're going to poison the schoolteacher, you just wait and see."

96

The old woman already had her hands back into the bread she was mixing. "Now, Zam, you knows Sod would never do nothing like that."

She could laugh, but the old man knew the difference. "Sod would do anything for revenge, and that Edwin Burton, he's game to do it. I knows he is."

The old man was looking across the harbour. "Looks like they just left the store. Edwin's on his way home. Sod's coming back by himself."

Hazel went straight to the old man and looked him directly in the face. "For the love of Mike, Zam, don't tell him I was inside his house, whatever you do." She was deadly serious. The old man perked up; he knew he had her where he wanted her. He also knew what kind of a racket Sod would kick up.

"If he sees your tracks going into his house and follows them here, I'm not going to get meself in trouble. You'll have to defend yourself."

The old woman was quick. "I'll tell him that he left his door open and the dogs were hanging around, so I went down and closed the door."

The old man shook his head. "You're still the biggest liar on Long Island."

Nothing else was said as Sod returned and went into his house.

It started to snow just after sunset on Boxing Day at Beaumont in 1928, and it looked as though there would be a storm. The wind turned around to the northeast and blew for about an hour, but then it cleared up. Although it stopped snowing, it remained overcast and the stars didn't appear. Some of the people from the surrounding towns didn't come to the soup supper for fear of the wind coming up again, but there was still a crowd present at the dance in the Lodge. The charge was fifty cents for adults and twenty-five cents for children. For this each person got a bowl of soup and a sandwich, with either tea or syrup, and a cookie or cake. Cuff and his boarding mistress, Mrs. Burton, were helping to collect the money. They started the soup supper at 7:00 p.m. The pots of soup were brought in and placed on the wood stove. It was warm and cozy in the Lodge and everyone there was in a good mood, with people singing and clapping their hands.

Some were talking to the schoolteacher while others were talking to Mrs. Burton. All was well, except Cuff noticed that Edwin wasn't around. He wasn't very happy and he didn't want to be there. If he could only have stayed at Lushes Bight with Lillian for tonight, he would be happy. How could he be happy, with her up there? *I suppose Edwin hasn't gone to Lushes Bight to meet Lillian. I haven't seen him around. No, I don't believe that.*

By nine o'clock, almost everyone was fed and they were itching to get out on the dance floor. Cuff saw Edwin and Jack Caravan come in. Jack kept his distance at the other end of the building, talking to some people. Edwin appeared to be in a good mood, and came directly over to the teacher.

"Willie, how are you? Are you busy?"

"I'm pretty good," he said. "I'll be glad when everyone is fed."

Edwin whispered, "Afterwards we'll take off somewhere—me and you and Jack. This old square dance isn't worth going to. I was never out to a dance in my life."

"Neither was I," said Cuff. "Yes, when all the soup and sandwiches are gone we'll go somewhere."

"Good enough," said Edwin. "Let me know and we'll meet you outside."

"Okay," said Cuff.

Fifteen minutes later, William told Mrs. Burton that he was leaving. "The dance is about to start and I don't feel like staying. I've never been to a dance in my life. I'm going to go with Edwin and Jack."

"Good night," said Mrs. Burton. She was glad that Edwin was Cuff's friend. She noticed that he had looked worried about something, but she dismissed the thought. She could rest easy; one thing for sure, Edwin wouldn't be drinking as long as Cuff was with him. She was glad that he wasn't going around with that Sod Mugford—that was her main concern.

She would have a good Christmas. So far, this was her best in years.

Before Edwin and Jack came to the Orange Lodge where the soup supper was in progress, they had been at Sod's house. While they were there it was clearly pointed out by Sod what they had to do. "Someway," he said, "get three or four good hot toddies down into him. Make sure he doesn't pass out. Then, bring him over here to me, supposin' you got to blindfold him. Make sure no one sees you."

Jack didn't say anything; he didn't want to be seen around Sod while he was at home in Beaumont. He knew his father would be mad if he was even near him.

Edwin, on the other hand, didn't care what his mother thought about his choice of friends. He was obsessed with getting even with Cuff for taking his Lillian away from him, and this would be the night.

"I'll have my part ready here. Don't worry," said Sod, "there'll be no mistake."

"Okay," said Edwin, "everything's all set."

"Well, boys," said Sod, "go on over to the Lodge and get that scruff out of there. I only wish Wes was home."

"So do I," said Edwin. Jack didn't speak. With that they left to fetch Willie Cuff at the Orange Lodge.

# Chapter 13

Sarah Roberts was married to Joe Brenton. She was the sister of Az Roberts, an upstanding lady with a large family, a member of the Methodist Church, and later, the United Church. She was one of the old-timers in Lushes Bight who stood hand in hand with Happy Tucker and Emily Jane Roberts, before they went to live in L'Anse au Pigeon.

Aunt Sarah was always involved in the Home League and the women's groups around the area, first in line to knit garments and make clothes for those who were in need.

During the First World War, she was head of a committee that put together packages to send to the men overseas. Aunt Sarah had a soft heart for everyone. She even used to say, "The poor Germans; so many of them are sent to war against their will for that old Kaiser. They are all some mothers' sons. We should pray for them."

It was after dark when her son Stewart harnessed up his team of dogs, settled his mother on the komatik and hauled her down to Beaumont to attend the time at the Orange Lodge.

She would go there strictly for the soup supper part. She would never attend a square dance.

On this evening she wasn't very happy. In fact, she'd had a funny feeling all day. She had told everyone of a dream she'd had the previous night.

Aunt Sarah was a firm believer in dreams.

Sarah dreamed that she was walking along a beach in the bottom of Beaumont and saw something on the sand. She walked up to it and saw that it was a man lying face down. Sarah rolled him over, but she didn't recognize him. She noticed that he was choking and had turned dark. His hands were clutching his throat, and he was trying to get his breath. When she looked at him closer, she saw that around his throat, like a collar, was an Orangeman's Red Cross ring.

The flesh on his face started to fall off, and then he spoke.

*I want to tell you to be aware that this Christmas will be a sad one, but next Christmas there will be a disaster. The ring won't kill me, but the ring will show a sign.*

The skull became visible through the flesh as it melted away. In a moment, the flesh had disappeared and all that remained was the white skull, with two bones crossed beneath it. A voice emanated from the skull. *Death in Beaumont. Death in Beaumont.* The Red Cross ring glittered in the sand.

She awoke with a scream.

"Why did I have that dream last night?" she said many times that day. "I've seen the face of that young man before, but I can't place him. Az has a Red Cross ring. I wonder if they're all right at the Pigeon?"

Her family had said to her, "It's just a dream, Aunt Sarah. You know very well that if we all had to pay attention to dreams, we would all go to bed and stay there."

She had replied, "This was different, really different."

The dream was still fresh in Sarah's mind as she sat at the table in the Orange Lodge in Beaumont. She didn't have to pay to get in because she was a member of the Home League in Lushes Bight, and she had been admitted through the side door. She was helping out with the things they were selling.

At 9:30 p.m., she was helping to pack away the items that weren't sold, when she heard someone say, "Has anyone seen Mrs. Rideout? I want to give her the money I collected." She looked up, and standing in front of her was a young man. Their eyes met.

*I've seen the face of that young man before, but I can't place him.*

Aunt Sarah dropped what she had in her hands. She felt faint. She closed her eyes and tried to maintain her balance. When she opened her eyes, the young man was walking out the door.

One of the girls said, "Aunt Sarah, are you all right?" Sarah didn't speak, so the girl asked her again.

"Yes, my dear, I'm all right. Who was that young man who was just here?" she asked.

"Why, that's the young schoolteacher, Mr. Cuff. You'd better sit down, Aunt Sarah," said the girl.

Sarah nodded and whispered, "Yes, Mr. Cuff."

A new wave of dizziness flowed through her. "Would you get me a glass of cold water?" she asked.

"Yes, ma'am," she said. The girl went into the kitchen, and in a few minutes she came back with Stewart. He looked frightened.

"What's wrong with you, Mother?" he asked.

"I took a weak turn. I'm all right," she said.

"Your lips are purple, Mother."

"I'm all right now. I'm starting to come around."

"Get a wet cloth and put it on her forehead," Stew said to the girl. In a few minutes she came back with the cloth. A crowd gathered around, anxious to know about Aunt Sarah.

"I'm fine now," she assured them.

"We're going home, Mother. Do you feel up to it?" Stewart asked.

"Yes my dear. Get the dog team ready."

"Okay," he said. Stew could see that his mother was now coming around fine, so he left. Ten minutes later, he came back. "The dogs are ready to go. Are you all right?"

"Yes, I'm fine," she said. She was dressed in her winter clothes and ready to go. Someone helped her outside, and in a few minutes the dog team left Beaumont and headed to Lushes Bight. About halfway there, Aunt Sarah signalled for Stew to stop. He saw her signal and stopped the dogs.

"What's the trouble, Mother?" he asked.

Above the barking of the dogs, she told him what was troubling her. "Stew, I have something to tell you. Remember what I've been telling everybody all day about my dream?"

"Yes," he said.

"Well," said Aunt Sarah, "tonight I saw the young man who was in my dream. It was the schoolteacher, Mr. Cuff. He's the one I saw, and the way he looked at me, it was as if he knew about it. I think something's going to happen to him, Stewart."

"Mother," said Stew, "don't worry about that. It's only a dream."

Stewart shouted at his dogs, and they were off.

Edwin Burton could hardly contain himself. He realized he was about to get himself involved in a murder, if their plans worked out and they were successful. However, he didn't for one moment think about the consequences. He only thought about Lillian and the jealousy and hatred he had deep down inside. It was like a monster that haunted him. He had to get revenge, and if it took killing Cuff with his bare hands, he was prepared to do it.

When the three men left the Orange Lodge, some people commented that they couldn't understand why Cuff the schoolteacher was going around with Edwin Burton and Jack Caravan. Everyone knew that Edwin and Jack were friends of Sod and Wes Mugford. They also knew that the Mugfords were determined to get even with Cuff for throwing Wes out of school like a dog. Most of the people, especially the old-timers around Beaumont, didn't trust Edwin and were sure that if he got the chance he would do something to the schoolteacher.

No one would comment on the matter to the schoolteacher to his face, but behind his back plenty was said. "I wouldn't give five cents for the schoolteacher's life after dark, alongside that Edwin Burton. He's just like old Sod." As they left the Lodge, someone said, "There goes the lamb to the slaughter." Many other similar comments were made, but none loud enough to be heard by Cuff or Jack and Edwin.

As they stepped outside, the stars were shining and the moon was soon to appear in the sky. To the east the reflection of it was already evident. "'Tis going to be a light night," said Cuff. "We should get some dogs and harness them up and go for a ride."

"Not on your life," said Jack. "I don't want to go handy to any stinking dogs on this night." Edwin laughed.

They went only a short distance when Cuff asked his two companions, "Where are we going, boys?"

Edwin thought for a moment. "Lets go jannying."

Cuff said nothing; he wasn't in the mood for jannying.

"I don't know," said Jack. "Lets go over to the house first and decide what we'll do afterwards."

"A good idea," said Cuff. Edwin was excited—the plan was on schedule.

In ten minutes the three men were at Jack's house.

"The old man has gone down to Lushes Bight, so there's nobody home," he said.

All lights were out. They went in, Edwin holding a flashlight. Jack lit a match and walked to the table. From a shelf above the table he took down a small lamp, removed the chimney and lit it. Each of the three men sat in a chair at the table. "Hey, Jack," said Edwin. "Is the kettle boiled?"

"No, but I think the water in it is!"

The three of them laughed. "Don't be funny, Jack," said Edwin. The three sat at the table for a few minutes and talked about the time at the Lodge, how much money they had collected, and about the square dance that by now was in progress.

"By the way," said Cuff, "who was that older woman there who was selling the stuff, the tall one with the white sweater?"

Edwin looked at Cuff, as if surprised. "Who? The one sitting at the table?"

"Yes," said Cuff.

"Why, that's Sarah Brenton. Why do you ask?"

"I went over to see your mother to give her the money, and this woman looked me straight in the face. I can't remember ever seeing her before, but there was something familiar about her. It's as if I had seen her somewhere."

"She's Lillian's aunt," said Jack. "'Tis funny they didn't take you over to see her when you were up to Lushes Bight. She's Stew's mother."

"Okay," said Cuff, "maybe I've seen her somewhere up there."

Edwin was furious, but he dared not show it. Being reminded of Lillian redoubled his determination to carry out the plan. "Have you got any of that 'shine left, Jack?" he asked, as if he didn't know.

"Yes, I have a little drop."

"Well, why don't we have a hot toddy each? 'Tis Boxing Night," said Edwin.

Jack had already fired up the stove, and the kettle was blowing steam. "Maybe we should," he said. He went into his bedroom and brought out a bottle that was half full. He placed it on the table and fetched three glasses, sugar, and a teaspoon.

Edwin picked up the bottle. "'Tis the best medicine in the world if you drink it like this, with hot water and sugar. Mom loves it," he lied.

Cuff said nothing, and Jack didn't ask him if he wanted a drink; he automatically poured him one, but one that wasn't too strong. The three men drank, discussing whether they should go jannying or not. They decided to have seconds. This time it was a little stronger. Cuff drank his first; in seconds it was gone. The two drinks seemed to affect him.

"Let's have a game of cards," said Edwin. They discussed having a game, but Jack wasn't interested.

Some time passed, and Edwin noticed that Cuff was beginning to get drunk. He mixed another drink for himself and the schoolteacher. They drank to Christmas. With the three drinks gone, Cuff could hardly stand without staggering.

"We'll have one more and go somewhere," Edwin said excitedly. He knew that Cuff was loaded. They mixed him another strong drink, and after this was gone, Edwin winked at Jack. They would go to Sod's house now, supposing they had to carry him.

Jack was getting cold feet. He thought about what was going to happen. He was afraid of Sod Mugford; he knew that if something went wrong he would be in deep trouble.

He said, "You can go on, Edwin. I'm going to stay here for awhile. I'll come later."

Edwin was fuming. "You have to come with us, Jack. We can't go without you."

"No, I'm going to stay for awhile."

Edwin knew it was no good to argue with Jack because it might make Cuff suspicious. "Okay, Jack. I'll see you later."

As Jack opened the door for them, he noticed that Edwin was very drunk. Jack was scared by now, and nearly sick to his stomach. If anyone saw them leave there and recognized them, and if Sod and Edwin happened to poison Cuff, only God knew what would happen. Jack was sober; he had very little to drink, only sweet water with a little moonshine.

Jack spoke to Edwin in a low voice. "I'll tell you what to do. Dress up—put a bedsheet over each of you. Nobody will ever know you. No one will ever know you or Cuff. Disguise him."

"That's a good idea," Edwin said.

Jack got two blankets and put one around and over the heads of each man and tied a scarf around their waists to keep the blankets in place. By this time, Cuff didn't know where he was going. He had to be led.

As he and Edwin went along the road, they met several people who didn't recognize them; they were just a couple of jannies who were out drinking or pretending they were drunk to hide their identity. Edwin led Cuff straight to Sod Mugford's house.

Jack Caravan knew exactly what was going to happen to Willie Cuff the minute Edwin delivered him into the hands of Sod Mugford. He was certain that if Sod couldn't get the flux down inside Cuff, he would strangle him instead. He watched as Edwin led the staggering schoolteacher away, wrapped in a blanket, their forms throwing dark shadows across the snowy road in the bright moonlight.

Jack shut the door and sat down at the table. He made himself another hot toddy and then thought about what was going to happen. It made him scared, though he knew it was too late to be scared. The plans were final, and if he interfered Sod would break his neck. He was scared of Sod and Wes, and even old Hazel, their mother.

"So be it," he said to the empty room. "Cuff had no business taking Lillian Brenton from Edwin anyway."

However, Jack now decided he wasn't prepared to take any blame; if he didn't follow them to Sod's house, nobody would be able to connect him with anything.

When he finished his drink, Jack left his home and went to the house of Arthur and Mary Rowsell. Uncle Arthur was a man who usually went to bed early, but tonight he was still up. He had a young daughter Emiline who Jack had taken out on occasion.

Jack entered the house, and Uncle Arthur was glad to see him. "Well," he said, "good evening to you, and Merry Christmas." The old man was very pleasant.

"Merry Christmas, Uncle Arthur and Aunt Mary." Aunt Mary also greeted him.

Uncle Arthur winked at him. "I bet you're here to see Emiline." Jack laughed.

"I s'pose he is!" said Aunt Mary. "But she won't see him now; she's gone jannying. But have a cup of tea with me. I haven't had my lunch yet."

Jack agreed. It was always said that Uncle Arthur Rowsell was an old saint. He was a hard-working man whom everybody loved; it was said that even the dogs loved him. He asked Jack about the woods work at the lumber camps and if he was going back. He had quite a conversation with the old man.

Jack Caravan now had an alibi. If anything happened to Cuff, he could say he had nothing to do with it—that he was at Arthur Rowsell's home until midnight.

Hazel Mugford had been sitting near her kitchen window all night. Old Sam was lying on the couch near the stove. He had the lamp put out, which was unusual. The only sign of any light in the kitchen was that on the wall behind the stove, coming from a crack in the fire box. When Edwin Burton and Jack Caravan had left Sod's house after spending only ten minutes there, she was more curious than ever.

It was now ten-thirty, and all evening she had noticed Sod anxiously going from window to window, looking around the harbour. She had seen several people walking the roads, especially over on the other side around the Orange Lodge, which had the lights blazing. The square dance there might go on until two or three in the morning. It was a bright, moonlit night. The snowy hills of Beaumont reflected the light around the harbour, making it almost as light as day.

As she sat there with her knitting, Hazel saw two human forms slowly coming around the harbour, arm in arm. As they got closer, she noticed that they were staggering around; one person appeared to be keeping the other up. As the two came closer, she noticed that they were two jannies.

Sod was also at his own window. They came to his door but didn't knock or make a sound. He was there to open the door. The two stepped inside and he shut the door. Hazel called to the old man, and he rushed over to where she was standing. She told him what she saw.

"Zam, I wonder who that is?" she said.

Sod had seen the two forms coming up the road around the harbour bottom. He watched as the two got closer.

"I wonder," he said out loud. "Is it possible? Yes, it's Edwin, with Cuff all dressed up."

He leaped to the door, just as Edwin put his hand on the latch. He opened the door and, to dispel any suspicion on the part of Cuff, played along with the janny charade. He said, "Yes, the jannies can come in."

Once they were inside, Sod knew for sure that it was Cuff, and that the young schoolteacher would never get out of his house alive. He had him now!

Sod knew that Edwin was drunk but still in possession of his wits. He asked the two of them to sit down. They sat down on the wooden bench, close together, Edwin holding Cuff upright. "Take off those blankets," said Sod. "I know you."

Edwin removed his own blanket. He motioned to Sod, and in a low voice said, "It's Cuff."

Sod stared at the blanket that covered the swaying form sitting on the wooden bench. He became excited and his eyes bulged in the light from the lamp. Sod was gasping for breath, and Edwin could hear him making a kind of hissing sound. Edwin squirmed uncomfortably and was about to say something, when Sod motioned for him to be quiet.

Sod spoke to the jannies. "I think I knows you. It's Edwin Burton and the schoolteacher."

Sod grinned at Edwin. Sod's skin was a ghastly white under a week's beard. He was shaking.

*At last,* he thought, *I got you.* His mind went back to the time when they had the racket, he and Bessie, the morning

Wes came home with his hands all swollen up. *But now*, he said to himself, *you'll never get out of here alive, Mr. Cuff. I am going to kill you.*

Sod meant it, but he didn't know if Cuff was as drunk as he appeared, because he still had the blanket over him. He had to be careful and use his words just right, so he pretended to be Mr. Good Guy while talking to Edwin. "Would you like to have a lunch, Edwin?" he asked in as calm a voice as he could muster.

Edwin almost laughed out loud. "Yes," he said.

"Better still, would you like to have a little drink?"

Edwin was quick to answer. "Yes, a small one with a little water." He winked at Sod in the pale lamplight.

Sod went into the pantry and got three mugs and brought them out, placing them on the table. He walked over to the teacher, who was barely able to sit upright. He lifted the blanket that was over his face, and sure enough, he was looking at Cuff, the very one he hated so much, only a foot away.

"Sod, you'd better get us that drink you promised us. If you don't, Willie here is going to pass out," said Edwin.

Sod let go of the blanket. He noticed that Cuff's eyes were almost closed. He didn't hesitate a moment longer; he rushed to the porch where he had the two bottles on the window bench. Sod had to make sure of what he was doing. He knew he had to be careful not to give the stuff to Edwin and poison the wrong man. He looked at the two bottles. The light was dull and he couldn't see the markings on the one with the flux. For a moment he couldn't remember which was which. "This is strange. It looks like someone's moved this stuff."

He lit a match and looked closer. He took up the bottle with the flux in it and turned it around. Then he saw the writings on the tape. "Someone's been tampering with this bottle," he said out loud. He removed the stopper and smelled it. Grinning, he said, "It's the right stuff, all right." He had a mug on the window bench, so he poured in enough pure flux to fill it halfway. He put the stopper back on. He took the stopper off the other bottle and smelled it—pure moonshine. He poured in enough 'shine to three-parts fill the mug. *If we can get this down into you,* he thought, *it's goodbye.*

His hands were shaking. Sod Mugford knew full well what he was doing; his eyes were burning like fire from the strain of his actions. He felt a little weak, but the thought of not going through with it never entered his mind.

He took Edwin's mug and filled it halfway with moonshine. He put the lid back on and put the bottle back on the window bench. With the match extinguished, he was again in near darkness except for a little lamplight and the flicker of light from the moon. He picked up the two mugs and walked into the kitchen again.

Edwin was nervous; he wasn't sure if he could trust Sod. He had made up his mind not to drink what was put in front of him. He took the blanket off Cuff's head and let it fall around his waist. He asked Willie how he felt. He got out an "all right."

"Sod has a drink for you that will do you good; gulp it right down." By now Cuff was loaded; he hardly knew he was in the world. Edwin handed him the mug but didn't let it go.

The blanket was in the way, so Edwin said, "Just a minute," and took the blanket completely off him.

"Okay, now, take her all down."

Cuff put the mug to his mouth, took a big gulp of the substance, and swallowed it.

"Take another," said Edwin.

Cuff suddenly let go of the mug and grabbed his throat. The remainder of the mixture poured down over the front of his coat and pants. He let out a groan and stood up.

Cuff staggered and fell down, letting out a chilling scream. He rolled over on his stomach, then onto his back. He kept screaming and clutching at his throat.

All of a sudden, the screaming stopped. Cuff couldn't get his breath.

Edwin looked at Sod and saw a twisted grin that he had never seen before, a demented grin that would haunt him to his dying day.

"We got him, Edwin, we got him. If Wes was only here to see this."

Cuff was still gasping for air. He was too drunk to realize what was happening. He started kicking his feet.

Sod stepped on Cuff's arm and grabbed him by the hair. "Edwin, go out and get the flux bottle as quick as you can."

For a moment Cuff got a gulp of air. He let out another scream.

Edwin ran out into the porch. He fumbled for the mustard bottle.

"Hurry up, Edwin! Get it in here!"

He found the flux bottle and ran back.

"Hand it over," Sod ordered. Edwin held out the bottle.

"Take the stopper off!"

Edwin removed the stopper. Sod held back Cuff's head and poured the entire contents of the bottle down his throat.

Cuff glutched it down and gave a big groan. He shivered from head to foot, and in a couple of minutes he was gone. He had stopped breathing. Sod kicked him.

"You done a good job, Edwin."

Hazel and Sam Mugford were staring across at the goings-on at Sod's house. "Wass that fool doin', I wonder?" Sam asked.

"Murdering the schoolteacher, that's what they're doing," said the old woman.

The old man blinked. "No he's not," he shot back.

"Oh, yes he is," she said. "Look, he's out at the poison, the flux bottle. Look at 'im lighting a match to see the right stuff. I'd say they're mixing a good drink for him."

The old man looked worried. "Is it possible that Sod would poison a man on purpose? What's he coming to?"

"Get back," Hazel snapped. "It seemed like Sod was looking straight at me then."

"If he saw you, he'll shoot you tomorrow."

"No," she said. "I think he was lookin' on the bottle."

Hazel fell quiet. Sod had gone back into the kitchen again. The porch seemed dark, so they moved closer to the window. The frost was rapidly forming from their moist breath blowing on the windowpane. The old woman ran to the washstand and grabbed a towel. She went to the stove, lifted the kettle and poured hot water over the towel. She ran back to the window and placed the hot towel against it. The old man was irate.

"If you break that pane of glass, I'll crack your skull," he said angrily.

"You mind your own business," she snapped.

In a couple of minutes the window was clear. The two sat back, looking closely. They could see movement inside Sod's house but very little of anything else.

In the silence of the night they heard it—a piercing scream. It came from inside Sod's house. It was a high-pitched sound.

"Hear that?" said the old man. "That's a screech."

The old woman's eyes were blazing as she stared. They heard another scream.

"Listen," she said. "They got it done. They got him murdered."

"Good God!" said the old man. "Sod wouldn't have the nerve to do that, would he?"

"Wouldn't he?" she barked. "I guess he would. He's just like you."

The old man grabbed her by the shoulder and hit her across the face. She fell off the chair and onto the floor. She pulled away at once, barely escaping the toe of his boot.

"Okay, okay," she said. "I didn't mean nothing by it."

The old man calmed down. "Don't you let me hear that come out of you again. They're all like you—possessed with devils, the whole lot of them."

Sod Mugford could only stare at the dead man on the floor. He knew that the schoolteacher was lifeless and would never breathe again; he also knew that there would be a lot of questions asked. Who was Cuff seen with last? Where had he been after he left the Lodge, and who was with him? He knew that if it was suspected that Cuff was so much as inside his door, he would get the blame.

Edwin could hardly believe his eyes. He appeared to be in shock as he stared at Cuff, who had a strange look on his face. "Is he really dead? Is Willie dead?"

Sod recognized the fear that was coming over Edwin. He knew he would have to take care to control and contain Edwin's bouts of panic. "Edwin, listen. It was the moonshine that killed Cuff. I didn't give him any flux. I was just making out. Maybe he's not dead—he could be passed out from drinking."

Edwin knelt down near Cuff. "I think he's still breathing."

Sod lost his patience. "No he's not, Edwin. He's dead as a doorknob."

Edwin was becoming hysterical; he was now sober, and his heart was thudding painfully in his chest. It was beginning to sink in; he had just helped to murder a man. What could he do?

Sod grabbed Edwin by the shirt collar and sat him down on the wooden bench. If Edwin panicked, both of them would hang. Therefore, a plan to cover this up would have to be put in place immediately.

"Now, Mr. Edwin Burton, we planned to murder this weasel a long time ago, and you played the biggest part. Now 'tis done, and you are scared, but let me tell you one thing— we won't get caught. At least I won't."

To Edwin, this Sod Mugford was everything—a giant as tough as steel. He loomed as a tower of strength that could do anything, but at that moment Edwin detected fear, and Sod knew it.

"Edwin, you listen to me," said Sod, looking straight at him. "Here's what we're going to do. After the dance is over and everyone's gone home, everything will be quieted down. We'll get the old man's komatik, put Cuff on it, haul him halfway around the bottom of the harbour and dump him off.

"In the meantime, you go on home. For sure your mother will ask you where Cuff is. You say he's supposed to have gone up to Lushes Bight looking for Lillian Brenton. Someone will discover him and spread the word. We'll never be tied in with this. I'll make sure the smell of moonshine is all over him. There'll be no mistake—everyone will believe that he was drinking."

This sounded pretty good to Edwin. He knew that they would have to wait until 1:00 a.m., and he knew that his mother wouldn't go to bed until he came home. It was a moonlit night, almost like day.

"Where's Jack?" asked Sod.

"Jack wouldn't come. He got scared I suppose."

"Scared of what?" said Sod. "When we were in the camp, he was the one who was going to do the big thing. He's involved in this too, you know."

Edwin didn't speak, for fear that Cuff wasn't dead and could hear them talking about it. The two men sat in the small kitchen, and every now and then they would look at the body on the floor. They noticed that it was turning dark. Edwin was shaking; Sod knew that he wanted to leave.

At midnight, the dance at the Orange Lodge was over and all the lights went out. Sod and Edwin watched as everyone went to their homes. "We'll wait until they have a lunch before they go to bed," said Sod.

It was one o'clock when they made their move. "Okay," said Sod. "Let's go." First they took the body and rolled him in the two blankets.

"Listen, Sod, we can't do that. How will that look like an accident?"

"You're right."

"I'll get rid of the blankets," said Edwin. "You get something to put Cuff in."

"Okay. Then I'll sneak up and get the old man's komatik," Sod said. After he found a large, sturdy bag, Sod dashed out the door.

Edwin took the two blankets belonging to Mrs. Caravan and stuffed them in the woodbox. He was afraid to stay alone with the body, so he stepped outside.

Hazel Mugford was watching the goings-on and saw Sod when he rushed out of his house. He looked around toward the window where his mother was secretly peeking out, and seeing no one, he ran for the woodshed. She saw Edwin come out and stand near the door.

She whispered to Sam, "I wonder what's going on? Sod's coming toward the house."

"You be quiet," he whispered back. They moved to another window where they watched Sod go into the woodshed. "What's he going in there for, I wonder?" said the old man.

Before Hazel could answer, Sod came out carrying the small komatik.

"They're getting the komatik ready. I bet they got him made away with, and they're going to haul him out and heave him over the edge of the ice."

Silently, the old man watched as Sod went to his own house. The window was beginning to frost over again, so the old lady took the towel to the stove and poured some more hot water on it. She could hardly hold onto it, due to the scalding hot water. She said unladylike words as she put the hot cloth on the window again. As soon as she touched the windowpane with the steaming towel, the glass cracked, but the old man was oblivious to it. He couldn't believe what was unfolding before his eyes.

"Hurry up," he said, "and don't let them see you." The old woman took the frost off the window again.

"Look!" Hazel shouted. "They're dragging him out. They're bringing the poor brute out."

"My God, my God," said the old man. "Is it possible Sod and Edwin have made away with that bugger? They'll never get away with it. They'll be hung!"

"Shut up," said the old woman. "Don't make a sound."

He obeyed, knowing that Sod was capable of doing them a lot of harm if he knew they were watching.

Sod left the small komatik near the door and went into the house with Edwin tagging behind him.

"You're frightened to death, Edwin!" Edwin didn't reply.

Pointing to the bag with Cuff's body in it, Sod said, "Now, grab holt to this bag of dog's grub and help me get it dragged out." He held Cuff's feet and was already dragging the body across the floor. He went directly to the komatik and put Cuff on it.

Sod decided to secure Edwin's silence under threat of serious harm. "Now Edwin," he said, as he grabbed him by the shirt collar.

Edwin winced in pain. "Let me go. I haven't done anything to you."

"Yes you have, sonny," he snapped. "You know what you've done to me; you got me to poison Cuff for you, for Lillian Brenton, and now you're frightened to death. You're the murderer, Edwin, but let me tell you something. If I hear one squeak out of you I'll cut your throat from ear to ear. Understand?"

Edwin was scared. He knew Sod Mugford meant what he said.

"Okay," he said. "Okay, Sod, I won't tell anybody."

Sod let him go. "Now Edwin, here's what you do; you haul him over to the bottom of the cove, where the road comes down from Lushes Bight. Dump him off by the side of the road. Then take the komatik over a bit farther, and push it out over the road. Then go home and go to bed. If you meet anyone between here and where you dump him off, say he's drunk, that he must have come from Lushes Bight. Now get goin'."

Edwin didn't hesitate; he stepped into the nose of the komatik, and away he went.

Sod laughed.

It didn't take Edwin very long to go around the cove, hauling the corpse behind him. He ran without looking back, as if he were running from a monster. When he got to the branch road leading out of town, he stopped. After a look around, he jumped to the side of the komatik, grabbed it and tipped it over, throwing Cuff's body off, face down. He then took the komatik and ran farther down the road. When he got near the shoreline, he pushed the sleigh over the edge of the road and ran for home. He noticed a couple of lights on in the kitchens of at least two houses but saw nobody looking out. Their windowpanes were frosted over.

When he got near his house he saw that the light was on. It took him a few minutes to catch his breath; his mouth was bone dry, so he picked up a handful of snow and put some in his mouth to moisten his tongue.

A voice inside him said, *Edwin, what have you done? What have you done, Edwin Burton? You have murdered a man. You have poisoned Willie Cuff.*

# Part 2

# Sod Mugford

# Chapter 14

Edwin was frightened. He opened the door slowly and crept inside, shutting the door behind him. He almost made it to the stairs leading up to his bedroom when he heard his mother. "Is that you, Edwin?" Virtue Burton said in a sleepy voice.

He hesitated before answering. "Yes, Mother."

"Oh," she said, "I'm glad you're home." He didn't answer, so she spoke again. "Have you seen William? Is he with you?"

"No, Mother. I haven't seen him since he left the dance."

"I wonder where he went? It's almost two o'clock."

Edwin knew he would have to answer her sooner or later. "I'd say he went up to Lushes Bight to see Lillian."

"I don't think so," she said. "If he did he would have let us know."

Edwin wanted to end the conversation about Cuff. "I don't know, Mother. I'm going to bed."

"Okay," she said. "I guess he'll be in soon."

Edwin ran to his bedroom.

He shut the door, undressed and got in bed. The voice inside returned to haunt him. The events of the last two hours were just a blur to him; the details escaped him. His thoughts were tearing him apart. *My oh my what have I done?* he thought. "I'll be hung, I'll be hung. What have I helped Sod Mugford do? We have killed a man."

He covered his head, as if the ghost of Cuff were already in the room. He was terrified. He knew deep down in his soul he would never get away with it. He was doomed.

Hazel and the old man were watching everything that happened. The old man saw Edwin when he took Cuff on his komatik.

Sam grabbed his coat. "He's going to get me involved in this," he shouted.

The old woman was frightened. "Quiet," she said, "Sod might hear you. People will only think Edwin's hauling a drunken man. You don't know if he's poisoned or not, so take it easy."

Sam went to the window. He could see Edwin in the moonlight; he was running with the schoolteacher's body on the sleigh. He saw Edwin when he tilted the komatik to dump the body at the side of the road.

"Look at what that fool is after doing. He's going to have me involved in it. He dumped Cuff, and now he's left my komatik down there!"

The old woman saw it too. "I zees it," she said, gleefully. The old man noticed the tone of her voice—she was enjoying it.

The old man didn't hesitate. He put on his coat and cap and dashed out the door; he walked around the cove on the trail. In ten minutes he was back with his komatik.

Sod saw his father when he went to get the komatik, but didn't make a move. "I wonder how much the old man's after seeing?" he mumbled. He followed him from window to window. "But he don't know about the flux."

Sod blew out the lamp and went to bed. "Now for a good night's sleep," he said, as he covered himself up, clothes and all.

At 3:30 a.m., Edwin heard a loud knock on the door. His heart stopped.

Someone called from the porch. "Jim! Jim! For God's sake, get up!" In seconds Jim Burton was on his feet.

Edwin heard his father say, "Who's there?"

"Jim, it's me, Cyril. For God's sake, come quick."

Edwin sat up but didn't get out of bed.

Jim pulled on his pants and shirt and hurried to the kitchen. Cyril Rowsell was in his early teens. Cyril and another young man stood staring at him. "Well, what's the trouble?" he asked.

"It's Cuff. We found Cuff." The two men looked frightened.

"You found Cuff—what are you talking about?"

"We found him up there on the road and, Jim, he looks like he's dead."

For a moment, Jim Burton didn't understand what he was hearing. "Boys, listen. Don't be funny."

"We're telling you the truth," they said together.

Mrs. Burton was up now, and she heard what was said. She dashed into the kitchen. "What's happening, Jim?" she said, looking from her husband to the two young men standing near the kitchen door.

"Mrs. Burton, Cuff is lying face down in the snow by the side of the road, not very far from the Lodge. His face is as black as a boot, and he doesn't appear to be breathing. He's still there; we came right here to tell you."

Virtue Burton could hardly believe it. She knew that Cuff wasn't at home; she also knew that he had never stayed out before without telling her. "Are you sure?" she asked.

"Yes," said Cyril, "it's Cuff all right."

Jim Burton had his boots on and was halfway out the door. "Grab the komatik, Cyril," he said.

Cyril's companion ran down the road ahead of them.

Mrs. Burton called Edwin a couple of times, but he didn't answer at first. She persisted. "Edwin! Edwin, get up, quick!" She was halfway up the stairs.

"What's the trouble, Mother?" he asked.

"Cuff has something wrong with him up there on the road. Cyril Rowsell says he's not breathing or something."

Edwin knew what he had to do. They had talked about it so many times, but the shock of it, now that the moment had arrived, made his blood chill. How could he lie his way out of a murder? He knew he would have to do it or face the gallows.

His mother pleaded. "Get up, Edwin, quick! Go help your father. Hurry!"

"I'm coming," he said.

He was too scared to come down, but he knew he would have to, eventually. He was fully aware of what he would see: the grief, the agony, the look in his mother's and father's eyes when they saw Cuff and how he had died. How could he lie his way out of it? How could he look at someone he had just helped to kill? Inwardly, he groaned in agony at the thought. Why had he brought this on himself? If only he could relive the last few hours.

The moon was still shining, making visibility good. Mrs. Burton could see up the road, where the men were coming with someone on the komatik.

*It must be William,* she thought. She prayed he wasn't hurt too badly. Who would hurt such a good man? Especially in this quiet little town of Beaumont? She could hear the crunching of snow under their boots in the frosty air as they neared her. With a hundred feet to go, she ran to meet them. She kept saying, "Oh my, oh my." She met the group with Cuff on the komatik, lying on his back. She looked at his face as it passed her, and she couldn't believe her eyes. She started crying as she walked behind the sleigh.

The community began to wake up with the noise and confusion surrounding the news that Cuff had been found on the roadside. Dogs started barking around the area, and Mrs. Burton could be heard crying. People in the houses nearby were beginning to awaken; lamps were lighting up their windows, one by one.

The towing party arrived at Jim's house and stopped near the door. "Bring him inside," said Jim.

"Where's Edwin?" he asked. "Get Edwin," he told his wife.

She again went to the bottom of the stairs. "Edwin, oh my, Edwin, there's something the matter with William. Come quick."

Edwin finally came downstairs. "What's going on, Mother?" he asked.

"They found William, and there's something wrong with him."

Edwin was shaking; his mother had gone to the door and was now out on the road.

"Edwin," called Jim, "come and give us a hand getting Cuff inside."

Edwin went outside where Cuff was. He had to pretend he didn't know what had happened; he knew at that moment he would have to tell lies about this incident for the rest of his life, or face the dreadful fate of a murderer.

It took only a few minutes for Mrs. Burton to prepare the daybed in the kitchen to put the body on. As far as she was concerned, William wasn't dead—he only had something wrong with him, and if it could be corrected he might be okay, she figured. Grief hadn't yet set in.

Mrs. Burton looked toward the door as they brought Cuff inside. When the light from the lamp shone on the face of the young schoolteacher, Mrs. Burton knew that it was too late— he was already dead. He had already turned dark.

She stared at him and put her hands to her mouth. "My God, Jim. My Blessed God. He's dead." She started shaking. She couldn't control herself.

Edwin knew he would have to put up a front, so he grabbed one of Cuff's legs. "Over on the daybed," said Jim. They carried the schoolteacher to the daybed and laid him down. They could smell the stench of moonshine on him. Jim Burton knew, that on his own, the schoolteacher would never drink enough moonshine to have it spilled all over him.

"He's drenched in moonshine. Where has he been?"

People were beginning to fill the Burton home. Everyone was asking questions and looking. By now, Mrs. Burton was weeping openly.

Everyone was in shock. Jim asked for a white sheet to go over the body, so Mrs. Burton went inside and came out with a white bedsheet. Jim spread it over him.

Edwin felt sick, so he left the kitchen and went back upstairs. He went into his room, shut the door, and fell on his face on the bed.

"What have I done?" he whispered. "I'm finished. I'm finished for good." He groaned in agony. He felt weakness coming over him as a voice inside said *You're a murderer, Edwin. You're a murderer. What will you do now?* The voices hit him and he wept. He was doomed—forever.

The word spread through Beaumont like a raging fire that no one could stop. The people went from house to house carrying the sad news: Cuff drank himself to death with moonshine. They couldn't believe it. Jim Burton's house was filled with people asking questions. "Where was he? Who was he with? What was he doing? Where did he come from?"

"I wonder if he really was up at Lushes Bight?" someone asked.

As people began to go back to their homes and the events started to sink in, they began to put the events of the night together.

"I told you," said one man. "When I seen Cuff leave the dance with Edwin Burton and Jack Caravan, I told someone he had better be careful."

Someone else said they heard Sod Mugford say that he was going to murder the schoolteacher during Christmas. "Sure enough," someone said, "he done it."

A lot of people saw them when they left the Lodge, but no one else saw them later that night.

Others said that they saw two jannies going into Sod Mugford's house, and one was keeping the other one up. "I bet that was them," they said, but no one knew for sure.

Before daylight, all of Beaumont was awake and all the adults were going from house to house telling one another, "Cuff is dead."

"Died drunk," some said. Others whispered among themselves. "He was murdered by Sod Mugford." Listeners would hush when these words were spoken. The schoolchildren were asleep, and Uncle Arthur Rowsell, a gentleman who was in his fifties, said, "What kind of a day will it be when all the youngsters hear about this in the morning? It will be very sad."

Hazel Mugford didn't go to bed at all and had not moved from her window, except to put wood in the stove and melt the frost from the window. She was shocked at what had unfolded before their eyes; she and her husband had seen everything. They knew that Sod and Edwin had poisoned the schoolteacher. "That Edwin Burton, he's capable of doing anything," she said to her husband.

"Listen, Haze. Sod's responsible for all that went on. Edwin's only a bedlamer. Sod is a grown man with a family; he should have better sense."

But the old woman was afraid of Sod and would say otherwise. "There's one thing for sure," she said. "Sod got to get out of town because the crowd will mob him; for sure they'll blame it on him."

"It serves him right," said the old man. "He won't get it bad enough to please me."

She looked at him. "You be careful Sod don't beat your face off."

"Not on your life," said the old man. "Sod better not come around here if he knows what's good for him."

The old woman laughed. "Sod can double you up and put you in his pocket, a dried-up rat like you."

Hazel continued. "I'm glad Wes isn't home because he would be involved in it for sure. I'd say that Wes planned the whole works that went on here tonight anyway, and you'll find that out if the truth ever comes out."

"It will all come out someday," said the old man.

"Don't you get Wes mixed up in this," she said to him sternly.

The old man was silent. They could see a crowd of people milling around Jim Burton's house. By now the moon had gone down and darkness was settling in around the town. However, the brightness of the snow and the lack of outside lights gave the eyes better clarity. Every house in Beaumont had their lamps lit. Hazel and her husband stood near their windows, staring. "There will be a lot of trouble, Haze, when daylight breaks. I can sense it.

"No wonder they called this place Beaumont," Sam murmured.

Beaumont had been called Cutwell Arm until it was renamed by the Newfoundland Government, in honour of the Newfoundlanders who died in World War I at Beaumont-Hamel, France.

"The same kind of a thing is going on here—murder," he said.

Hazel looked at the old man scornfully. "Don't be silly. What, are you frightened to death? It's good you wasn't at that Bomot, whatever you calls it. If so, you would have dropped dead with fright."

The old man walked over to the couch and lay down. He pulled a blanket over him, and as he gazed at the light from the flickering fire, he said, "Why didn't I stop them? I saw it going on. Why didn't I stop it?"

He groaned and turned to the wall.

128

# Chapter 15

A t the dawning of the morning of December 27, 1928, Beaumont was beginning to cloud over. One of the old men said that a storm was brewing; the wind was coming from the northeast. Someone else said they wouldn't be surprised if fire started falling from the sky and burned up the town, but the big talk was "What happened to Cuff?"

Cuff was never known to take a drink, let alone drink enough to kill himself. Others said he hadn't even drunk a stain, that he had been choked and moonshine was poured over him to make it appear that he had been drinking. One man came to Jim Burton's house and wanted to talk to him. Jim sensed trouble and wouldn't come out.

As anger and rumours travelled from house to house, things began to take on a very nasty tone. A lot of people had seen Edwin and Jack Caravan leave the dance at about 9:30 p.m., with Cuff, heading over to Jack's father's house, but no one could recall seeing them after that.

A dozen men got together and went to see Jack Caravan. He was out of bed; he had heard the commotion around town long before daylight. He was sure that Sod and Edwin had poisoned Cuff, and now the whole town was in an uproar.

As the men came to his door, Jack opened it and invited them in.

"Have you heard the news?" one man said.

"Yes," said Jack. "I was next door just now."

"And what do you think of it?" another asked.

"I don't know what to think of it."

Another stepped forward and said, "Jack, we want to ask you a question." He said nothing, and the man continued. "Where did you go when you left the dance at the Orange Lodge—you, Edwin, and Cuff—about nine-thirty?"

Jack looked at him then said nervously, "The three of us came over here."

The man spoke again. "Did you have any moonshine to drink, Jack?"

Jack didn't know if Edwin had told them a story or not. However, he knew he couldn't hide the fact that he had moonshine and that Cuff was drinking. "Yes," he said, shaking. "The three of us had three drinks each; we made it into hot toddies."

"Oh," they said. "Cuff had been drinking, is that what you're saying, Jack?"

"We had three small hot toddies before we left. As for Cuff and Edwin, I don't know where they went and I never saw them anymore. Besides that, all I know is the time; it was about ten-thirty."

"Jack," one man said, "it looks like someone choked him. We were just looking at him; he's as black as a boot and his eyes are bulging right out of his head."

Another man said, "And there's marks all over his throat." They were angry; some didn't know what to say.

Jack could hardly believe what he was hearing next. "We're going now to Jim Burton's and have a talk to Edwin. He'll have to tell us where they went when they left here."

Jack said nothing more. The men left as they came—angry. He sat down at the table, worried; he knew full well that Edwin and Sod were determined to poison Cuff.

Especially Sod—he lived for it night and day. Jack also knew that if Sod got alone with Cuff, he was capable of killing him with his bare hands. He hoped this wasn't the case because it would be harder to cover up than poisoning him. He would have to talk to Edwin.

He dared not go handy to Sod's place just yet, since everybody would be watching their houses. Jack felt guilty; he knew he was just as much involved in it as the others. If the police ever came and did an investigation, Sod and Edwin would hang him, too.

He was frightened.

"I wonder what they did with Mom's blankets?" he said out loud, as the thought struck him that the blankets that Edwin and Cuff put around themselves were enough to tie him to the murder.

He started pacing the floor.

Edwin was in bed with his head covered up; he hadn't gotten any sleep. The words rolled over and over in his head. *If only I hadn't done it. If only I hadn't done it.* But the same voice would say, *It's too late, Edwin. It's too late.* The room was beginning to show signs of the dawn.

He heard the sounds of people who for hours were moving around and talking about the death of Cuff. He heard one person say, "It was Sod Mugford and Edwin—that's just who choked him." Everyone thought Cuff had been strangled by someone, but they were wrong.

Jim came into his room. "Edwin, get up. Some men are here. They want to talk to you."

Edwin was nervous. "What do they want to talk to me for, Dad?"

"I don't know. They were over to see Jack Caravan and now they're here to talk to you."

"What do they want to talk to me for?" he repeated.

"Edwin," his father said, "they want to know where you and Cuff went when the two of you left Jack Caravan's."

Edwin thought for a moment, then said, "Cuff said he was going to Lushes Bight to see Lillian, and I went over to Sod's. I didn't see him afterward."

Jim was reassured by Edwin's response. He was satisfied with the answer, but deep down he had a feeling Edwin was mixed up in whatever went on. Everyone else had the notion that Sod Mugford was behind Cuff's death.

"Get up, Edwin, and come downstairs and talk to them," said his father.

"Okay, Dad." He got out of bed and went downstairs.

They had Cuff's body laid out on the living room table. He was covered by a white sheet. He was dressed the same as he was when he had been at the dance: none of his clothing had been removed. One old man who helped to lay Willie Cuff out was quite upset and remarked that he was just a youngster. "Oh my, what someone's done to him," he said. As Cuff lay on the wooden table, a heated argument started in the kitchen, just a few feet away.

"What about Edwin?" asked a man who was in his shirt sleeves. "What does he know about the goings-on here last night? We saw him leave the dance with Cuff and Jack."

Edwin was scared, but he knew he would have to face those questions. He told them that he had gone to Jack's father's place and had three drinks of moonshine—hot toddies—and Cuff left and went to Lushes Bight or somewhere. "I darted over to see Sod after I left Jack's. Ask him. Then I came straight home from there."

That was all he knew, he said, until Cyril Rowsell came and reported finding Cuff on the road. "I was in bed when Cyril came knocking. Now, I'm not going to say anything else to you. I'm going back upstairs." He turned and left the room.

Over his shoulder he heard, "We're going to wire for the magistrate to come and look into this—someone has murdered Cuff."

Edwin didn't look back, but those words frightened him. If that happened, he would be hanged.

Jim Burton was a very quiet man, but he wasn't prepared to allow a group of men to come into his house and harass his son about the death of Cuff. Next, they would be accusing Edwin of something he didn't do. "Okay, boys," he said, "I want you to leave us alone. My wife is having a rough time."

Hearing this, they all left out of respect for Mrs. Burton, but it was obvious to Jim that the men were still outraged. He wanted the wagging tongues to cease, because as the news travelled from town to town, many people would be coming to pay their last respects to Willie Cuff. He didn't want Edwin's name tangled up in it. He would have to get to work and control the situation; it would be a trying time.

Around midday there was an awful uproar in Beaumont. Most people believed Cuff had died of drinking too much. It was a proven fact that he had been drinking and the stench of moonshine coming from him was evidence enough. However, they couldn't understand why this respectable young man would drink himself to death, especially with moonshine. They were stunned at the thought.

But others were convinced that something more had taken place. "Cuff didn't drink himself to death," they said.

"Something else killed him."

# Chapter 16

Bob Huxter decided to go over to Jim Burton's house and lend some help. He knew his friend would need words of comfort because William Cuff was like a son to Jim. He went into the house, and after talking to Jim decided to look at the corpse. On entering the living room, he could smell the moonshine, and he saw the body on the living room table. Cuff was wrapped in a white bedsheet. He went to the body and pulled the sheet back, exposing the head and shoulders. It wasn't a pretty sight. He noticed that Cuff had turned completely black. He said afterwards that he had seen a black man.

Bob reached down and pulled on Cuff's shirt-collar to have a look at the neck. The front of his shirt fell apart. "Oh my," he said, "his clothes are all burned up with something. I wonder what he was drinking? It was something more than moonshine."

In shock, Huxter realized that the teacher had been poisoned. "God help us all," he said, and pulled the bedsheet back over Cuff's face.

When Bob told everyone what he had seen and how the clothes were burned up with some kind of substance that looked like acid, the rumours began in earnest. Everyone was now convinced that Cuff had been poisoned. It was decided to get Nurse Simmons to come over and take a look at the body.

When summoned by the people of Beaumont to come and take a look at young William Cuff, Nurse Simmons made it very clear that she wouldn't put anything on paper. Her thoughts on the cause of death would only be a theory, but the townspeople were looking for a reason or a cause and were quick to agree to her terms.

Leander Rowsell said that Nurse Simmons was a very stern woman whom everyone respected. She was a war veteran and a medical professional. The Simmons family lived next door to him, and Nurse Simmons was a close friend of his mother.

Stan Simmons had joined the Royal Newfoundland Regiment in 1914 and had spent four years in the trenches of France. While on leave somewhere in England, he met a young nurse. Stan brought her back to Newfoundland and married her at Beaumont (then Cutwell Arm), and she was known simply as Nurse Simmons.

The nurse sent a note to Jim and Virtue Burton to inform them that the citizens of Beaumont were requesting that she come to their home and look at the body of the young schoolteacher, William Cuff. She asked their permission, requesting that they let her know in writing. She asked this because they were dealing with the death of a public servant, and things would have to be done in proper order.

Virtue Burton read the note from Nurse Simmons out loud to Jim. He knew that there was something more to this matter than just a drink of moonshine, and he had a strange feeling that Sod Mugford was involved. He could bet Cuff wasn't drinking moonshine. But deep down in his soul he was wondering if Edwin was also involved. "My God, my God," he groaned, "I wonder what this will come to, Virtue?"

Though he was fearful of what might come out of it, he said, "I want you to drop a note to Nurse Simmons and tell her to come and take a look at him right away."

"Okay," she said, and got her pencil and paper. When the note was written, she gave it to a young girl who delivered it to the nurse.

Edwin had heard the conversation between his father and mother down in the kitchen after they received the note from Nurse Simmons. He had been listening to the commotion all day, and everyone was saying that Sod had choked Cuff to death. They were calling it murder.

Edwin knew all too well that it was true. Cuff was murdered, but it was poisoning that caused the death, not choking. He lay in bed, scared, his mind racing, searching for a way out. "What a fool I've been," he whispered, "what a fool."

He couldn't banish the thought. At two o'clock in the afternoon, he got up and dressed and went downstairs. He could smell the stench of death. His mother and father were in the kitchen, and his mother's eyes were red and full of tears. As Edwin entered the kitchen, Virtue put her arms around him and started crying, "My, oh my, Edwin. I can't believe it. I just can't believe William was out somewhere last night drinking moonshine. I just can't believe it."

Edwin said nothing.

Jim came over to him. He could hardly talk. After awhile he said, "Have you any idea, Edwin, where Cuff went last night, after he left Jack's place?"

When Edwin didn't answer, Jim spoke more to the point. "The last time anyone saw him alive was when he left the Lodge with you and Jack Caravan. Now, where did he go?"

Edwin hesitated. He didn't know what Jack had told everyone. "We were at Jack's house for a little while, then Willie said he was going up to Lushes Bight to see Lillian. I told him that Uncle Walter Brenton wouldn't let his daughter come to the dance here in Beaumont, and for sure she wouldn't be allowed out courting."

His mother looked at him and said, "Well, Edwin, what did he say then?"

Edwin's story was well rehearsed. "He said that if Lillian didn't come out with him, this would be the night that he would get himself drunk. Jack asked him what he was going to drink, and Willie said moonshine."

Jim Burton could hardly believe it. Could it be possible that Willie would go drinking over a girl? He was stunned.

Edwin knew he couldn't answer any more questions before talking to Jack first, to get their stories straight.

"Have a cup of tea, Edwin," said his mother.

"No," he said, "I'm going over to Jack's."

His father saw the look in his eyes. "Someone saw Jack just before daylight with a packsack on his back and a suitcase in his hand, heading for Lushes Bight. Last night he told Uncle Arthur Rowsell he would go back to the lumber camps this morning. Didn't you know that?"

Edwin couldn't believe it. "No," he replied, but then quickly added, "Yes! I thought I heard something about it."

Jim looked at Edwin and said, "'Tis goin' around that you and Jack and Willie went over to Jack's house when you left the Lodge."

Edwin had to be careful. "We just walked with Willie so far, and then Jack and I went to Jack's place. Willie didn't go; he left us after saying what he intended to do."

Nothing else was said as the door opened and Nurse Simmons walked in. Edwin ran upstairs.

Jim and Virtue Burton greeted the nurse with tears in their eyes. She knew that they were grieving over the loss of the young schoolteacher who had spent four months with them. Virtue often said that he was like a lamb. She often wrote letters to William's mother, Harriett, and his father, Wilson, telling them about their son, of how she loved him just as much as her own Edwin.

Nurse Simmons went to work right away. She asked to see the body.

Jim took her into the living room and removed the white bedsheet. She looked at the body from a distance at first, then from two different angles. She first examined Cuff's hands, paying special attention to his fingernails.

Nurse Simmons opened one of Cuff's eyes and took a close look. The smell of moonshine was strong, and she could see that the front of the schoolteacher's shirt had disintegrated.

"Oh, my," she said, "this young man's been in contact with a strange substance, not only moonshine or alcohol."

"What do you mean, Nurse Simmons?" asked Jim.

"He's been in contact with something that has burned up his clothes, something like acid. He must have been drinking it because it's all around his neck and shoulders. His lips and tongue are burned up. I've seen dead soldiers in France very similar to this. This young man drank something strange that has taken his life."

Jim couldn't speak as he looked at the unrecognizable face of young Willie Cuff. When he found his voice, he said, "Do you know what it is, Nurse Simmons?"

"I can't say for sure," she said, "but it's not common around Beaumont."

She was careful not to get involved, and Jim knew it. "In other words," he said, "the schoolteacher's been poisoned."

"All I can say, Mr. Burton, is this young man has been drinking something unusual. Are you able to get him ready for burial?"

Jim knew that she wouldn't commit herself as to the cause of death.

"Yes, nurse," he said.

# Chapter 17

Sod Mugford awoke at 8:00 a.m. His head was throbbing and he could still taste the moonshine. His thoughts flashed to the events of the night before. He and Edwin Burton had committed murder by poisoning the schoolteacher. Although his head was splitting, his thoughts went to Wes. How delighted Wes would be when he heard the news! This made him grin. Although Bessie and the youngsters had gone down with Az Roberts in the Pigeon, he still had some satisfaction this morning. He had been the death of Cuff.

He reached for the bottle of moonshine that was nearby. It was just about empty. He finished the remainder of its contents and threw it across the floor. He could see his breath as he sat up. "This house is like a cold storage. I think I'll go up to the old man's, fight or no," he growled.

Sod was fully clothed; the only thing he had to put on was his winter boots and cap. As he opened the outside door, the hinges made a squeaking noise with the frost, and out of the corner of his eye he saw his mother's face peeping through a frost hole that she had made in a windowpane. He noticed another hole thawed on another window that would have been made by his father.

Sod swore. "Those nosy rats!"

As he stepped outside, his boots slipped on the icy road and he had to struggle to keep from falling. As Sod neared his father's house he noticed the small komatik near the door, the komatik that he had taken from the woodshed last night and on which he and Edwin had put the body of Cuff.

He unlatched the door and went inside his parents' house, where it was warm and cozy. His father was sitting at the table and his mother was sitting in the rocking chair. Neither spoke as Sod entered. He went over to the stove and put his hands close to the dampers to get some quick heat.

He rubbed his hands. "I see the kettle's boiled, old woman. How's about a cup of tea?" It was more of a plea than a request.

"Oh, you're hungry, hey, Sod," said his father.

He looked at the old man very suspiciously.

"And cold," he replied. His mother continued rocking. She watched her son closely.

"How come you got no fire in this morning?" asked the old man.

"Got nothing to light it with, old man," said Sod.

"Wass wrong, Sod? No trees on Long Island? You should have plenty of wood."

Hazel answered for Sod. "That old Bess sold the wood Sod had cut for the winter, to get enough money to buy a ticket on the *Prospero*."

Sod sensed a little sympathy in her voice. "Come on, Mom. How about a cup of tea?"

Hazel put down her knitting and stood up. She went to the pantry and brought out a cup and saucer and a plate and spoon, and she placed them on the table. She took the teapot from the stove and poured a cupful of strong tea. She went back to the pantry again and brought out a molasses jar and part of a loaf of bread.

Sod went to the table and sat down. He put a spoonful of molasses in his tea and stirred it. He tasted it, and felt the hot liquid flow through his body. He picked up the bread but there was no knife. His father was watching him.

The old man put his hand in his pocket and took out his pocketknife and threw it to him. Sod caught it and opened the blade. It was as black as tar, and dirty from cutting Beaver tobacco. He cut off two slices of bread. His mother took the remainder of the bread and carried it back into the pantry. Sod quickly spread molasses on the two slices of bread before his mother snatched the jar away. He started to eat.

The old woman was like a fox. She was looking at him from the corner of her eye, and it made him nervous. He was swallowing the bread as if it were his last meal.

"What was you doin' all last night, Sod?" she drawled.

"Nothing," he said through a mouthful of bread and tea.

"Is you sure, Sod?"

Sod stopped eating and looked around at her. "I'm sure," he said.

"Have you looked across on the other side this morning?"

"No. I just got up."

The old woman stopped knitting. "There's an awful goings-on over on the other side. Everybody's in a fuss. I wonder wass happening?"

Sod knew that by now there must be an awful confusion around Jim Burton's place. He kept quiet.

"I seen something last night, Sod," said the old woman in a witchy tone. Sod stopped chewing and glanced at her. He didn't speak. She knew that Sod heard her and that the words had registered. By now the old man had moved near the stove; he was sitting on a bench against the wall.

"You put some wood in the stove, Zam," said Hazel in a loud voice. Sam obeyed. Sod resumed eating.

Hazel was in a mischievous mood. "What time you goin' away from here, Sod?"

He wasn't sure what to say. He swallowed what he had in his mouth. "I never mentioned I was going anywhere. Do you know any reason why I should go?"

The old woman pretended she hadn't heard him. She got up from the rocking chair and went over to the window. The heat in the kitchen had melted some of the frost off the panes, and half of the window gave a clear view of the outside.

"Zam," she said, "come and have a look across at the other side." She picked up the binoculars and put them to her eyes. "There's an awful racket going on over at Jim Burton's house. Zam," she squeaked, "it looks like a crowd getting their guns out. It's funny for them to be goin' out birdin' this morning."

The old man didn't move off the bench. He knew that she was up to something. Sod finished the bread and had the mug of tea up to his mouth.

"Oh my, Zam," she said. "Do you know what's wrote down on the side of Jim Burton's house? There's four big letters."

Sod looked at her.

"I'll call them out to you, Zam. F-L-U-X."

Sod almost choked on the hot tea; he blew it right across the table. He knew that his mother and father had been watching last night.

The old woman spun around when she heard Sod cough up the tea. "Wass the matter, Sod? The hot tea burning your t'roat?"

Sod was silent. He knew that his mother would have more to say.

"There'll be more than hot tea that'll burn your t'roat, Sod. I 'lows it'll be brimstone."

He knew he was caught, and he knew that his mother would tell on him if he didn't do what she wanted. She went into the pantry with the dishes Sod had used, and when she came out she was angry. "When is you leaving, Sod?" she asked.

"I don't know," answered Sod in a shaky voice.

The old woman sat down again. "I knows when you're leaving, Sod," she said. "You're leaving as soon as you can get your dirty duds packed and your snowshoes on."

"I'm not leaving here this winter," he argued.

The old woman knew what was going to happen if Sod stayed at Beaumont. Edwin Burton would confess what he and Sod had done, and eventually the magistrate from Twillingate would come and investigate. If the people found out the truth, they would burn down Sod's house and theirs.

"Sod," she said loudly, "we zeen everything last night, how you and that Edwin Burton poisoned the schoolteacher. We watched youse from the beginning to end. We zeen the flux bottle and the moonshine—we zeen it all, Sod, we zeen it all."

"Now, me son, you might as well leave right now for L'Anse au Pigeon. Dass the safest place to go, down there with your wife and youngsters and Az Roberts."

Sod said nothing, but he knew it was the truth; he would have to leave. He looked at his mother, sitting in her rocking chair. He stood up and hit the table with his fist, then walked over to his mother. The whiteness of his face and the black beard exaggerated the viciousness in his eyes.

"I hates you, old woman, and if I had a knife I'd cut your t'roat from ear to ear." With these words, he struck her with the back of his hand. It was such a blow that he sent her flying backward, chair and all. He then turned and walked out, slamming the door behind him.

A group of men went to the home of Nurse Simmons to inquire about what she thought caused the death of the young schoolteacher. They were in a very angry mood. In fact, it appeared that they were ready to lynch someone in Beaumont. Nurse Simmons wasn't afraid of any mob, however. She had spent three years as a nurse on the battlefields of France and had seen more blood and death than anyone could even care to imagine. A group of men didn't frighten her.

She greeted them. "Hello, gentlemen. It appears to me that you blokes are hot around the collar." Actually, they were scared of her.

"We're here to find out from you if the schoolteacher was murdered," said one of the men.

"Listen, my man," she said in her English accent, "tomorrow morning I'll tell you what happened to the schoolteacher."

No one spoke. She then added, "Now, be like gentlemen and go back to your homes. Let the authorities look after the matter." With that, she dismissed the group.

It was a hard day for Edwin Burton; he didn't leave the house all day. He spent almost all of his time in bed, but he heard people talking outside. Most people blamed Sod Mugford for murdering Cuff; others said that Edwin was mixed up in it, that Edwin knew what went on.

Edwin was scared. Every time he closed his eyes he would see the face of Cuff, gasping for air, dying.

Edwin agonized. *What have I done? What am I going to do?* He would get up and walk around the room, fear gripping every part of his body, cold sweat running down his back. The worst torment of all was to see his mother crying as if Cuff were her own son.

If only he could relive last night. What a fool he'd been to have anything to do with Sod Mugford. He pounded the bed with his fist.

"When I see Old Sod again I'll tell him what I think of him," he said in a whisper.

But Edwin would never see Sod Mugford again.

# Chapter 18

It had been a great Christmas so far in L'Anse au Pigeon. Az Roberts had killed a cow and a pig a few days before Christmas Day, and there were lots of shore ducks, or eiders, around every morning. Evenings, the guns could be heard as the men who were hunting killed as many of them as they needed. The women did the picking at night when the men brought the ducks home. Bessie received her share of everything. The doors of Az's warehouses were open to her to take whatever she wanted. She was treated the same as the rest of the family, including Uncle Happy, her father.

That fall, Gideon Hancock had brought the Salvation Army's message to L'Anse au Pigeon. He had arrived in the little town in early summer with a songbook in one hand and a concertina in the other. He was also a wonderful singer.

Gideon stayed with Az and Aunt Emily Jane and their two daughters, Winnie and Grace. Whenever it was possible, Azariah Roberts permitted him to hold services in the cookhouse. This was usually Sunday morning, and Sunday night Gideon would play the concertina and sing. Aunt Emily Jane thought she had landed in heaven when she sat and listened to him sing and play.

Az would have no part of this, and usually spent his weekends at the lighthouse with the Fontaines, drinking rum, or he would go to one of the small towns nearby.

Eventually, a religious revival came into full bloom, and people came from everywhere to hear the young Salvation Army officer sing and play.

The cookhouse, which had been vacant since the fishing crew had gone home for the winter, was now full. Az didn't like it, since his grocery store and warehouse were attached. His house was on a slight rise, and the cookhouse where the revival meetings were held was nearby, down on a flat reached by several steps. He decided it was time to firm up the plans for constructing a new church.

He called the crowd together and told them that they would have to start planning to build a church as soon as the snow was gone in the spring. "I'll give you the complete materials and the land, but it has to be used as a school, too," he said. Those at the meeting agreed.

A Christmas tree was made ready in the cookhouse. It was decorated, and a costume was made for a Santa Claus. There were gifts for all the children, and a great lunch followed by a concert. Gideon led everyone singing carols, and a good time was had by all. It was the first Christmas tree party ever in L'Anse au Pigeon.

Az Roberts had a new trap skiff timbered out. It was the tenth of January, and he knew that by spring he would have it completed and ready for the cod trap season. He was about to leave the workshed for the day when one of the men said, "Hey, Skipper, look. Someone's coming over the Middle Hill."

Az squinted and looked. He could see a tiny speck in the dying sunlight. "You're right, someone's coming. He must be half a mile away," he said.

"Whoever he is, he's walking fast," said a man standing nearby.

The man got closer. "A stranger," said someone else.

When the person was about a thousand feet away, Az spoke up. "Well, 'pon my socks. If it ain't the devil himself."

The men looked at the skipper, and one asked, "Do you know who it is, Skipper?"

"Yes," said Az, "it's Sod Mugford."

Everyone looked and they all agreed. "Yes, sure enough, 'tis Old Sod," said one of them.

Sod saw the men near the shed and went straight for them. "Uncle Az," he said as he neared.

"Sod, where did you come from?"

"I came from the lumber camps—walked all the way," he said as he caught his breath.

He was in a sorry state. He was carrying a packsack that had a worn-out pair of snowshoes hanging from it, and an axe was in his hand. His clothes were grimy and worn out; his boots were full of holes. He had a black beard that covered his face; ice candles hung frozen on his beard.

"You're carrying the mail, hey, Sod?" asked one man in a joking manner.

Sod didn't appreciate it, but said nothing. "You must be pretty worn out," said Az. "Come into the house."

"I sure will, Uncle Az." It was the first kind word he had heard in months. Some of the men wanted to ask him questions, but he quickly left with Az.

When they entered the house, Az called to his wife. "Emily Jane, come and have a look at who's here."

Emily Jane stood in the kitchen and looked at Sod. He was unrecognizable to her at first, but after a second look there was no mistake. She frowned. She knew there would be no more peace in the Pigeon this winter.

"Sod," she said, "for goodness sake, where did you come from?"

"I walked down from Badger, Aunt Emily Jane."

"My, you poor man, you must be nearly gone. Take off your clothes, Sod, boots and everything."

Sod knew this woman and her reputation for a kind heart. She came to him and put her arms around him and gave him a hug.

"Come over near the stove, Sod," she said. "Winnie, get a chair."

"No, that's all right, Aunt Emily Jane. I'm all right," he replied.

"No, you're not all right. Sit by the stove. My, Bessie and the children will be very surprised to see you, Sod," said Emily Jane. He removed his coat and sweater and his boots.

"Haul off your socks, Sod, before the dogs break into the house and attack you," Az said, laughing.

Emily Jane gave him a clean pair of socks. He hadn't been treated this well since the last time he was in L'Anse au Pigeon.

"Supper will be on the table in half an hour. Do you want a lunch now, Sod, or will you wait until then?" Winnie asked.

"I'll wait for supper," he said, as politely as possible.

After Sod was settled in the chair near the stove, Az asked him a few questions.

"How is everybody around Long Island, Sod?"

Sod was a little uneasy because he didn't know if anyone had heard the news about Cuff. "Everybody's all right as far as I know. I came from Badger to Deer Lake on train and came right from the lumberwoods to here," he lied.

"You never went home, then?" said Az.

"No," said Sod.

"Then you have no more news from Long Island than we have ourselves," said Az.

"No more news than you got," Sod replied.

"I guess we won't find out from you who's sneakin' in through the back doors when the lamps are blown out," said Az with a laugh. He winked at Sod.

"Enough of that, Fred," said Aunt Emily Jane in a stern voice.

Sod was afraid to make another comment. It was getting too close to supper, and he didn't want any wisecrack to stand between him and the only sensible meal he'd seen since the lumber camp at Badger in December.

Word soon went from house to house that Sod Mugford was in the Pigeon. Finally, someone ran into Bessie's house and announced, "Sod just arrived and is gone to Uncle Az's."

Bessie was startled for a moment. She was thinking, but her thoughts came out as words. "I wonder what drove him down here, now? For sure it's not love for me or the youngsters."

Her heart sank. She knew there would be no more peace for her now with Sod around. She'd had such a wonderful Christmas; it was "heaven below." But now!

It was the moonshine can that she dreaded; he hardly got in bed with her on the best of times, anyway. Bessie sat down and tears filled her eyes. She looked out at the ocean and her thoughts raced. How she hated him. She knew that the word "hate" was a bad word, but she also knew that the young devil himself would soon follow—young Wes. The only thing that she could say through her tears was, "God help L'Anse au Pigeon." She knew she would have to accept him under her roof, but she would never let him come near her bedroom. She shuddered at the thought of him.

She mused, "I wonder why he's here? I wonder what he's running from?"

The door opened and the oldest girl came in and said, "Dad's here, Mom." She was old enough to know about the problems her father always created at home when he was drinking, and her mother's misery whenever her father got drunk or had a hangover. "What are we going to do now, Mom?" she asked.

"I don't know, my dear," Bessie replied. "I'd hoped your father would change his ways." The child didn't answer. "Anyway, don't worry, my dear. You go on out to Aunt Emily Jane's and see him."

The child put on her boots slowly, as if to say, "I guess so, Mom."

After she left, Bessie said to herself, "I thought I was going to have a great winter here, but now I feel like running away." She wiped her eyes with her apron and continued her work around the kitchen.

It took until the first week of February before word of the tragedy at Beaumont reached L'Anse au Pigeon. It came in the form of a letter to Winnie from Lillian Brenton. In it, she told about the death of the schoolteacher William Cuff. She didn't give any details, but it stated that there were rumours around Long Island that some of the men had poisoned him. People were calling for an investigation. Lillian told Winnie that she had been going out with William.

Winnie looked over the letter before reading it slowly to her mother.

"My, oh my," said Emily Jane, "what next is going to happen in Beaumont? I wonder who did that?"

Az was told the news. He read the letter and told the women not to tell anyone because he suspected there was something more to it.

"Just keep that to yourselves," he said. "Don't get blamed for starting a rumour here in the Pigeon, because I've got a feeling Sod's mixed up in this mess."

Bessie had told Az earlier about the incident between Wesley Mugford and the young schoolteacher Cuff, and how Sod wanted to shoot him. She had also told him that Sod and Wesley vowed to murder Cuff that winter, and that this was the main reason she left Beaumont and came to L'Anse au Pigeon.

Az would wait for more reliable information. "We'll wait 'til the next mail comes, Winnie. I'm guaranteed to have a letter from Sarah," he said.

Az knew there was something strange about Sod Mugford. He was awfully quiet. He had moved in with Bessie and appeared to be a changed man. He hadn't gone out drinking, and he was now working on the new trap skiff for the skipper.

Az was glad Sod was there to give a hand, and of course he was credited for every hour against the bill for groceries and clothing that Bessie and the children had gotten from the store.

When the mail came two weeks later, everything broke loose. Az's sister Sarah informed him of the events of Christmas past. Four or five other people also received letters, spelling out in detail the goings-on in Beaumont, and all fingers pointed to Sod. "You got a murderer under your roof, Az," one letter said. Another letter asked the question, "Why are you hiding a murderer under your roof, Az Roberts?" Another one said, "Sod Mugford and Jack Caravan made away with the schoolteacher and ran."

Nobody mentioned young Edwin Burton; this was because he hadn't left Beaumont and swore he didn't have anything to do with it. Some people believed him, due to the fact that Sod and Jack Caravan had disappeared.

Everyone who ever knew Az Roberts over the years will tell you that he was a very lovable kind of man, but when he was mad he was like the devil. There was never a man that set foot inside L'Anse au Pigeon who wasn't in dread of vexing him. Az was now very concerned. He called for Sod, and the two of them went to the cookhouse.

Sod wasn't in a pleasant mood; he had heard about the news that came in the letters from Lushes Bight. He hadn't yet commented on them, but now he knew he would have to have some kind of a story for the skipper. He also knew that Bessie would hear all about it sooner or later, and this made him very upset. Since he had come here over a month ago, things had been very good. Bessie had allowed him in her bedroom on several occasions, but after the arrival of these letters, he knew that would be the end of it.

After they went into the cookhouse and the skipper had closed the door, Az was the first to speak. "You lied to me, Sod," he said very sternly.

Az was tall and strong, with a well-built frame and huge hands. Sod was very much aware of this and was scared of what Az might do. For a moment, Sod didn't say a word, but he knew he would have to face his accusers. He had a story rehearsed and was ready for Az Roberts or anyone else. He would never be able to deny that he said he had come from the lumber camps.

"Yes, I lied to you, Uncle Az," Sod admitted.

"I know the reason why you lied to me. It was because you made away with the schoolteacher."

Sod pleaded, "Uncle Az, you've got to listen to me."

"I knew there was something wrong with you more than hunger pains when you came staggering in on that cold evening. I could see it in your face."

Sod let the skipper talk.

"It's been said for some time now, that you and Wes would murder someone—and now you've done just that."

Az was walking around, but Sod sat down and took out his tobacco and started rolling a cigarette.

"What are you going to do now, Sod? What will you do now?"

Sod lit his cigarette, then replied. "Uncle Az, I want you to listen to me now. Will you listen, Uncle Az?"

The skipper stopped pacing and said, "All right, Sod, what have you got to say? You had better not lie to me this time. If you do, you know what you'll have to do, and that is get out of the Pigeon, and I won't be worrying where you go."

"Uncle Az, I never had anything to do with making away with that schoolteacher Cuff. I had nothing to do with it, so help me."

Sod took a long drag from his cigarette, and before he had a chance to say anything else, Az asked, "Why did you say that you came straight from the lumberwoods at Badger to the Pigeon? You said you hadn't been home and had no news."

"Uncle Az, I didn't want to bring a big yarn here to the Pigeon and get everyone upset or all riled up. No one made away with that schoolteacher. He made away with himself."

Az looked at him. "How?"

"He went out drinking moonshine with them two hard tickets, Jack Caravan and Edwin Burton, that's Uncle Jim's son. They were on the 'shine and gave him too much; it was his first time drinking. I knows all about it—Edwin told me. He told me he was going to get even with Cuff for taking Lillian Brenton away from him. I had nothing to do with it."

Az was furious. "Listen, Sod, I don't believe you, and I know you're in deep trouble, because Bessie told me all about the racket you and Wes had with the schoolteacher last fall. You wanted to go to the school with the shotgun and shoot him, and you vowed that you would murder him someway."

"But Wes wasn't even home when I left Beaumont for here. I told you about how he cut himself and was in the hospital at Grand Falls."

"Then why did you run from Beaumont, Sod?"

"Uncle Az, I knew I'd get blamed. The people went crazy up there. They had to blame it on someone."

Az was no fool. "Sod, I'm going to find out the truth about the whole incident, and if you're involved in this racket in any way, I'll be sending a wireless to Magistrate Walcott at St. Anthony. I'll even handcuff you myself and deliver you to him."

Sod was uneasy. "I'll leave, Uncle Az. I'll go on back to the lumber camps."

"Sod, the safest place for you now is right here and you know it, but if I find out for sure that you murdered Cuff, then by Harry, this will be the most dangerous place for you."

# Chapter 19

After Sod Mugford left Beaumont, everyone's frayed nerves began to settle, but the talk was loud and clear in every house that he and Jack Caravan had murdered the schoolteacher. They knew for sure that Edwin Burton was mixed up in it, but due to the fact that he had stayed around home, and the fact that Edwin and his father had convinced some people that he had nothing to do with it, things got a little better for Edwin—until the night of the card game.

One night in early March, Hazel Mugford was playing cards with a crowd of women, and the conversation was about Az Roberts. Soon the talk led to Bessie and Sod.

One of the women playing cards was named Bella, who said, "Az Roberts is down in the Pigeon, hiding away that murderer, Old Sod." She had forgotten that Hazel was Sod's mother.

One of the other women was Edwin's aunt. She was an old girlfriend of Az, and she spoke up for him. "Don't go talking about Az Roberts, whatever you do," she said.

"Why?" Hazel asked.

"I can guarantee you one thing. If he knew for sure that Sod murdered Cuff, he'd kick him out of the Pigeon."

Bella spoke up again. "I'd say that Jack Caravan's also down there hiding. His father and mother don't know where he is. I'd say that he's down there too—the two murderers."

Hazel Mugford wasn't one to be fooled with. Everyone there could see that she was ready to explode. She put down her cards and put her hand to her mouth. With her tongue, she rolled the large wad of tobacco she was chewing, pushed it out of her mouth into her hand, and tossed it at the front fender of the Waterloo stove.

She then focused her stare at Bella. "Now, you listen here, Beller!" She shrieked in a witchy voice that came from deep down inside her chest. "I'm the one who zeen the murder happen, and Jack Curvin had nuttin' to do with it. But Edwin was there."

She was so possessed that she could hardly talk. This was the first time she had talked about it to anyone except her husband. "I zeen how they planned it and I zeen it happen right before me eyes," she said.

"You did?" asked Bella.

There was no way of keeping Hazel quiet; she had to talk. She pointed at Edwin's Aunt. "Imagine you! You, talking about my Sod. Sure, Sod helped to poison that Cuff, but Edwin Burton was with him, too. Jack Curvin wasn't even there."

Hazel's hands were clenched on the table; they could see the whites of her knuckles, huge from hard work, fishing side by side with Az Roberts's crew in L'Anse au Pigeon. Az had once said that he thought more about her than he did of either man that ever worked for him.

Hazel told them that they had given Cuff moonshine spiked with flux, and how Edwin took their sleigh and hauled Cuff over and dumped him off by the side of the road before he ran home. "We zeen it all, Zam and me. We zeen the whole works."

She was furious, and jumping up, she almost turned the table over, but the others barely noticed. They were so shocked at what they heard that some held their hands to their mouths. Hazel scrambled into her coat and scurried out through the door, slamming it behind her.

The women who were left behind sat and looked at each other; they couldn't believe their ears.

Finally, one woman spoke. "There's no doubt that Az has a murderer under his roof all right, and he'll be knowing about it as soon as I can get someone to write a letter."

Another woman spoke up and said, "There's no need of that, because in a couple of weeks or so, Stewart Brenton's going down to the Pigeon for the summer season. I'm going to tell Stew the whole story myself, and he'll tell Az in person. That's when trouble is going to start for Mr. Sod."

They all agreed that the truth was finally coming out. One woman asked if they should tell the people what they had heard. "If we spread this around, what do you think will happen to poor Virtue and Jim?" asked one.

"What about the truth?" said another. "People are blaming it on Jack Caravan, but it wasn't him at all."

Another asked, "Then why did he run from Beaumont as if the place was on fire?"

"I know the reason," said another. "He's mixed up in it—just you wait and see."

"I know one thing," another woman said. "It's time the truth came out, and who would know any better than someone who saw the whole thing—Sod's mother."

They all agreed that tomorrow would be a very interesting day in Beaumont.

Bessie heard the news about the Sod racket from her stepmother, Mary Tucker.

"I have to tell you something, Bessie," she said. "You're going to hear about it anyway, so you might as well hear it from me first." Mary had sent for Bessie to come to her house. She had heard the news from Beaumont through Winnie, Az's daughter.

"What is it, Mary?" asked Bessie.

"It's about Sod."

"What about Sod?" asked Bessie, anxiously.

Mary then continued. "When he came here he told everyone, including you, that he came directly from the lumberwoods. Well, Bessie, that was a lie."

Bessie stared at her stepmother. She knew that she had important news to tell her. "What is it, Mary? Tell me."

Mary tried to be calm. "Remember what you told us first when you came here—that Sod and Wes were going to kill the schoolteacher if it was the last thing they ever did?"

"Yes," said Bessie, sitting down near the table.

"Well, my dear, according to the letters from Lushes Bight and Beaumont, they did the job on him. They poisoned him."

"Oh my God!" said Bessie.

Mary continued. "Winnie got a letter from Lillian Brenton, who told her all about it. Lillian said the likes was never known on Long Island. What an uproar!"

Bessie was shocked, even though deep down she had known Sod was capable of doing it. She put her elbows on the table and her hands to her forehead. She knew that Sod had never told the truth in his life; he had been a liar from the first day they got married. He was still a liar to this very day. But why would he bring his troubles to the Pigeon for her and her three children? When she thought about it, though, she realized that there wasn't a better place for him to hide than right there, especially if he was running from the law.

Bessie started to cry. The tears ran down her face. "Can you imagine?" she said through her tears. "That schoolteacher was just a young man who never hurt anyone in his life. It's hard to believe. Imagine, Mary, someone with the nerve to kill another person. It's too hard to believe. I guess it's like they say, 'what's in the cat is in the kitten.' It's a wonder his mother, old Hazel, hasn't murdered someone before this. Well, Mr. Sod will not be staying under my roof one more hour."

Mary looked worried. She was sure that her husband Happy didn't know anything about this, but he wouldn't be surprised when he found out. He had left early that morning with their son Roland to go over to the Clue. The Clue was a small cove about two miles away, where the men were cutting firewood for the winter. Happy wanted Sod to go with them, but Sod refused. He said he was going to Quirpon to see someone.

Mary knew that Happy would be distressed at hearing the news, because for the first time since Sod and Bessie were married there had been a little peace in their daughter's home.

"I knew there was something wrong all the time, ever since he came to the Pigeon," said Bessie. "He looked worried, and that's not like Sod. He even told Aunt Emily Jane that he hadn't been home to Beaumont before coming to the Pigeon. How could he tell such a lie?"

Mary laughed. "Tell such a lie? Sod telling lies? I know how he could tell such a lie. It's because he's just like Haze and Sam. They're the two biggest liars on earth."

Mary appeared to be ready to tear Sod apart, and she could do it. Once, Mary had chased a Ranger with a fish prong. If he hadn't run, she would have stabbed him with it.

"Well, Mary," she said to her stepmother, "if you were me, what would you do?"

"I know what I would do. I'd go to where he is right now and I'd tell him not to show his ugly face in my house ever again. Believe you me, I'd mean it!"

"I wonder what Uncle Az thinks about it? For sure he's heard about it by now."

"Az has known about it for close to a month, according to Winnie," said Mary.

"He has? Why didn't he tell me about it?"

"Well, my dear, I'll tell you the reason why," said Mary. She paused for a moment. "Winnie had a letter from Lillian Brenton telling all about it, but Az wouldn't let her tell anyone else, until he confirmed it himself. You know what the skipper's like." Mary rolled her eyes.

The turmoil in L'Anse au Pigeon lasted for about a week. The people began to get used to the talk about Sod. Everyone was curious. Why does Az Roberts let him stay in the Pigeon? It's funny why Uncle Az would let him stay around. What is he waiting for?

Az was being patient. He knew that if he kicked Sod off his property and out of the Pigeon on the strength of a few letters from Lushes Bight, it would only create more talk.

One day he called all the men in the Pigeon together with Sod. He told the assembled crowd that if anyone came looking for Sod, especially the law, Az would personally turn him in. And he made Sod promise that he would co-operate.

Sod and Bessie had quite an argument—it was clear to everyone. She wouldn't let him stay in the house with her, at least for awhile. After that he moved in with an acquaintance by the name of George Oake.

The people of Beaumont were not surprised to hear that Sod had gone to L'Anse au Pigeon. They knew he had to run and get out of Beaumont and off Long Island. He had nowhere else to go. If he went to the lumberwoods at Badger or Millertown and talk got around about him, he would be closer to the law than down on the tip of the Northern Peninsula, which in those years was total isolation.

Edwin Burton was the only one of the three who stayed home in Beaumont. He took the full impact of the Cuff murder. For days he stayed in bed.

Everyone heard what Hazel had said, how he and Sod had given flux to the schoolteacher. They knew it was true, because they had seen the clothes Cuff was wearing, and heard how it was burned up. Some people came to Jim Burton's house to see the clothes, but Jim had burned them long ago. He had dressed Cuff in fine clean clothes before putting his body in the coffin.

He never dreamed there would be questions about the way the schoolteacher died.

When the clothes were gone, some people accused him of covering up for Edwin. All fingers and remarks were aimed at Edwin. It was impossible for him to go anywhere without someone making a disturbing remark, and by now it was getting difficult for him to withstand the pressure. It was said that he was beginning to lose his mind.

Jim and Virtue Burton were having a rough time. Mrs. Burton tried to persuade Edwin to start seeing Lillian Brenton again. "You should write her a letter, Edwin," she told him. "It's not your fault that Cuff drank himself to death." She hadn't yet heard the story that was told by Hazel. She was told that Cuff had died from drinking too much moonshine, and by now she was feeling sorry for Edwin and bitter towards Cuff.

Edwin wasn't surprised that his mother believed his story, but his father was different. It appeared that he suspected something. After a little coaxing, Edwin decided to write Lillian. With a heavy heart, he sat down in the chair that his mother had given him when he was a small boy. He began to write.

*"Dear Lillian,"* he began. *"I don't know how to even begin to write you, because you seem to be like a stranger to me. It was only like yesterday when we were going out together and you were telling me that you loved me. When I think about it, I realize how foolish I was to even have anything to do with Sod and Wes Mugford. I guess this was where I made my first mistake.*

*"But now the two of them are gone, and even if they were here I wouldn't have anything to do with them again. I guess you have heard about the yarns that are going around about me. Well, Lillian, that is nothing but a pack of lies. Can you imagine me doing a thing like that? And above all they're saying that I gave him poison to drink. What a lie! As you know, Willie and I were the best of friends, although he took you away from me. You can ask Mom and Dad."*

Edwin knew he would have to be careful not to sound too foolish, or Lillian would have nothing to do with him.

*"Anyway, Lillian,"* he concluded, *"I would like to see you, and maybe we could meet in the same place near the pond by the side of the hill. I'm longing to see you. Please write me and let me know as soon as possible. Edwin."*

He folded the letter, put it in an envelope and sealed it. He boarded their small boat, rowed up to the post office and mailed the letter.

Sod Mugford behaved himself for the rest of the winter. In late March and early April he spent almost all his time sealing. Being in the seal fishery kept him busy. There was no time to even think of the Cuff incident. The dangers of working from land on the moving Arctic ice, with all of its narrow escapes and hard work, put everything out of his mind.

Az controlled the hunt from the land. He carefully watched all the hunters on the ice from the high cliffs that towered near the shoreline. If anything happened, he would signal for someone down below to signal Ned Fontaine, and Ned would blow the foghorn, telling the sealers what to do. This would depend on the weather, of course. There were no major incidents regarding men getting lost in that area, but there were many narrow escapes.

That spring, Az had finished his twenty-eight-foot trap skiff, and when Art Windsor came in the spring with his schooner, the *Almeta*, he brought a new 8-h.p. Acadia engine for it. During the summer he used it hauling the cod traps, and it proved to be very seaworthy, although when he launched it after the engine was installed, the blades were partly out of the water. It had been built too wide in the stern.

Az and Happy poured a thousand pounds of cement in the rear to get it down enough to put the blades underwater.

"What do you think of her now, Az?" asked Happy.

Az said, "She looks all right, but if she ever fills full of water, God help us. She's gone to the bottom with all that cement aboard her."

Happy laughed. He knew the chances of the boat filling full of water were slim, especially with Az in charge. "She'll be all right. There's always lots of boats around." Az said nothing, but he was concerned.

"There's one thing about it, Skipper," said one man. "If she ever fills with water, you can kiss the world goodbye, because whoever is on board will be living with the crabs."

Everyone laughed.

Sod spoke up. "What, are you fellows scared?"

Someone said jokingly, "Living with the crabs doesn't bother you, does it Sod?"

For the benefit of those nearby, the joker continued. "Certainly, if he went down where the crabs were, he would have to write them an invitation to come near him."

They all laughed again. "I would say that before it's all over, Sod will be looking for a few crabs," he said.

Sod didn't like the remark, but he was in no position to start an argument. He knew that this was part of the price he had to pay for what he had done. However, he registered the remark and who had made it. It was Allan Hillier.

For the fishing season at L'Anse au Pigeon, Az contacted his men and had them report to the Pigeon early. As requested, his foreman Art Windsor brought five new men with him.

In May, the coastal steamer *Prospero*, which was a Newfoundland railway ship, came to the small town of Quirpon, about five miles from the Pigeon. The *Prospero* discharged her cargo and passengers. Az sent a boat to the town to pick up the freight and the five men. When the boat returned, Az and Emily Jane went down to meet them.

"Look, Fred, there's six men coming instead of five. I wonder who the extra person is?"

Az recognized the other person. "Emily Jane, for the love of mercy, just look at that. Why, it's the devil himself."

The boat wasn't yet close enough for Emily Jane to see. "I can't get a good look at him," she said. "Which one is it?"

Az burst out laughing. "Emily Jane, we got the pair all right. And I'll tell you one thing, that if you and Happy can get the two of them to join the Salvation Army, then I'll join immediately." Emily Jane said nothing. She knew there must be something wrong.

Az said, "All we need now is old Hazel, and we'll be ready to tackle the Germans."

Startled, Emily Jane replied, "You don't mean to tell me, Fred, that young Wes Mugford is down here?"

"He sure is, or it's his ghost."

Emily Jane gave him a withering look and said, "Why don't you ever take things seriously?"

# Chapter 20

Edwin didn't attend the memorial service that was held for Willie Cuff. He peeked through the upstairs bedroom window at the huge crowd that had gathered. It appeared that everyone on Long Island had come to pay their last respects to the young schoolteacher. He watched when it was over, and still peeking he saw the crowd follow the coffin to his father's storeroom down near the water. The body would stay there until spring when the first coastal boat came.

"What have I done? What have I done," he whispered in agony. The words burned like fire in his brain.

Through the window, he saw seven or eight men carry the coffin inside the storeroom and shut the door behind them. He knew what they were doing. He visualized them shovelling the salt in around the corpse of young Willie Cuff. His imagination was as clear as if he were there. They were covering Cuff's face with salt, pouring it in his mouth, and sprinkling it inside his shirt, making sure it went down around his arms. In his mind Edwin saw them fill the coffin to the top, and a man took a board to smooth the salt level with the top, leaving just enough space for the cover to be placed on and nailed down. He thought about what the men were saying as they did this horrible job. Maybe some of them would have nightmares for weeks afterward.

Edwin knew they were blaming him and Sod. If only Old Hazel hadn't seen them, he might have gone and hidden in a place where nobody knew him.

One man had told him, "You'll be caught, Edwin Burton—you'll be caught, sonny boy, and you'll pay for what you've done."

Edwin was beginning to believe it. Those words continued to echo in his head and ring in his ears, like a broken phonograph record. He spent the winter lying around the house. On the few times he did go out, he wouldn't look at anyone or speak to them.

"Edwin, my dear," his mother would say, "why don't you tell me what your trouble is? I'm so worried about you."

He wouldn't even answer her, as if he didn't hear her talking to him.

Edwin began to lose weight. He looked like a skeleton. "He looks like someone dying," everyone said, but no one took pity on him. When the ice was gone from the harbour of Beaumont, Edwin's father took him out in the boat with him a few times, hoping this would make a difference. It didn't. As soon as the boat got back he would head straight for bed.

It should have been very clear to his family that Edwin was going out of his mind.

It was a sad day when the coastal steamer *Kyle* came into the harbour of Beaumont. It was the first ship to call there that year. Under usual circumstances, it would have been a time of great excitement, because after many months of isolation everyone welcomed the arrival of fresh produce and other foods—but not this year. The steamer was on a different mission.

The wharf was crowded with people, young and old alike, as the steamer came close to the wharf and her lines were thrown ashore. When she was fastened, the winches secured her tightly. The crew then put the walkway ashore.

As the people stared in silence, Captain James Snow, one of that area's most famous seamen, came ashore. He knew what was facing him at Beaumont. He had received a wireless telegram telling him that he had to pick up the body of a young schoolteacher who had died there that winter. The captain noticed all the schoolchildren on the wharf. Many were crying. He heard the drums of the Orange Lodge beating in the distance.

The night before, a group of men was summoned to go to the fish store and prepare the body of young Willie Cuff for shipment back home. It was a job that the men didn't like. The problem was, it was at night. It had been difficult to get volunteers, but eventually enough were found to do the job.

Each man carried a lantern, and leading the group was an elderly lay reader carrying a Bible. They unlocked the door of the fish store, went inside, and closed the door behind them. They were wary of what they had to do: take the salt out of the coffin and prepare the body for shipment. Most of the salt had to be removed to make the coffin easier to lift. All stood waiting and wondering what the body was going to look like. Would Cuff still be recognizable? One man took a hammer and removed the nails from the cover.

When the cover came off they were surprised. A lot of the salt was gone and most of the man's head was visible. They took the coffin down off the table and put it on the floor, where they tipped it to one side to carefully roll out the remains. They were appalled at what they saw. Most of them cried out when they viewed what remained of the young schoolteacher. One man said Cuff didn't look like a human being at all. Another said that he resembled old salt bulk codfish that had been left in the salt all winter.

The men shook the salt from Cuff and removed all his clothing by cutting it off with scissors. Taking a bucket of water they had brought with them, they washed his entire body. Next, they rolled him in a white sheet.

They washed out the coffin and put cologne in it to help remove some of the odour. They then placed his body in the coffin and stuffed wool from an old mattress around it to prevent it from moving around while being transported. This done, the lay reader opened the Bible and started to read. It was a very solemn moment for everyone. After cloth and handles were put on the coffin, someone nailed the cover shut.

One of the men took out a letter addressed to Mr. Wilson Cuff, Ochre Pit Cove, Conception Bay, Newfoundland. He took out four small nails and was going to nail the letter to the coffin when one of the others spoke up.

"Men," he said, "I'm not satisfied for that letter to be nailed to that coffin before we read it."

The man holding the letter said, "The nurse told me not to let anyone open it."

His companion said, "Ever since this mess started, all that I've heard is 'don't do this' and 'don't do that.' Some say that he died drinking moonshine, some say he was poisoned with flux, and others say he died from the cold. I want to know, and I think the answer is in this letter. I want it opened right now."

It was a tense moment. The man holding the letter remembered the nurse's instructions, and he intended to follow them.

Another one of the men spoke up. "I think we owe that much to young Willie. Let's have a show of hands." All except the old lay reader and the man holding the letter agreed. "It's six to two." A decision was made to open the letter.

The man who first spoke took the letter and opened it. He couldn't read, so he asked the old lay reader to read it. The old man took the letter and with trembling hands slowly started to read it.

*"To whom it may concern. Mr. William Cuff quietly passed away on April 20. The cause of his death was pneumonia. He had been suffering for some time with the disease, but finally succumbed to it."*

This was all the letter said, and there was no name signed to it. Those present were shocked to learn what was in the letter. Cuff had died on Boxing Day, not April 20, and it was obvious that he had died of something other than pneumonia.

The men groaned and swore at this deception, but the old man spoke. "Listen, boys. Maybe it's better this way. We don't know what his people want done or what they requested, so the best thing for us to do is leave the whole thing as it is."

The nurse's letter was resealed and tacked onto the coffin.

In the morning, before they moved the coffin from the shed, the lay reader asked everyone to bow their heads while he prayed. The children and women started singing as the men brought the coffin down the dusty road.

*Amazing Grace, how sweet the sound, that saved a wretch like me...*

The crew and passengers on the ship had tears in their eyes as they watched the funeral procession come onto the wharf and proceed to the gangway. When the singing stopped, the lay reader then took the Bible and read a psalm. He was careful not to say anything else, especially after reading the letter the previous night. He was still reeling from the message in the letter.

The men picked up the coffin. A new hymn was begun.

*I will meet you in the morning, just outside the Eastern Gate over there...*

They carried the coffin on board and stored it on the upper deck. The young man who had come to Beaumont, so full of life, was going home in a box, murdered.

# Chapter 21

The sun looked boldly through its bloodshot eye as it peeked over the boiling ocean, and the breath of the toiling men mixed with the salty spray to give a pinkish hue as they hauled the huge cod trap. Giant swells slammed into the solid granite only a few hundred feet away. Soundings were made, and it was determined that the trap was full of codfish, about three hundred barrels—enough to load all the boats around the trap, and more.

The men weren't expecting the trap to be hauled this morning, due to the heavy sea that was rolling in from the angry North Atlantic. They had come only to inspect the trap for damage. However, the fishing skipper, Az Roberts, standing on the engine house, gave the orders to his men to haul her up. As soon as the cod trap came to the surface of the water, codfish could be seen everywhere.

"I would say," said Az, "that when this storm is over there won't be a thing left out there on the rock. The cod trap and everything will be gone."

This was the most productive cod trap berth on the coast, directly under the lighthouse on Cape Bauld. It was said that every codfish that went through the Strait of Belle Isle went through this cod trap berth. When every other berth failed along the coast, there was always fish to be caught in Az Roberts's cod trap.

As dawn was breaking on this chilly June morning, Az and his crew had slowly steamed to the trap berth under the towering lighthouse. Ned Fontaine saw them and gave a few loud blasts on the foghorn. Az and the men waved in appreciation; its sound could be heard for ten miles or more. Not far from where this cod trap was set there was a huge iceberg that looked like it was getting ready to founder. As they got closer to the cod trap, the engineer shut down the 8-h.p. Acadia engine. The man with the gaff, who was standing on the cuddy, hooked the small buoy that was attached to the span line of the trap, which was fifty feet under the surface of the water.

"The sea is mountains, Skipper," said one man.

"I don't think there's very much that can be done," said another.

Az had a good look around and called to Art Windsor, the man he generally went to for advice.

"What do you think, Art? Should we haul her up?"

"I'm not sure, Skipper," he said as he looked around. "Maybe we should. I've seen us haul her up before in conditions as bad as this, and worse."

Az nodded and said to his men, "Haul that rope tight, someone. Haul that rope tight!" When the rope on the span line was tight, the boat was directly over the centre of the cod trap.

"Someone, let down a jigger to see if there's any fish in her, boys," said Az. One of the men started to let down the jigger.

"I'd say that she's right full," another said. "Look, you can see the water rippling from their tails."

"You could be right," said Az. In a moment, the man with the jigger confirmed it. "She's right full. I can't even get the jigger down. I got one on now, and a big one it is."

As he hauled it in over the side, one man remarked, "What a fish!" The sea was mountainous but there was no tide, which was a big factor in hauling the cod trap in this place.

"All right, boys, we're going to haul her up, so get the capstan ready," Az ordered. The capstan was a winch made of wood that was placed in the centre of the boat. There was a three-foot round pin through it, and when the rope was placed, two men turned it and lifted the trap. There were two like this in the boat. The haul-up rope was placed in the block in the stem-head. Four men started hauling, but it became too hard for them, so the rope was then placed around the capstan, and two men started winching.

"Play the swells, boys, play the swells," said Art Windsor. The men obeyed. When the boat went down in the huge waves, the rope became less taut, so the men would haul until the rope came tight again. When a wave lifted the boat, it pulled the rope and trap up with its contents. When the boat went down again, they began winching again. In less than fifteen minutes, the span line was up and across the middle of the boat. When the big wooden floats on each corner came to the surface, the ripple from the codfish in the trap made the water under the boat boil. It wasn't very long before all the smaller boats that were fishing with hook-and-line gathered around the cod trap. This is where they got most of their fish anyway, so now they came to help.

The crew untied the two doorway ropes from the span line and put them around the capstans and started twisting. This pulled up the doorway bottom, weighted down with heavy chains. Pulling up the doorway closed it, preventing any fish from escaping.

"Skipper," said Art, "we're going to have to be extra careful with the corners because the weight of that fish could split the bottom open, or tear the foots from the back."

Az knew he was right. "Lift her easy boys—lift her real easy," he said to the hook-and-liners who had positioned themselves at the back of the trap. Although they weren't his crew, these men were as good as his own, well-experienced fishermen who knew what they were doing.

They quickly hauled in the skirts of the doorways, preventing any fish from escaping. The huge waves were lifting the whole armada, including the cod trap full of fish, every time it rolled under them. By now, the whole cod trap was completely surrounded by boats, everyone eager to help.

"Skipper," said one man, "she's right full, and what ogis gaffers!"

Az laughed. He was enjoying this moment. He had spent a lifetime at the very thing that he was doing right now. He was fifty years of age and had never had a sick day in his life. In fact, there was never a morning that he couldn't get up at four o'clock and help get breakfast for his crew.

Now, as he stood on the top of the engine house and held onto the rail, he was glad he was alive. With the sting of the salty spray in his eyes, it made him fully realize that he was someone who belonged to—and was part of—the Great Atlantic Ocean.

The men tried to get the bottom corners up but were unable—the fish was dried up already, concentrated in one area of the trap. "Hurry men, the tide could turn any time and sweep the whole works away," he roared above the noise of the sea, pounding like thunder as it slammed against the cliffs only a few hundred feet away.

"Look, Skipper," said one of the crew. "There's undertow coming right out to the doorways of the trap."

"Sure enough, I see it," Az said.

He then looked around at the men in the boats surrounding the bloated cod trap. If enough undertow were to start boiling, combined with the heavy sea that was rolling in, it could sweep away the whole cod trap, its moorings and contents.

"Listen, men," said Az, "you'd better start dipping the fish in right away, and make sure the cuts are wrapped tightly around the pins. Don't let the boat get too far away from the doorways. Hey," he yelled from the top of the engine house, "tie up that span line and don't let her go out any farther. Hold everything fast; I'll watch the swells."

"Okay," said Sod Mugford, who was holding onto the span line.

Then the skipper yelled at the top of his voice, "Tie everything on solid, and hold her fast. There's a huge breaker out there and it's coming straight at us."

Everyone saw it and froze for a moment, holding onto the part of the trap where they were. They held their breath as the great breaker rolled in under them, lifting everything as it passed. There was a fourteen-year-old boy with them, helping to haul the trap and keep the net in the boat. He wasn't fully prepared when the wave lifted the boats and their contents.

As the wave rolled in, the huge bag of fish was slow to rise with the wave, causing the boat to dip low in the water, as if it were going to roll over. With this sudden movement, the part of the trap that was on board started to get pulled out. The young boy saw it and started to panic; he grabbed it with his arms, and before he knew anything the trap twisted around the buttons of his rubber coat. It started to drag him out of the boat.

The men in the other boats saw what was happening and started yelling. The skipper, who was standing on the engine house, heard them yelling and saw them pointing.

Then he saw the young boy.

"My Great God," he whispered, and leaped from the engine house. The young boy was just going over the side of the boat, entangled in the cod trap, when the skipper grabbed him and tried in vain to pull him in. Then Az saw what had happened; the buttons on the boy's coat had hooked in the linnet. He reached down into the water and started to untangle the buttons while someone held onto the boy's legs.

"Get a knife! Get a knife and cut off the buttons," Az screamed.

Sod Mugford reached into the engine house and grabbed a knife. As quick as a flash, he cut the collar at the neck of the boy's oilskins and ripped the coat down the back. He then pulled the young boy back into the boat.

Before anyone could say a word, Sod heard another scream from the men around him. "The skipper's got his hand caught in the linnet!"

Az realized with mounting horror what had happened. He was wearing his Red Cross ring on his index finger, and while trying to unhook the buttons of the rubber coat, the ring had become caught in the linnet. He was helpless, and he knew he had only a few seconds before he would be pulled under.

Sod jumped to the skipper's aid. He grabbed the skipper's arm and gave a pull with all his strength. Az felt as though his fingers were being pulled from his hand, and the next thing he knew, he landed in the bottom of the boat with a terrible pain in his arm.

Az looked at his hand and saw blood coming from his fingers. He noticed that the ring was missing. "My ring is gone," he said. "Listen, boys, my Red Cross ring is gone. Has anyone seen it?"

The men looked at him and shook their heads.

"Your ring is gone, all right, Skipper," said Sod. "I saw it come off your finger and pop right out into the trap. You should consider yourself lucky that your hand isn't gone, or that you never went under yourself."

Az couldn't believe it. He felt his finger—it was cut to the bone.

Sod watched the skipper put his handkerchief around his finger. Az was nearly in tears. "My ring, my Red Cross ring," he moaned, as he held his arm and looked out into the trap.

"Skipper," said Sod, "you shouldn't worry about that old ring. There's lots of them where that one came from."

Az gave Sod a sour look. "Listen, Sod, there are twenty-two fathoms of water down there where my ring went, and if you make one more remark like that I'll make you go down and pick it up."

Sod was about to say he thought he saw a codfish go after the ring once it hit the water, but given the skipper's present mood he decided against it.

Az Roberts climbed back onto the engine house and shook his head. "My ring," he said, "is gone forever."

Soon the cod trap was hauled and every boat had a three-quarter load, as much as it was safe to carry. There was still a lot of fish left in the trap. Everything was released, including the span line, and the cod trap slowly sank back to its box-like formation.

The 8-h.p. Acadia engine slowly pushed Az and his crew with a full load of fish out of Lighthouse Cove heading toward the Pigeon. Az sat very quietly in the back of the boat, near the tiller. His thoughts were far away. His ring, the Red Cross ring, was gone forever. He felt his finger.

*Don't join the Lodge, Az. Don't join, a curse may fall on you. Remember what your father told you.*

*Az, what you've done is something I'll never forgive you for. You broke your promise to me.*

*Why are you hiding a murderer under your roof, Az Roberts?*

Az owned the little fishing town and everything in it, so naturally everyone looked up to him. If anyone was hungry he fed them, and if anyone wanted clothing but had no way of getting any, he gave them clothing. When the boat landed and it was sounded around that he had had a narrow escape, it was big news.

Gideon Hancock, the Salvation Army officer, would have big ammunition for his sermon on Sunday morning. There would be no doubt that he would be telling his congregation to take a warning from this incident, or else.

Aunt Emily Jane cried when they told her that Az came close to being drowned.

"You would be gone now, Fred, out into the lost world of the unsaved."

Az laughed. "This is a lost world now, Emily Jane, and if the Depression gets any worse in Newfoundland, we'll all be better off in the lost world."

"Don't joke about it," she told him.

When they were alone that night, Az told Emily Jane that he was going to resign from the Orange Lodge at St. Anthony. She was glad to hear it. "One good thing about it, Fred, is that you won't have to give back your ring because it's on the bottom of the ocean off Cape Bauld, and the only sound it will ever hear again is Ned Fontaine blowing the foggle horn."

Az laughed. "That will be good," he said. "Wait 'til Old Neddy hears he's playing a tune to the Red Cross ring."

# Chapter 22

The little town of Beaumont was buzzing with activity as the codfish was brought in and processed into what was called shore fish. This was fish that was split, the sound-bone taken out, and then salted. After five days in light-salt it was washed and dried in the sun. By the first day of June, all the cod traps were set in the water and fish was being brought ashore.

Jim Burton was no different than the rest—he was fishing full out. He was what they called a hook-and-liner, meaning he was fishing with a cod jigger and baited hook. However, he was getting most of his fish as excess from the cod traps that were set out all along the shore of Long Island.

Edwin was fishing with his father, but preferred working in the fishing stage most of the time, where he would wash out the fish and put it out on the flakes in the sun to dry, depending on the weather. This was a busy time for him, but the hard work wasn't enough of a distraction to snap him out of his depressed mood. Sometime around the middle of June, the word went around that the magistrate was going to investigate the death of Cuff. It frightened him.

It was said that Edwin had taken a turn for the worse after watching the men carry the body of Cuff on board the *Kyle* to ship it home. He had been watching from the upstairs window. He saw all the people on the wharf, including all the children. It appeared that almost everyone from Long Island was there, and when the people began singing, Edwin started to cry. His mother had come upstairs to see him sitting near the window, tears streaming down his face. He looked like a small child.

Virtue looked out the window and saw the *Kyle*. It was slowly moving out the harbour, and its steam whistle blew three times. She knew what it meant; it was a farewell to Beaumont and the people, from their schoolteacher. William was the one Mrs. Burton had loved as her own. She could almost hear him whisper, in the voice she had loved to hear. *Goodbye, Mrs. Burton, goodbye. I'll never be back again. I'm leaving forever.* She burst into tears.

Edwin didn't look away from the steamer. It was flying its flag at half-mast.

In a few minutes, Mrs. Burton's concerns turned to her son. "Edwin, my dear, what's the matter?" she asked. He didn't answer. She sat next to him and put her arms around him. He was in the depths of despair, but what could she do? What he needed was someone to console him, to cheer him up.

Virtue couldn't understand why Lillian wouldn't answer Edwin's letters. She wanted to go and talk to her about it, but Jim wouldn't permit it.

"Edwin," she pleaded once more, "what's the matter? Now, I want to know. This has gone far enough. I'm your mother and I want to know."

He wiped the tears from his eyes with her apron and looked up at her. "Mom, I'll be all right, really, I will," he said through his sobbing.

They heard the sound of a motorboat coming in the harbour. "Your father's coming, Edwin. You'd better go help him; it looks like he has a lot of fish."

Edwin didn't lift his head as he replied. "Yes, all right, Mom."

Lillian had received the two letters from Edwin and had read them to her mother and father. They knew of the sad state Edwin was in. Uncle Walter Brenton had always been a personal friend of Jim and Virtue Burton. He had sat many times with Jim in the Methodist Church and had admired Virtue's musical talent, but he wouldn't let his daughter have anything to do with Edwin after he started going around with Sod and Wes Mugford, and especially when he heard what Hazel Mugford had told the women at the card game.

What more could be said? Hazel had seen them poison Cuff, and she had made it public. Mr. Brenton had said to his daughter, "My dear, he could be gone out of his mind by now, judging from what people are saying. He could kill you if he got you alone."

Lillian was also afraid. Even if her father permitted her to meet him, she wouldn't go to the place where Edwin suggested. Her father said one day, "Lillian, imagine if you started going out with him again and the police came and took him away—what kind of talk there would be."

As a result, there would be no replies to the letters.

Az Roberts was a changed man after his ordeal with the cod trap, when he almost got dragged overboard and had lost his ring. One night shortly after, Az confessed to Emily Jane that he felt as if a heavy load had lifted from his shoulders. Emily Jane was surprised to hear him say that, but she knew he meant it. She almost told him that he was undergoing a conversion, but she kept her peace.

"I feel like a free man, Emily Jane," he said. "It's as though I've been guilty of something or another. I feel like whistling and singing. Make sure you don't tell anyone. It's our secret." He knew she wouldn't tell anyone, not even Winnie or Grace.

Plans were made to build the new Salvation Army barracks in the Pigeon. Az and Happy went across a small bog near a hill and planted four wooden pegs. "This is where we'll build the barracks," Az proclaimed.

Happy Tucker had always said that he would never live to see a church service held in L'Anse au Pigeon. "Maybe, Az, I had the wrong feeling after all. Maybe, just maybe, I am going to see it."

Az laughed. "Don't count your chickens before they're hatched; if the fish get scarce, we might all end up on the dole, and if that happens, the church won't be able to help us.

Happy looked at Az and said, "God will supply all our needs."

· Az grunted and said, "Lets go back to the house for a cup of tea."

From the moment Edwin Burton decided to kill himself, he appeared to be a changed man. To his mother, it seemed that he was starting to get a little better. He was more active, more pleasant, and he was even sleeping better. There were times when he was depressed, though. Every few days there would be a new rumour floating around about the Cuff incident, the latest being that the police were coming to Beaumont to arrest Edwin.

He got up one morning late in June. The weather was clear and warm. Most of the men had gone fishing, but others were left on the shore to spread the fish on the flakes to dry. In their spare time they had to saw firewood, and Edwin was left ashore to do the same.

During the night, Edwin had written another letter to Lillian.

"*Lillian. It's obvious that you don't want to see me again. This is the third letter that I've written to you. You haven't replied to the others and this is the last. Today I am going away, and I won't be coming back. I still love you. Goodbye, Edwin.*"

He neatly folded the letter and placed it in an envelope and sealed it. He wrote another letter, this one to his father.

*"Dear Dad. You may not understand what I am going to do, but Mom will. I've always loved you, but I can't take it any longer. I have to go away. Goodbye, Edwin."*

He placed the note on the highboy in his parents' bedroom.

At nine o'clock in the morning, Edwin went down to the stage, where hidden under a wheelbarrow there was a ten-pound rock with a rope attached to it. Looking around and seeing nobody, he picked it up and carried it out to the front of the wharf and put it down near the edge. From the wharf, he saw several people; some were spreading fish, while others were sawing wood and going about their general work. He thought there was no one watching him; they were too busy. There wasn't a breath of wind, and the hustle and bustle of the activities of people in the town was loud in his ears.

When he was satisfied that there was no one watching him, he pulled the small rowboat close to the wharf and jumped into it. He looked around again. Satisfied, he reached up for the rock and rope and quickly put them down into the boat. *Don't do it, Edwin*, said a voice deep inside him. Another voice said, *It's your only hope, Edwin Burton, your only hope. It won't hurt, it will only be a second, just go on and do it.*

He pushed the small rowboat off from the wharf and started rowing. He had one more thing to do, and that was go to the post office and mail the letter to Lillian.

*This is the last thing I'll ever do on earth,* he thought.

A young girl stood not far away, spreading fish on the flake with her mother. Seventy years later, she can still recall that day in late June of 1929.

"We watched Edwin come out on the wharf and look around. I said, 'Look Mom, Edwin isn't out fishing today. He must be at the fish.'

"Mom looked and said, 'I wonder what he's doing this morning out there on the stagehead?'

"We then saw him looking around, kind of suspicious-looking. He went back into the stage, and in a few minutes he came out carrying something in his arms.

"'What's that he got there?' asked Mom.

"'I don't know,' I said.

"He pulled in the small rowboat that was tied to the wharf and got down in her. He reached up and took something down—well, we know what it was now, it was the rock with the rope tied to it, but we didn't know then. He then put out the oars and started rowing the boat toward the bottom of the harbour, and landed. He pulled it partly up, where it wouldn't drift away with the waves, and walked up to the post office. 'Aunt Virtue must have sent Edwin to the post office for something this morning,' I said to Mom.

"He was only in there for a few minutes when he came out again. Edwin had gone in the post office and given the letter to the postmistress, with the money to post it. We found out later it was addressed to Lillian Brenton, Lushes Bight, Newfoundland.

"He left right away. He got in the boat again and started rowing back toward the wharf where he came from. This was all we thought of it. We went back at the fish. In a few minutes, we heard someone singing. I said to Mom, 'That's Edwin singing, isn't it?' It looked like he was rowing straight towards us. She said yes. We were silent as we listened. For years I never did get the sound of Edwin singing that morning out of my mind—it haunted me. And poor Mom, she never forgot it either, 'til the day she died.

"'Listen, Mom, can't that young Edwin sing?' I said.

"'Yes, he sure can,' Mom said. 'I guess he learned to sing from his mother, Virtue.'

"We all knew that Aunt Virtue used to play and sing in the church. We listened to him as he got nearer; there were other people listening and watching him as well. I can remember what he was singing, just the same as if it was yesterday. He was singing *Nearer my God to Thee, nearer to Thee.* He wasn't looking around—he was just looking straight back as he rowed.

"I said to Mom, 'Isn't that the same song that they sang on the *Titanic* when it went down?'

"'Yes, dear, that's the same hymn.'

"We never did talk about it, only among ourselves, because it's too hard to talk about. Uncle Jim and Aunt Virtue were so kind. For years, the people saw a light in that very spot when the wind was a certain way, or when a storm was brewing. Uncle Jim and Aunt Virtue never got over that, especially Uncle Jim. He always said that the people drove Edwin to do it."

Mr. Bert Parsons was ninety years old and sitting up in his bed at the intensive care unit at the Bella Vista home in Springdale, Newfoundland, when he told the story of that day. Both his legs were gone, with only six inches left on each one, but his memory was perfect and his sense of humour was amazing. He joked and laughed as if he were getting ready to take a trip into the woods.

When asked about the Cuff incident at Beaumont seventy years earlier, the incident involving Edwin Burton and Sod Mugford, he said, "Yes, I saw it all happen."

"My brother and I were sawing firewood with an old crosscut. It was about nine-thirty in the morning, not a cloud in the sky. We had just finished spreading a flake full of fish. 'Twas waterhaus fish, codfish that just had the salt washed out of it and was going on the flake for the first time. When we finished we went up to the house and had a cup of tea and a smoke. We watched the fish in case it would sunburn.

"Then, as we were sawing, my brother said, 'Good grief, Bert, I think I hear something making a sound, like singing.' I laughed at him.

"He said, 'Don't laugh. Look out there.' He nodded his head in the direction of the water.

"I looked out and saw a small rowboat. We knew it was Uncle Jim Burton's boat, but for a moment we didn't know who was on board it. 'There's Edwin, in that boat,' my brother said. We just looked for a moment and my brother said, 'I knew he would go out of his mind.'

"We laughed, but we never dreamed that he was going to do what he did. If we had only called to him, maybe it would have changed his mind, but we didn't. He kept on rowing and singing. He was singing that hymn, *Nearer my God to Thee.* I said to my brother, 'He should be careful he don't strike an iceberg!'

"I was facing the water. We started sawing again, but we still heard Edwin singing. He came on along, just out clear of where we were, about two hundred feet from us. We saw some women out on a flake not far from where we were. They were watching him too.

"My brother, who was older than I was, said, 'It sounds awful weird to me, if I got to say anything.' I said that he'll sing a different tune when they put a noose around his neck. We noticed he was just looking straight back and rowing real hard, and singing at the top of his voice, *Nearer to Thee.* We put down the saw and watched him—something was wrong. He rowed on past the houses and the stages. Then he kept clear of the shoreline. I could see him real plain. When he started to shut in from view, we stood up on the flake and watched him. Then he stopped.

"I saw a large trap skiff come into view out around the point at the entrance of the harbour. Edwin then stood up. He was wearing a pair of bib overalls and a woollen shirt. I saw him as plain as day, and so did my brother and the people that were on the other flakes.

"What the fellow did next was hard to believe. He reached down and picked up a piece of rope, or he caught hold of a piece of rope, and sat down again. We didn't know what it was then, but we know now. We saw him when he put the loop of rope over his neck. It was attached to a rock about ten pounds.

He then took the rock up in his arms and stood up. People said later that he had his coveralls filled with rocks, but he didn't. He made no hesitation. He just jumped over the side of the boat.

"'Dear God,' I said. 'He's after doing it now.' We looked at each other. 'Edwin's after doing it. He's after drowning himself.' We stood there dumbfounded for a moment. We called out to the people who were on the next flake and told them. With that, we ran to our stage and the two of us jumped down into our rowboat. I wasn't long getting the oars out, and we started rowing toward the empty boat that Edwin had been in. We knew the water wasn't very deep where he had jumped overboard.

"In a few minutes we were at the place. My brother stood up as we neared the small boat. I reached out and grabbed the rope. I started looking around, then I saw him—he was legs up. His feet were about six feet from the surface of the water. We didn't have a gaff or a jigger or anything to hook him with. I tried to hook him with the oar, but couldn't. Then I saw the trap boat coming in. It was getting closer, so I waved to it. It then came over to where we were.

"The skipper of the crew said, 'What do you want, Bert?'

"I said, almost screaming, 'Edwin Burton's down there; go astern, quick.'

"They reversed their engine to avoid running over him. Everyone in the trap boat was shocked to hear what I said. I then shouted to anyone who would listen, 'Get the boat hook, get the gaff.' Someone grabbed the gaff and reached down and hooked Edwin's clothes and pulled him to the surface of the water. I reached down and grabbed him and pulled him into our rowboat. My brother pulled in the rock. Everyone there then knew what had happened—it was a suicide, sure enough.

"'What's the world coming to?' said the old skipper.

"By now there were other small boats around us, and the people on the shore were calling out and asking what had happened. 'Take him on board the trap boat, Skipper,' I said.

"It was then that the men reached down into the rowboat and lifted him into the trap boat. They put him on the gangboards. I took the rope off his neck; it appeared that no one wanted to touch him. Just then we saw another boat coming in the harbour. We waved to it. Within a few minutes the boat pulled up alongside. This was a certain skipper who had a terrible dislike for Edwin and Sod Mugford after what they had done. In fact, he had said many times that winter that they should be shot. He still had the bitter feeling. When he saw Edwin's body, he became very upset and angry.

"He said, 'Bert, you can just cast that dirt overboard. Throw that dirt back into the ocean.' This was an example of how much most of the people in Beaumont hated Edwin."

Bert Parsons moved around in his bed. "It was one of the worst things that I had ever had to deal with.

"There's only so much that a person can get away with. He's guaranteed to get caught one way or another, especially when it comes to taking the life of a person."

The news spread like wildfire around Long Island and all throughout Notre Dame Bay. In every home and stage, in every grocery store, from the youngest to the oldest, they were all saying, "Have you heard the news about Edwin Burton, how he drowned himself?"

Then they would say, "I wonder if Sod Mugford will drown himself next? When will Sod drown himself?"

In their conversations, they would say that they wouldn't be surprised if Sod did it, because of what they did with the schoolteacher. It was the talk everywhere.

But there was no pity for Edwin.

Jim and Virtue were in a state of shock. When Jim read the note left by Edwin, it finally sank in. It was true—their son had helped poison the teacher. With saddened hearts, they kept quiet, but there were still many unanswered questions. Why did William Cuff go out drinking moonshine with Edwin Burton, especially at Sod's house? As Hazel Mugford had said, the teacher didn't drink at all. Maybe they held him and poured the moonshine and flux down his throat. Virtue would say to Jim, "We may never know the truth."

Jim would answer, "Maybe someday the truth will come out and everyone will know it."

After the funeral, Jim took all of Edwin's clothes down to the beach and burned them, but the memories of his son would always be fresh in his mind. The blazing heat of the fire could not destroy them.

# Chapter 23

Long Island was in an area of Newfoundland that had many
schooners going to Labrador for the codfishery, and before
they crossed the Strait of Belle Isle they usually went into
L'Anse au Pigeon to deliver freight or to get the news and share
the latest gossip. This summer they were mainly interested in
the gossip, especially the "Sod Mugford racket." With the
comings and goings of these schooners the residents had full
access to all the news and gossip from other areas of the colony.

The news reached the Pigeon that Edwin Burton had
jumped overboard with a rock around his neck. It caused quite
a stir, and by the time it circled the town a couple of times, it
was said that he had made a confession before he did it—that
he and Sod had murdered Cuff. The exaggerated rumours also
stated that he tried to get Lillian Brenton into the woods to
murder her, and that it was only because of her father that he
didn't do it. And so the stories went.

Hearing all this, Az became furious. He had made up his
mind that this was enough. He called in some of the people
who were on the visiting schooners and asked them about it,
but he couldn't get a clear answer. Each one would say that he
heard someone else say this or that, but the facts weren't clear.

Again, Az called Sod in the cookhouse to have another talk with him. When Sod was confronted, he denied everything.

"But your mother saw you, Sod," said Az.

"Listen, Skipper," Sod said. "You know all about that old woman. Uncle Az, she's the devil."

Az knew all about Hazel Mugford. She had worked there in the Pigeon one year, working in the stage, salting fish. She was a great worker that year, but he wouldn't let her come back again for fear of trouble.

"But Sod, do you know that Edwin made a confession before he drowned himself, saying that you and he had poisoned Cuff?"

Sod pleaded. "Listen, Uncle Az, do you think that if I had anything to do with poisoning Cuff that I'd come here and crawl under the wing of old Bess? Not on your life would I do that."

Az knew that Sod was lying, but what could he do? He wasn't a judge. All he could do now was warn Sod that when the time came—and it would come—he wouldn't get any kind of help from anyone in the Pigeon. For the moment, Sod just wanted to get away from the skipper; he didn't like to be questioned.

When he left, the skipper sat down with his daughter Winnie and the second cook, Emma Bridger. "Winnie, I want you to go up to the barracks and tell Gid to come down. I want to talk to him."

In ten minutes, Gideon arrived. He was wearing his work clothes. "Get Gid a cup of coffee before he drops," Az joked.

When Gideon finished stirring his coffee, the skipper began. "Gid, I'm the Justice of the Peace here in the Pigeon, as you know. I want something done about the goings-on concerning Sod. It's gotten to a point now that people on Long Island are starting to drown themselves and blame it on me, thinking I'm hiding Sod."

Gideon had heard the news about Edwin, but it was the stories brought in by the schooners that were more disturbing.

Gideon had never had a quarrel with Sod. He was aware that he had a drinking problem and was having many fallings-out with certain people, but Sod hadn't said anything to him. In fact, there was a bit of an improvement in him.

"I know, Skipper," Gideon said, "there are a lot of ugly stories going around about Sod murdering the schoolteacher. I've heard them."

Az was concerned. "I'm afraid people are saying that I know the whole story. They say I know the truth, and therefore I must be hiding Sod Mugford from the law. You know what I mean—covering it up."

"Who did you hear that from, Skipper?"

"Skipper Peter Parsons told me about an hour ago, just before he left for Battle Harbour."

Gideon knew that the skipper was deeply concerned. "What do you want me to do about it?"

"It's hard to say. The problem is, I don't want to accuse Sod of something that he may not have done. It's based on rumours, but all the people are accusing him. I'm convinced that there's something to it, especially after young Edwin Burton jumped overboard with a rock around his neck. He made a confession before he did it, so they say."

Gideon shook his head. "I don't know what can be done, for sure."

"I know what can be done," Az said. "I want you to write the magistrate's office at St. Anthony and ask him if he'll come here and carry out an investigation. He can start by interviewing Sod. That way, if the axe falls, whenever that will be, I won't be accused of hiding him."

Gideon scratched his chin. "Skipper, I think there's a better way to do it than that."

"What is it?"

"Maybe I should write the Methodist minister at Little Bay Islands for you. You can ask him to confirm or comment on some of the rumours that are rampant in the community regarding the suspected murder of Cuff by Sod and the late

190

Edwin Burton. Also, you can make it known that Sod Mugford is in your employ and that you would like to have a reply at his earliest convenience. I can impress on him that Beaumont is part of the Little Bay Islands parish. This letter would be a request for him to notify the authorities in the Notre Dame Bay district and have a proper investigation started immediately. You can make it clear that you would like to have your letter go on record."

Az nodded. "There's a schooner leaving for Little Bay Islands this evening. We could send it by her."

Gideon agreed to write the letter immediately. Az started to feel much better about the whole mess.

From the day Sod Mugford heard the news that Edwin Burton had drowned himself, he started having a rough time. Wherever he went, especially if he was drinking—Sod did a lot of that—the first topic to come up was Edwin's drowning himself. Next would be the schoolteacher being poisoned. He was becoming a very violent man, worse than he had ever been. He realized that he would never be able to spend another winter at L'Anse au Pigeon, no matter what happened.

He would have left earlier that summer, but Wes pressured him not to leave. Wes was crazy about young Susie Tucker, Happy Tucker's daughter, even though she had a boyfriend.

Susie was going out with Allan Hillier, and when Happy heard that they were planning to get married, he was delighted.

Happy said that he would never let Susie have anything to do with Wes Mugford, due to the hard life his other daughter was having with Old Sod. One day Happy told Wesley, "Not as long as I'm alive, Mr. Wes, will you ever have Susie."

Of Wes and Sod, he said, "They're hard workers, but they can't be trusted, especially when they're around the moonshine can."

One night when Sod was drinking with his buddies, he told them that he didn't see any other way out than to do what Edwin had done.

"Maybe Edwin did the right thing," he said. "Wherever I turn, someone's bringing it up to me about Cuff; even old Bess don't want to see me. The youngsters don't want to hear talk of me, and even Uncle Happy seems to give me the cold shoulder. Above all, Uncle Az is turned against me. I just don't know where to go or where to turn."

The fellows laughed. "Sod, when are you going to drown yourself?"

Half drunk, he replied, "When Old Sod goes, he won't be like Edwin. He'll be taking more people with him, don't you worry about that."

Most people took it for a joke, and very soon a lot of his acquaintances tormented him whenever they had the chance. "Sod, when are you going to drown yourself?"

Sometimes Sod would get angry, and other times he would just shrug it off, but deep down inside he knew that he would have to take his medicine, one way or another. He was sure that Az Roberts's patience was growing mighty thin, and that he would eventually do something about it. When that happened, Sod knew that the law would catch up to him.

Sod vowed that he would never let any magistrate or constable come here and take him—he would never go to the gallows. If it took a shootout, then a shootout it would be. His buddies joked to him all the time that he was going to the gallows, but Sod took it seriously—it was always on his mind.

He was living under the same roof as Bessie again, but he was sleeping on the couch in the kitchen. The reason he was there at all was to keep up appearances for the children. He was spending most of his time at the house of his friend, George Oake. He was afraid to complain or kick up a racket with Bessie, because he was warned that the next sound he made would get him fired and sent out of the Pigeon. He was also tormented because Uncle Happy practically lived under the same roof—only four feet of space separated their houses.

Then there was the Salvation Army officer. Sod said that he didn't trust him any farther than he could throw him.

Sod told Wes one day, "I don't stand a chance. I'm caught between my two biggest enemies—Bess's father Happy, and Uncle Az. 'Tis like living between the devil and the deep blue sea."

Wes laughed. "Old Bess knew where to go, didn't she?"

Sod knew what he meant. "If I can only punch the winter in here, by the spring things might be cooled off, especially with that Edwin gone."

"Yes, that Edwin Burton, the murderer."

Sod laughed, then said with glee, "Wes, my son, you should have been there. 'Twas the best moment of my life when I saw the last breath going out of that young Cuff."

Wes laughed as Sod continued.

"You should have seen the pair of legs on Edwin go that night. Just like the squid, Edwin was, darting all over the road with Cuff's carcass on the old man's komatik."

They both laughed.

"But, Sod," Wes remarked, "you made one mistake. Why didn't you make Edwin go out and throw Cuff over the edge of the ice? If you'd done that, nobody would have ever known his whereabouts. They would still be looking for him now."

Sod took a big draw from his cigarette and flicked the ashes with his forefinger.

Wes stared at him. "The next one you murders, Sod, I'm going to make sure that I'm there."

"I wouldn't bet on that if I was you, Wes, because I's got a plan up my sleeve."

Wes narrowed his eyes. "Don't let anyone here in the Pigeon know anything about that, Sod. The skipper would break your neck if he ever suspected anything. But you could tell me."

Sod just shrugged him off. "You'd better keep your little mouth shut too, Wes."

Sod took the cigarette out of his mouth and had a coughing fit. When he caught his breath, he wiped his mouth and grinned. "Wesley, my boy, I'll never go to jail."

# Chapter 24

During the summer of 1929, there were lots of codfish around the shores of L'Anse au Pigeon. Az was able to fill all his stages with salt fish twice, and both harvests had been shipped before the last of August. His two schooners were used to send the cod to Little Bay Islands and return with more bulk salt. The harbour was so full of fish guts and fish bones thrown from the stages that the boats coming in from the traps had a job getting in to the wharves. In order to solve this problem, they put down heavy anchors on top of the fish waste and had the large boats pull the waste out to deeper water. They would also start up the 8-h.p. Acadia engine and the tide from the propeller would move the fish guts away. This was done at least twice a week.

The fish that year was trapped until the middle of September. Then it was gone, or the fish moved offshore. During this period, the crews would do the work onshore. This year there was a big job to do, and that was to build the Salvation Army church. The Salvation Army officer Gideon Hancock was in charge of the project, and whenever there was a blowy day, the men could freely go to work on the barracks.

One rainy summer afternoon, Az walked up to the construction site for the church. It had poured for more than a day and the ground was flooded. In order to get to the site, he either had to walk across a little bog or take a much longer walk around. He decided to take the shorter route, and as he crossed the bog, he sank down and got his feet wet. He made a promise. "I won't get these feet wet anymore on this bog!" he exclaimed.

He inspected the bog and decided to construct a road across it. While they were eating that evening, he told the crew what he had in mind. Everyone was more than glad to give a hand building a new road to the church. The next morning, the work began.

All twenty-two of the crew, with shovels and picks and wheelbarrows, were there in the area of the new church, eager to give Uncle Az and Uncle Happy Tucker a hand. The main job was to construct a road across the wet bog. Az divided them into groups. Some were chopping the sod with axes, and another group carried the sods away.

"The road will be eight feet wide, with a ditch on either side so the water can run off," he told them. "Then we'll get the gravel from the beach and spread it between the two ditches to make a good road for walking—at least the water will be gone."

On one side of the road, there were two or three men shovelling out the ditch, two feet down in the wet bog. At three feet, one of them struck something hard with his shovel. "I struck something. I think it's a rock," he reported.

The worker next to him said, "There's no rocks there where you're digging, my son. We're too far out in the bog. You would have to go down about four feet before you struck a rock there."

The man removed some of the material from around the hard object and looked closer. "It doesn't seem like a rock," he replied.

He scraped the object with the shovel and said, "It's shining."

The man next to him became interested and looked also. "It looks like brass or copper to me." This got everyone's attention.

"Look, there's something else here," said the man.

Az went over to where they were digging and said jokingly, "What have you found, men? Your fortune?"

"Hey, look here," said the digger, excitedly. "There are some bones here."

Az immediately called a halt to all the digging. "Listen, boys, maybe someone is buried here. We've got to be careful."

Az got down into the ditch himself and carefully examined the things they had found. He picked up the round object they had uncovered and lifted it up out of the ditch. It was the size of a soccer ball and was black in colour. Az took out his pocketknife and scraped the object. To his surprise, it was shining inside.

"It's copper or brass," he said. He went over to a hole filled with water and washed it as everyone looked on. When the mud was washed away, each man was shocked at what they saw.

It was a brass helmet with a funny design, and in the helmet was a man's skull. Az didn't wash all the mud out of it; when he realized what it was, he took it back to the ditch.

"We've dug up a human grave," said Uncle Az. "Some poor soul's been buried here and we have opened up his grave."

Happy Tucker took off his cap and said, "May his soul rest in peace."

Az thought for a moment. "Now that we have him partly dug up, we'll dig him up completely and take him outside the road. Let's have Gid give him a proper burial."

The young Salvation Army officer listened to their story and agreed to hold a service. Everyone then went back to the spot where they had found the grave in the ditch.

"Now, boys, be very careful and save every bone and everything else that's in the grave," Az warned.

As they dug, they made another surprising discovery. They opened up a large hole and very carefully moved all the dirt from around the body area. In doing so, they found a large round plate, about three feet long, covering the chest and abdomen of the skeleton.

"Look at that," said one man.

"A fighting shield, I think they used to call it," said someone else.

They took up the shield and washed it off, revealing strange letters on it. Uncle Az was educated and could read, but the letters made no sense to him. It looked like the letters, some of them anyway, were upside down.

Azariah Roberts had had a lot of dealings with Dr. Wilfred Grenfell, and he said that the doctor once told him that there had been Vikings around the Pigeon at one time. He said that he saw some maps that looked like the Pigeon area, indicating that this is where they came ashore. He called them Vikings, and maybe this was one of them who died or was killed somehow.

They started digging again, cleaning all the mud and dirt from around the bones, until someone said, "Stop. I see something."

The man in the ditch looked closer. He hauled out a sword, about three or more feet long. It was made of solid brass.

Norman Pilgrim was in the work crew. He said, "I don't guess we'll bury that. We can use that to make keys for the shafts of the engines, to keep the blades on, Skipper."

Az agreed. He figured it had nothing to do with the man or whoever it was in the grave. When they continued digging, they came across more material, but no one wanted to handle it. They were a superstitious lot, and they had become afraid after Az spoke about the Vikings. He had to move it all himself from that point on.

They dug a big hole five feet away from the ditch and put all the bones and everything else into it. Gideon Hancock read for the burial and prayed, and they sang a hymn, just like any other funeral. Then they covered the remains.

Az said that the Viking shouldn't have anything to worry about. He figured he got a better send-off than the first time.

# Chapter 25

By the end of September, 1929, all the fishing was over and the cod traps were dried, repaired and stored away for the next year. The rope and grapnels were all stored and most of the boats were pulled out of the water and turned over. Az knew how much fish he had brought ashore and had processed—it was his biggest year. He paid his men, and those who didn't live in the Pigeon went back to their homes on Long Island, or other places around Notre Dame Bay. They returned home on the schooner with the last load of fish going to Little Bay Islands, then they went to Lushes Bight, where the schooners would be pulled up for the season. Any winter work on the schooners was supervised by Art Windsor.

In mid-October, Az and Emily Jane went to St. Anthony, a town twenty-five miles south of the Pigeon. They went there to join the coastal steamer the *S.S. Kyle,* to go to St. John's and acquire their winter supplies and get straightened up with the fish merchant, the Strong firm of Little Bay Islands.

Before Az left for St. John's, he had a meeting with Happy and outlined what he wanted done in the way of repairs and renovations. One job was to repair the roof of the fish-salting shed behind the cookhouse. He also took Happy's order of supplies for the winter, and a written shopping list from Mary and Bessie for special things that they wanted. In fact, Emily Jane had a shopping list for every woman in the Pigeon. It was said that Christmas came in October at the Pigeon, when Aunt Emily Jane and Uncle Az came back from St. John's.

Az and Emily Jane went to St. Anthony a day before the *Kyle* arrived. They wanted to visit some of Az's relatives there, and to mix with some of his old buddies who were members of the Orange Lodge. Most of them commented on the loss of his Red Cross ring. They told him that he should immediately order a new one. They said that at their next meeting, they would have replacing his ring on their agenda, so that a motion could be made that the Lodge pay for it as a gift to him.

Az made it very clear to them that he would flatly refuse their offer. He said, "Listen, boys, I lost my ring trying to save a young man from drowning. It went down in over twenty fathoms of water in the North Atlantic, and for some reason I feel good about it, kind of relieved, as if something lifted from my shoulders, and I don't miss it."

His friends dropped the idea, and it was never brought up again. The next day he joined the lightkeeper Ned Fontaine and his wife Anastasia on the *Kyle,* bound for St. John's.

It was early in the morning when Happy Tucker got up on the scaffold to do the work of putting the black jack felt on the roof of Az's salting shed. It was a glorious, sunny morning— not a cloud in the sky. Happy took out his pocket handkerchief and wiped the sweat from his forehead. "It's a hot morning for the middle of October," he said, talking to himself out loud. There was no wind and the tide was out, making the water in the harbour just like a mirror.

The usual sounds of activity around the little town were loud in his ears, giving him a sense of belonging. This morning, he was glad to be alive. While he listened, he could hear men chopping wood, children crying and laughing, roosters crowing and sheep bleating.

"What a world," he said as he worked. "The problems I have are minor. I have plenty of food on my table, we have lots of clothes to wear, my children are around me, and we're building a new barracks."

He gave God thanks for it all.

At ten o'clock, Winnie Roberts called out to him. "Uncle Happy, come up for a lunch. I have baked beans and fresh bread on the table."

"I sure will, Winnie, my dear," he said. He put down his hammer and started to work his way down from the top of the building. When he got to the bottom scaffold, which was close to the water, he turned to walk in off the wharf. As he turned, his keen eyes caught sight of something shining in the water. He stopped and leaned back as he looked in the direction of the shining object.

"Something out there is shining very brightly," he said.

Happy backed up a step or two and shaded his eyes with his hands for a better look. "Yes sir," he said, "there's something out there among those old fish bones. I wonder what that shining object is? I think I'll have a look to see what it is when I come back from my lunch."

Happy looked toward the house, then back to the water. The tide was low; he estimated the water to be about four feet deep. He changed his mind about lunch and decided to check it out right away. "If I wait, the sun might be in a different direction or it may be blowing."

The shining object was about ten feet out from the wharf, so he got the small dory nearby and boarded it. He then leaned over the dory and shaded his eyes with his hands, his face about three inches from the water. He slowly pushed the small dory out, keeping his eyes on the shining object. When he saw it quite clearly, it was lying on top of a heap of bones, but still he didn't recognize it.

"It's something, for sure," he said. "I know what to do."

Happy stuck an oar into the harbour bottom to mark the position of the object. He went back to the shed and got a can of hard grease that was on the shelf and took some out on his hands. He smeared it on the end of a prong handle. "This should do," he said, as he walked back and got in the dory.

Happy pushed the dory out to the marker, and sure enough he saw it. He very gently put the prong handle into the water and carefully pushed it down, keeping his eye on the object. He held his breath as he positioned the handle over the object. He pressed a little to make sure that the grease stuck to it. He slowly lifted it up and pulled it back.

"I've got it, whatever it is," he said, as he lifted it in over the side of the dory. He sat down and examined the object.

Happy Tucker was never known by anyone to as much as let a swear word come into his mind.

"Goodness gracious!" he said. "It's not possible!"

He pried the lump of grease and the object from the prong and sat down. His eyes bulged out as he examined it.

"It can't be. No, it can't be," he exclaimed. "It's Az's Red Cross ring!"

He held the ring between his fingers as he wiped it clean with his pocket handkerchief. With trembling hands, he held it closer to his eyes. He saw the red cross on it, and, turning it over he saw the initials AFR in Old English letters. "It's your ring all right, Azariah Frederick Roberts," he said, smiling.

"Uncle Happy! What's keeping you so long? Your beans are getting cold," called Winnie from the shore.

"I'll be there in a moment, my dear."

Happy marvelled at his lucky find. Still smiling, he pocketed the ring and rowed for shore.

Uncle Happy Tucker was still shaking when he went to his house at noon for lunch. He told Mary that he wasn't very hungry because he had eaten a big feed of beans and bread at the cookhouse two hours earlier.

When Mary shook her flaming red hair, she wouldn't take any nonsense and usually won out. She stood out in a crowd of women; she had good looks and was built with a strong body and large hands. She always wore good clothes that were very neat and clean-cut. Happy loved his wife very much.

He sat at the table with a cup of tea in his hand. He was very quiet.

"What's on your mind today, Happy?" Mary asked her husband. He laughed. He knew he couldn't fool her.

"I'm shocked, to say the least," he said. That got her attention. She looked at him.

There was no one else in the house, since all the children were in school. "I'm going to tell you something, Mary, and I know you wouldn't believe me if I didn't have the proof to show you. I've been so shaken-up about it that I haven't been able to work since this morning, and I'm still shaking my head."

"Well," she said, "you must have seen the end of the world!"

"It might not be the end of the world, but I think that it's the first time it has ever happened in the world!"

Mary looked at him, her forehead creased in a frown. She knew her husband was serious; he had something important on his mind. Happy reached into his pocket and took out his handkerchief that was rolled up and tied with a string. He put it on the table. She looked at it and knew at once that there was something in it.

"Now, Mary my dear," he began, "before you see what's inside, I want you to promise to keep it a secret."

She smiled and said, "You know I will if that's what you want."

He handed her the cloth bundle and told her to go ahead and unwrap it, to take a look at what was inside. She picked it up and said, "Can I guess first?"

"No," he said. "It will take too long. The children will be home soon and we don't want them to know."

Mary unwrapped the handkerchief and found a package wrapped in brown paper. She then removed the paper and something fell into her lap. She picked it up and held it up to her eyes. At once, she recognized it.

"The ring!" she exclaimed. "Az's Red Cross ring!"

She knew the story of how Az had lost it, but this was impossible. She looked across the table at Happy. "It's Az's ring, isn't it? Where in the world did you get it?" she asked.

"Yes it is, Mary."

Happy went over the events of the day when Az had lost the ring, how he almost got pulled overboard and came close to being drowned. This discovery was beyond anyone's wildest dream. It was a puzzle to him. Ten men had seen it when it was lost in the cod trap, but there was no attempt made to pick it up, because all were concerned about saving Az and not the ring. In a split second it was gone in over a hundred feet of water.

He then told her how and where he had found it.

She asked, "What do you think we should do with the ring, Happy?"

Happy scratched his chin. "I've been thinking about that ever since I found it. I think we should give it to him on Christmas morning as a present. I wonder what he would say? Like I said, we have to keep it a secret."

Mary laughed at his suggestion. "I know it will shock the daylights out of him if we do that," she said.

"But Mary, the only problem is there's a piece broken out of it. He won't be able to put it on his finger."

"Why don't we send it to the jewellers at St. John's and have them put a piece in it to make it the same size as his finger? They can easily do that in there."

"I was thinking about that," said Happy, "but it will cost a lot of money—the ring is gold, you know."

"You're right."

"I've been thinking," said Happy. "You know about that sword we dug up in there by the church, the one belonging to the Viking?"

"Yes."

"Well, that's almost the same colour as the gold ring—I was over in the forge comparing it. There's still a piece left there yet. I was thinking that we should send away a piece of it with the ring and have the jewellers splice a piece into it. That will be cheaper."

Mary said, "I think you've got a great idea, Happy."

"Okay, then," Happy said, "that's what we'll do. We'll keep it a secret—no one will know but the two of us."

She smiled. "I won't tell a soul."

Happy felt better. "Okay," he said, "tomorrow, try and get it in the mail. It should be back by Christmas morning."

Mary took the ring from him and carried it into the bedroom.

Wes Mugford was spending a lot of his time hanging around Bessie's house, because Susie Tucker, Bessie's younger sister, spent most of her time there. Although Susie and Allan Hillier had plans to get married, young Wes was determined to have her, and he wouldn't give her any rest.

Bessie was determined not to let Wes have anything to do with Susie. On one particular evening Bessie, Susie and Allan were just about to have a cup of tea. The children were in bed, and of course, Allan was sitting with Susie on his knee. Around 9:00 p.m., young Wes Mugford came in uninvited. He had been drinking. He immediately started mouthing off to Allan, throwing false accusations about Bessie.

"You only came down here because Uncle Az wanted you, Bess," he said.

Allan was a quiet man who said very little to anyone, but he'd had enough. He stood up, walked over, and with hands like a vise, grabbed Wes and lifted him off the chair. In his hands, Wes wriggled and squealed like a child.

"You'd better get your frame out of here, you vermin, or I'll squat you like a fly," Allan warned.

"Let me go," Wes said. He was in pain.

"I'll let you go, but I'm warning you Wesley, don't you ever speak to Susie or Bessie again. If I ever catch you under this roof again, I'll knock out every tooth in your gob."

Wes started to speak but was cut short. "Susie and I are planning to get married right after Christmas, so you stay away. I also want to tell you that I'm not Cuff the schoolteacher. You fellows might have made away with him, but you won't make away with me."

Allan was angry, and he threw Wes toward the door as if he were a rag doll.

As Wes stood in the doorway, he turned and said, "Don't you be too sure of yourself, Allan Hillier. The schoolteacher said the same thing, but look what happened to him. There are ways of doing everything." He gave a loud laugh as he shut the door.

When Wes was gone, Bessie said, "There's no doubt that the two of them are criminals, and if I was you, Allan, I'd never turn my back on either one of them, night or day."

"I won't," said Allan.

The year 1929 was a bumper year for the fishery. Az's voyage of salted codfish almost doubled compared to other years. The price for salt-bulk fish was also up slightly. As a bonus, he received cash for ten percent of his voyage. The other ninety percent had to be taken up in goods, either in foodstuffs or hardware and the like. This didn't matter, because most of it was distributed as trade to the people of the Pigeon and the surrounding area. No one used cash.

Sod was into the moonshine whenever he could get it. If he wasn't drinking, he was quarrelling with Bessie and the children, or anyone else he could draw into a racket. Bessie had driven him out on two occasions, and for this reason he told her that she could expect the house to be burned down any night. She was living in fear.

Sod's presence in the Pigeon was also affecting Az. He knew there were whisperings behind his back, rumours that he was hiding Sod Mugford from the law. On the contrary; he had tried on two occasions to have an investigation carried out, but nothing happened. He had even talked to Dr. Curtis, the head of the International Grenfell Association at St. Anthony, but was advised by him to wait a little longer. A lot of things were going backward or "in reverse," he would say.

# Chapter 26

One day in November, Az and Happy were working on the floor of the new church. There was no one else around. While they worked, Az told Happy that he had a funny feeling that something was going to happen.

"What do you mean, Az?"

"It's just that I have an uneasy feeling, that's all."

Happy was surprised to hear Az talking this way. Generally, nothing bothered him. He was a mature man, tough as nails, who feared nothing. But Happy knew that Az was troubled about the Sod Mugford racket. Happy admitted to Mary that he himself was having a problem sleeping at night, trying to cope with the thought of having Sod and Wes Mugford in town. He feared what they might do.

Happy was kneeling on the floor. He looked at Az and said, "Sit down, I have something to tell you."

Az teased him. "You'd better have something good to tell me," he said.

"I know that when you hear this you're going to call me crazy, and I won't blame you, but you must hear it. I've received a message."

Az sat up straight. He looked at Happy and said, "A message, Happy? I hope it's not one of those that comes along in a dream like Sarah has. And if it's about my ring bringing me back luck, don't tell me about it. I don't want to hear it."

"No, no. This is about myself. You know, we have to hurry and get this barracks finished. It's important."

"It will be finished by the spring. Remember what we said? We said if we could get it opened for Easter, we would be lucky," said Az.

"It has to be finished by the end of the year."

Az frowned. "Are you saying that it has to be finished before the last day of December?"

"Yes," said Happy.

"What's the rush? We have the cookhouse. We can use that for this winter."

Happy had been looking at the floor where he was kneeling. There was a long silence. He looked up at Az, and there were tears in his eyes.

"What's wrong, Happy?" asked Az.

Az helped him stand up. He hadn't seen tears on Happy's face since the day they talked about Az and Emily Jane adopting Truman, and that was many years ago. But now—

Az asked him again, "What's wrong?"

Happy took a deep breath. "I want you to listen to me, Az. A few nights ago I had a dream, and in my dream someone came to me and gave me a message. He told me to tell you to make sure that the barracks is completed by New Year's, because the first service to be held in it is going to be a memorial service for me."

Az stared at him in disbelief. "What in the world are you trying to do to me, Happy? You must be trying to destroy me altogether!"

Az looked down at his close friend, the man he called his right arm. Ever since he had gone fishing in his early teens, Happy had always been at his side, but now he was having a rough time. Happy was predicting the end, and on top of it all, the end of himself.

"What's this all about, Happy?" Az was sick with worry.

He believed Happy, because he had never known him to tell a lie. He had read in the Good Book, where it said "mark the perfect man." Well, Happy Tucker was the man.

"Az, I'm sorry I had to tell you this. You're the only one I've told. I don't want you to mention it to one soul. I haven't even mentioned it to Mary."

Az shook his head. "Why did you tell me about this dream, or whatever it was? Why wouldn't you just tell it to Gid? He's the Salvation Army officer here. This stuff should be told to a clergyman, not to the likes of me. I've had enough strain for one year, Happy. I can't take much more. The load is too great for me."

"Az, you're strong. They call you the steel man. The burdens of the Pigeon have to be carried on your shoulders. Mary or Aunt Emily Jane can't carry them—they are for you."

Az was visibly shaken. He headed for the door, but before he went out he turned to Happy and said, "I suppose the next thing you'll tell me is that your memorial service has something to do with my Red Cross ring." Happy was about to say something, but Az shut the door.

Once outside, Az looked up at the sky. "When will this all end?" he said.

George Roberts was Az's younger brother. He had never married, and he lived with Emily Jane and Az after their mother died suddenly of a heart attack. George was a good fisherman, and when not in the stage or in the trap boat he did most of the work in the forge, working with iron and repairing engines. He shaped the ironwork for schooners and worked with lead. He was also a tinsmith, using sheet metal to make kettles and cod oil lamps. George was a key man around the firm of Az Roberts at L'Anse au Pigeon.

The Pigeon couldn't function without George. Whenever there was firewood to be cut, he was there. If there was any firewood or saw logs to be brought home by boat, George was the one who was called upon. Az always put him in charge of the boat when the fishing was over in the fall, when the cold weather came and ice started to form. George would always get the job done.

Around the sixth of December of that year, 1929, it was decided that they would go to Pistolet Bay, an area about twenty miles to the west of the Pigeon, and bring home their firewood and logs for the coming winter and following summer. The wood and logs were cut in October of the previous year and had been drying all spring and summer.

The weather was clear and fine, and the boat could make a round trip in a day. Otherwise the dogs would have to haul it all the way on sledges. George took charge of the project and in less than three days they had the material landed in the Pigeon. Shortly after this, the weather turned bad. The wind came in from the southeast, but the storm wasn't bad enough to have to haul up the large trap skiff. They had it anchored safely in the small harbour and ran lines to the shore and attached them to the ring bolts driven into holes drilled into the cliffs.

By the twenty-third of December, the storm that had been raging for more than a week was over. Az called some of the men to his house and told them that they should pull the large trap skiff out of the water before another gale of wind hit the area, or before a blizzard struck. "If we get a batch of snow, we might have a hard job trying to get her up over the bank of the shoreline." They all agreed.

George said that perhaps they should go over to the Clue and get Happy's firewood before they pulled the boat up. When there had been spare time, Az had sent a group of his sharemen to cut firewood for Happy over in the Clue, a small cove located to the southwest of the Pigeon, where small stunted trees grew.

"If we use the boat, it will save us a lot of work with the dogs," George said.

Az agreed. "The tides are on now, and if you're going to do that, the best thing is to go over and carry the wood out to the edge of the water first. When the water is high tomorrow morning, go over and put the boat right into the beach and load it aboard. It shouldn't take more than an hour. George, can you manage that?"

"Sure, Az," George said.

It was decided that the group would go over right away and get the wood gathered, to be ready for the next morning when the tide would be high at nine o'clock. It would only take them about half an hour to put the wood on board the boat.

However, George and his crew didn't get going until after lunch at noon, due to extra work that came up. At 1:00 p.m. they left for the Clue. It was just before dark when the men returned; the firewood had been taken down to the shoreline, ready for the next morning.

At the home of Az and Aunt Emily Jane, it was obvious that it was Christmas. Every part of the house was decorated. Winnie and Grace had spent days hanging up decorations around the house and putting up a Christmas tree. They were also preparing for their usual party on Christmas Eve. This was the time when Az and Emily Jane took all the children at the Pigeon into their home for Christmas. Cakes and cookies were baked for them, and strawberry syrup was popular with the children. They knew that Aunt Emily Jane had gifts for them that she had brought back from St. John's earlier. They were stacked under the Christmas tree.

Happy and Mary were disappointed that the ring didn't come back in time for Christmas. The last mail had arrived a couple of days earlier, but the ring didn't come, and it was the last mail for the season.

The beautiful decorations did not make Az happy on this evening. His troubles started in the afternoon, just after the men left to go to the Clue to gather the firewood. He was getting ready to butcher a pig for the Christmas season, and he was down in the forge sharpening some knives when he saw someone through the window, staggering along outside by the cookhouse. There were two men. He stood and opened the door to get a better look to see who they were.

"Hey," he called, but they didn't turn. Neither did they answer. They were only about fifty feet away.

"Hey, there," he called a second time. The two stopped and turned towards him.

"Well, it didn't take you very long to get back from the Clue," he said with sarcasm. He knew that Sod and Wes hadn't gone over to the Clue.

"'Tis Christmas, Uncle Az," said Wes. He was cocky, and would mouth off at anyone.

Az opened the door wide and glared at Wes. "You know 'tis Christmas, but you also know that there's work still to be done. And when did you become a spokesman for Sod?"

He stared at Sod. "Come into the forge. I want to talk to you."

Sod knew it was no good for him to go any farther toward Bessie's house, because Az wouldn't let them. He motioned for Wes to go on into the forge ahead of him.

Az could sense that they were afraid of him, despite the fact that they were criminals. He also knew they were very drunk.

"Didn't you get word that I wanted you to help get the firewood over in the Clue?"

Sod didn't answer.

Az lost his patience. "Wes, you get out and shut the door behind you. I didn't invite you in. Get out or I'll throw you out."

Wes knew better than to stay. In fact, he was glad to get away. He stepped outside.

Az shut the door. "Sit down, Sod." He went over and put more wood in the stove. Sod sat down on a pile of boards. "Sod, methinks the time has come for you and me to tell one another the secrets that we know about. If we don't, we're both going to get into trouble."

Sod had been drinking, and by now he wasn't only drunk, but half crazy. Wes had talked him into going over to Bessie's house because he wanted to see if Susie was there. He knew that Allan had gone over to the Clue with Uncle Happy and the others to collect firewood.

Sod watched as Az sat on a wooden bench near the stove.

Az was tired of the goings-on that were haunting the little town, and he was wondering what Sod's attitude was toward coming to some arrangement. He knew he would have to try some strategy on Sod in order to solve the problem, but how? He wasn't very good at using honey or butter on people, but he was so desperate to get this problem solved that he was prepared to try anything.

"Sod, my son," he said, "I know you're having a rough time of it, and you're trying to put the best side out. You're just like me, trying to cope with the impossible, but there's one thing about it. You can trust me and you know it."

Sod was staring at the floor, and for a moment it looked like he was going to fall off the pile of boards.

"Uncle Az," he began, "I don't know where to look to. My mind's almost gone. What can I do now, Uncle Az? I'm finished. I can't see nothing left for me, only the pen."

"Sod, I think you should tell me all there is to tell, because I'm the one who took you in last winter when you had nowhere to go. For God's sake, tell me the truth. It's only then that something can be done about it."

Sod shifted around on the loose boards. He put his hands to his face and started to cry. Az couldn't believe it—Sod Mugford was crying!

"Uncle Az, I made a mistake. I should have done the same as Jack Caravan done, took off out of the country or somewhere. Everything would have been all right by now, but instead I came down here and brought all my troubles on you. I might've known what was going to happen."

"Listen, Sod," Az said softly. "What part did Jack Caravan have in the goings-on with you and Edwin Burton?" He knew he had to be careful in his questions for fear of frightening Sod, now that he had him talking.

"The only part that Jack was involved in was where he and Edwin got Cuff drinking moonshine at his house. Jack's mother and father was gone up to Lushes Bight. They got Cuff drunk and dressed him up, and Edwin led him over to my house as a janny."

Sod was so unsteady that he fell off the lumber onto the floor. He sat up on the floor not far from the stove. "I was on the 'shine, Uncle Az, when Edwin brought in Cuff. He had him all done up, just like a bale of hay."

Sod's face softened a little. "I couldn't believe me eyes when Edwin took the blanket off him."

He laughed crazily. "Uncle Az, I just gave him a little bit of flux in a drop of moonshine, just a little drop." Sod held his thumb and forefinger up to Az. "Just enough to make him a little sick, not to hurt him. Now, Edwin wanted to give him a lot. I don't know what Edwin gave him when I wasn't looking."

Sod had finally done it. He had admitted to someone what he had done with the schoolteacher. "Cuff then started throwing up, and before we knew anything, he started choking on his own vomit. I did everything I could to help him, but he choked."

Sod was staring at his feet. He knew he had said too much already, but he couldn't stop; he was on a crying jag. "Edwin put him on the old man's komatik and hauled him over to the other side and dumped him off. That's where Cyril Rowsell found him sometime that night. The old woman was right in what she said."

Az fixed Sod with a steely gaze. "Stop crying, and tell me something. What do you intend to do now?"

"I don't know, Uncle Az. If I had the money, I'd go to the States or up to Canada somewhere."

"Listen to me, Sod. There's one thing that I know for sure, and that is you're getting out of the Pigeon, or at least off my land. For good. From what you just told me, you and Edwin murdered the schoolteacher. It's only a matter of time, and time is getting short for you. There will be police here with a set of handcuffs, and they'll snap them on your wrists and take you to the pen. And you know what that means—a rope around your neck."

Az had Sod where he wanted him. "And it won't be a noose like the one Edwin Burton had around his neck, either."

Sod had a frightened look on his face.

"That won't happen to me, Uncle Az. I'll shoot myself first."

"Sod, I'll tell you what you're going to do. Right after Christmas Day, I'll give you and Wes the money to take you to Badger, to go to the lumber camps to work. I'll leave the trap skiff in the water, and right after Christmas Day I'll send her to St. Anthony with the two of you on her. There'll be a coastal boat going south. You can get passage on her."

Az stood. "If you don't do that, Sod, then tell me something. How do you intend to stay here in the Pigeon after what you just told me?"

Sod knew he had made a mistake, and he knew that from that moment on he would have to run for his life.

He stood up. His speech was slurred as he said, "All right, Uncle Az, all right. Let me have Christmas Day with the youngsters, then I'll take off."

He staggered toward the door, then turned and looked back at Az. He knew that Az was desperate to get rid of him. He said, "Uncle Az, it all depends on you. I want you to make a promise to me. What I just told you about the poison, you are not to tell one living soul. If you do, I'm not going."

"Sod, I'll keep this to myself for so long. I'll tell what you told me to one person, and that is to Happy, and if I am ever asked about it by the authorities, I won't lie."

"When can I have my money to leave?"

"When you arrive in St. Anthony, I'll have someone there hand it over. The deal includes Wes, too. He has to go with you."

Sod didn't like it, but he had no choice. "All right," he grumbled, "I'll take Wes with me, if that's what you wants."

Az opened the door to let Sod out and found Wes with his ear to the outside part of the door, listening. It was obvious that he had heard everything.

Wes swore, then said, "Sod, what a fool you are. What a fool. You've just hung yourself."

Az had to restrain himself from punching Wes square in the mouth.

Az went to Happy's house just as they were sitting down to supper. It was a beautiful sight, to behold Happy and Mary with their children, all sitting at the table, enjoying a hearty meal. Az looked around, and everything he saw was sparkling. The Waterloo stove was polished and clean. The wooden boards on the floor were scrubbed white, and there wasn't a speck of dirt anywhere. Hooked mats of all colours covered most of the floor. There was a Christmas tree near the table that Mary and the children had nicely decorated and had made ready for Santa. He noticed that some of the stockings were already hung by the tree.

"Merry Christmas, Uncle Az," they all said.

"Merry Christmas," he said, as he took out his pipe. "Mary, I'd like some supper, if you have enough cooked."

At the Pigeon, every house was the same as your own; wherever you went, the doors were always open.

"There's plenty of supper for you, Uncle Az, if you're going to sit by me," said Susie, as she winked at him.

"You be careful now, Susie. Allan might find out." They all laughed.

"There's plenty of supper for you, Uncle Az," said Mary. Susie moved farther to the side, and Az sat at the corner of the table, next to her.

"The best-smelling grub in the world is here in this house. Right here, you got the best cook on earth, Happy," said Az, laughing as he sat down.

"You knew that before I married her!" said Happy. Mary laughed, shaking her head. "I'd say that Winnie and Grace got a grand scoff cooked, too, especially this close to Christmas."

"Yes, you're right," said Az. "I can't eat too much now, because they've got a feed of saltwater ducks on for supper. I'm having a piece of salt beef and one potato, though, and I've got to have a doughboy." Mary put the food in front of him.

Happy sensed that Az wasn't really there to eat supper with them. Az wanted to talk to him.

Az picked at his plate and said, "I've got to go, or Emily Jane will kill me." He got up from the table and winked at Happy.

"Thanks, Mary. That was wonderful. Listen, when you get your work done, come out to the house, you and Happy. Gid doesn't usually play that squeezebox when you're there, Mary."

Everyone but Happy laughed. He thought that the young Salvation Army officer was a gift from heaven, concertina and all.

"I'll be out in about ten minutes to see you, or just as soon as I get my supper finished. We have to make our plans for tomorrow," Happy said.

"Great," said Az, and he stepped outside.

On that evening of December 23, 1929, Happy joined Az to plan the following day's activities. It was a cold evening with no wind, and a bright moon lit the evening sky. They commented on the smoke from the stovepipes, how it fell to the snow.

While they walked along, Az spoke. "I got Sod in the forge this afternoon and really put it to him. Guess what? He confessed to me that he and Edwin killed Cuff last year by poisoning him with flux, just like everyone's been saying."

Happy wasn't surprised to hear it, but he felt bad. He knew that if this ever got out around, it would ruin Christmas for everyone.

"What are you going to do about it, Az?"

"I made a deal with him, that if he and Wes left the Pigeon right after Christmas Day, I would give them enough money to take them to the lumberwoods at Badger or Millertown. At least they would be out of the Pigeon. I told him that, except for you, I wouldn't tell anyone what he told me unless I was asked about it."

Happy shook his head. "Can you imagine, someone confessing to a murder? I have a feeling that this isn't going to be the end of it yet. But Az, when he told you that he and Edwin Burton had poisoned the schoolteacher, how did he act? Did he appear to be sorry, or show any sign that he wanted to change in any way?"

"No, Happy, he didn't show anything. He had tears running down his fáce, and for a moment I thought he was feeling sorry. But when I saw him outside with Wes, I was convinced that it was just a crying jag that he had. As far as I'm concerned, it was lucky that I was here this afternoon to stop the two from going to the houses. There's no telling what they would have done."

Az lit his pipe. "Maybe I should go right now, get some men, and go over to George Oake's house to grab Sod and tie him up, and tomorrow morning have him delivered to the magistrate at St. Anthony. What do you think?"

Happy held up his hands. "No, Az, wait 'til after Christmas Day and see what happens. If he isn't satisfied to do what he agreed to do, then you should take other steps."

Az wasn't satisfied with the answer his friend gave him. "Happy, how much trouble can the two of them cause here between now and next week? It's dangerous to have them around."

"I'll tell you what, Az, leave it 'til after Christmas Day."

"All right, Happy. On your say-so, I'll leave it 'til then." They turned to walk back. "Oh, about tomorrow morning— what have you got planned for the wood at the Clue?" Az asked.

"We'll be leaving at about eight o'clock. By the time we get over there the tide will be top high. It's only a twenty-minute run in the boat, and it won't take us more than half an hour to put the wood aboard. We should be back here again not later than ten-thirty, eleven at the latest. Sod told me he's going. We need him to drive the engine. If he can't, due to his drinking, or for some other reason, then we'll have to get Stew to go. He knows about the engine. Truman's coming along to give us a hand, and so is Allan Hillier."

Az said, "Truman has the flu pretty bad, and a sore throat. It might be better for him to stay home. Anyway, we'll see in the morning. If he's sick, we'll send someone else."

"Five men is plenty. If we have any more than that, we'll be in each other's way," said Happy.

"Fine. By the way, the crowd did a lot of work today on the barracks. They got everything ready for the Christmas tree party tomorrow night. I didn't think they would be that far ahead, but they did it."

Happy smiled. "That's wonderful."

The two men walked back to Az's house, their breath rising into the air like miniature wisps of fog.

In Lushes Bight, more than a hundred miles from L'Anse au Pigeon, Sarah Brenton awoke with a fright and jumped out of bed.

Her husband, Joe Brenton, was a big man. He knew his wife was having a rough time, but over what? He was beginning to tire of hearing his wife talk about his brother-in-law, Az Roberts, and his Red Cross ring. When was his wife going to get over this foolishness?

Joe got up, put on his pants and socks and went out into the kitchen. He would have to light the wood stove. He lit the oil lamp, placed the chimney on it, and adjusted the flame. He heard his wife crying. He went into the living room and saw her sitting with a heavy blanket over her. In the dimness of the lamplight he saw tears running down her face.

Joe loved his wife and family, and he couldn't stand to see her like this.

Softly, he said, "Sarah, my dear, what's the matter?" She shook her head and continued crying.

He put his arms around her. "Sarah, tell me, did you have another bad dream?"

"Yes," she said, sobbing. "I saw a boat on fire. There were six men in it and one of them was the young schoolteacher, Cuff. On board the boat was Happy Tucker. I saw one man push the schoolteacher into the fire. I know him but I can't call him by name. Then Happy turned to me and held out his hands. In one hand he had Az's Red Cross ring. When I looked up I saw Az standing on the beach, crying. Then I heard this music—it was a concertina—and a man started singing, and I know what he was singing. He was singing *The night is dark, and I am far from home. Lead thou me on.*"

Her husband looked at her with pity. She started crying again and covered her face. "What am I going to do? I wonder if Az and them over in the Pigeon are all right?"

"Everybody's all right, Sarah. Everybody is all right."

"Are you awake, Mary?"

Mary Tucker opened her eyes and looked at her husband, the man with whom she had seven children. He'd been so good to her. They had seen poor times, but were much better off than most families on Quirpon Island. They always had lots of food on their table and plenty of clothes to wear. Although Happy was a church-goer, he never pushed religion on her or tried to have her do anything against her wishes.

"What's on your mind this morning, Happy?"

Happy lifted himself up on one elbow and looked down at her.

"I was just thinking about Az's ring, of how we didn't get it for him in time for Christmas. I want you to promise me something, Mary. I don't want you to tell Az about his ring. I want to be the first one to tell him."

"My son, you must be off your rocker this morning. Imagine, lying in bed on a Christmas Eve morning, thinking about Az's ring."

Happy laughed. "Anyway, I know that you won't tell him. You'll leave that to me."

"You know I will," she said.

# Chapter 27

The sun came up on December 24, 1929. The little town of L'Anse au Pigeon reflected itself on the edge of a mirror-like sea under the bluest of skies. Long before dawn the men and women were out of bed and the lamps were lit, glowing through the windows. The smoke from the stovepipes was reaching to the sky on this frosty morning. Some women were washing clothes, others getting ready for Christmas, baking cakes or wrapping gifts. Some were making clothes for the families, and busy with all kinds of duties before the children got up. One old-timer, Uncle Gus Bridger, was up early. He was getting ready to help Az kill a pig and dress it for the Christmas dinners.

Truman Tucker lit his fire long before daylight. He went back to bed while the house warmed up. He had been in the house for a week with the flu and a sore throat, but now he felt better. This morning he was going over to the Clue with his father and a few more men, including Sod, to get firewood.

He had been upset with Sod for not going with the crowd yesterday, and seeing him and Wes staggering around the Pigeon had turned his stomach. When he saw Az take Sod into the forge yesterday afternoon, he had hoped that something was finally going to be done with him. Despite that, he also hoped that Sod would be sober enough to go and help them at the firewood this morning. Sod was as strong as an ox and he didn't mind handling a yaffle of wood. It was only right that he should go, because his family would also be burning the wood this winter, the same as Happy. Last night, Truman had told Sod that he should only be too glad to go.

Truman's wife Lydia got up early and started washing clothes. As the day was dawning, Lydia was out hanging sheets on the clothesline. Her fingers grew cold as the white sheets froze. At about seven-thirty she heard someone coughing. She looked behind, along the icy road that was worn smooth by people walking and pulling sleighs.

As she looked through the early-morning rays of sunshine, she saw a man bent over. He had his coat over his arm, and a five-gallon gas can in his hand. The man straightened up after his fit of coughing, and he took a long drag on a cigarette.

"Oh, Sod, my dear. How are you on this beautiful morning?"

Sod stopped and noticed Aunt Liddy there for the first time. She was a person above all the rest, one to whom he could tell his troubles, and he needed someone like her to talk to this morning. He knew she would never betray him, no matter what. Although Lydia was younger than himself, he always called her Aunt Liddy. She was a member of the Salvation Army in the Pigeon and took part in everything that they did; it was said that she was an angel, if ever there was one on earth.

"I'm not very good this morning, Aunt Liddy," Sod said in a hoarse voice.

"Oh my, Sod. What's wrong, my dear?" she asked as she stood at the clothesline, her fingers almost frozen.

Sod started coughing again.

"Are you sick, my dear?"

"Yes, Aunt Liddy, I'm sick. I'm sick of livin'. The world is a storm and it's all against me."

She had heard about the goings-on involving Sod, and how he had poisoned the schoolteacher, or at least he had been blamed for it, but she never made it her business to have anything to say about it. "Come in the house, Sod, my dear, and have a cup of tea. Trum has the kettle on the stove."

"No, Aunt Liddy, I don't have time."

"You should be saved, Sod."

He knew what she meant. She was referring to joining the Salvation Army. "Saved," he said. "I don't think that I could get saved after last night."

Lydia looked surprised. "What happened to you last night, Sod?"

"Well, Aunt Liddy," said Sod, "I had a bad dream last night."

"Oh my, Sod. What was it?"

"I dreamed that I was way out on the ocean and I was lost in the fog. There was people all around me, and it was like I was choking or something. I could hear voices all around me, calling me, but I couldn't answer."

He took another drag on his cigarette. "Then I heard something, Aunt Liddy."

Lydia stared at him. "What did you hear, Sod?"

He put down the can and his coat. "As I stood there on the water, I heard old man Fontaine out there on the Cape, playing a hymn on the foggle horn. It was so clear, Aunt Liddy. He played out every verse, and then I heard Gid join in with his concertina, and he sang every word. A voice said, 'Listen, Sod, to that great horn. This is for you, and the souls that are with you.'"

Lydia saw that Sod had tears in his eyes. "Can you remember what the hymn was?"

He looked like a little child who needed help.

"Yes, Aunt Liddy, I can remember it just as clear as day. He was playing *The night is dark, and I am far from home. Lead thou me on.*"

He frowned, then asked, "Aunt Liddy, is that a hymn?"

"Yes, it is, Sod, my dear." She put her arms around him for a moment and they cried. She knew that Sod was in a desperate situation, but could she reach him? She knew how, but at the moment there was no time. The boat would be leaving soon. She let him go as he wiped away the tears.

"Aunt Liddy, I love my children, but I may never—"

Truman appeared in the doorway.

Sod picked up the can of gasoline. "Aunt Liddy—" He was going to say something, but Truman called for Lydia to come into the house.

Sod started walking away.

There was a strong smell of gasoline in the air as Lydia said, "Sod, I think something dreadful is going to happen today. That dream is for a reason. It's a warning. Make sure you are ready. Oh, and Sod—"

He didn't answer. Either he didn't hear her or he chose not to answer. Lydia was going to tell him to be careful, that his cigarette would ignite the gas, but he was already out of earshot.

Winnie Roberts got up early that morning. She was going to the little town of Quirpon, which was about five miles away. She would be using a dog team to haul chairs for the concert and the Christmas tree party being held that night at the new barracks. She would take Gladys Hillier with her on the trip.

Az had been up early. He already had the fire going, and the house was warmed up. Gideon was sitting at the table. When Winnie came downstairs, Az said, "Good morning, Winnie. There's not a cloud in the sky. This is going to be a great morning. Would you get my breakfast for me, my dear?"

"I certainly will," she said. "We have baked beans for breakfast this morning."

Az laughed. He already knew it, because he could smell the aroma coming from the oven.

"How many trips will it take for you to haul the chairs over, Winnie?" he asked.

"I don't know," she said, "but we figured it may take about three trips, if we could take twenty a trip. Why do you ask that, Pop?"

"I want you to make sure that you're back before two o'clock, because I didn't like the look of that sky last night. It looked windy to me, although it's a great morning, and the glass looks good now. But I have a feeling that we may get weather before this afternoon."

"It might not take us very long. We may take them in two trips if we can get them on the sleigh. They're not that heavy."

"Good," he said. "Gideon, put up the window and call out to Happy. Tell him to come over for some breakfast."

Gideon Hancock always said that he truly admired Az Roberts. He lived with him for seven years as a Salvation Army officer and later as a son-in-law. He said it was true that the skipper drank a little rum on occasions, and that he smoked his pipe regularly, but, he said, there was never a morning that he didn't have someone read from the Bible and ask a blessing before each meal. He would always say that "if we can keep this up 'til we die, we'll never die hungry."

Gideon was in a good mood. He was going to work at the barracks this morning with several men. It was on his mind that within a couple of weeks he was going to have a service in the new barracks. It would be finished enough for that. He called for Happy to come out, and he told the skipper that Happy and his son Roland were on their way.

Az was glad that young Roland was coming. He was only sixteen, but he was fishing with Az that summer as one of his regular crew, and was as good as any man that Az had with him. Roland was a reliable worker, and very smart. He even knew how to split fish as well as Az's most experienced splitters. That morning, Roland was on standby to go to the Clue with his father if someone didn't show up. Az sat at the table with George, his brother, who always went in the boat wherever it went, and this morning would be no different. This morning he was rarin' to go.

Winnie carried a steaming platter of beans to the table.

Az dug in and talked while he chewed. "Winnie, I'm going to send one of the boys up to tell Norman to come down around nine o'clock to harness the dogs for you and Gladys, and to get them straightened out."

"Okay, Pop," she said.

After the men had their breakfast, they went down to the wharf. It was a clear morning. There was some slob ice in and around the harbour, but not enough to cause any trouble for the boat. Sod and Truman were already on board, waiting for the others.

Allan Hillier arrived at the same time as Az and Uncle Happy. He was beaming with energy. He was always pleasant and full of humour. "Good morning, Uncle Az," he said with a grin.

"Good morning, Allan," said Az.

Allan looked at Happy, then laughed. "And a good morning, Dad," he said. He winked at Az.

"Good morning, Allan," said Happy. "I won't call you son yet, not 'til it happens. I've seen too much of that change hands at the last minute."

Az laughed. He knew what Happy was talking about. He was referring to the time when Allan was supposed to marry Gladys Pilgrim, but she had married his brother Tom, instead.

Allan grinned. "I guess I put my foot in that one."

"Trum," said Az. "What do you think you're doing this morning? You've been in bed all week with the flu and a sore throat. You must be trying to get pneumonia as a Christmas present. Listen, get up out of the boat and let Roland go in your place with your father. We have enough trouble here now. You stay here with me and Uncle Gus. We're going to kill a pig. You can boil the water for us in the forge. Roland, you jump aboard."

Truman didn't hesitate. He climbed out of the boat, and young Roland got on board in his place.

"Sod," said Az, "the tank is full. It holds nine gallons, as you know. That's enough to take you to St. Anthony and back."

Sod waved.

"Make sure you take the punt with you. Just a minute," Az said. He went into the shed and brought out a sixty-pound grapnel and a hundred feet of rope. "Happy, go in and get one of those haul-up ropes and tie it on the claws of the grapnel. Get one with the small white buoy attached."

Happy got the rope and tied it on. Az handed the grapnel down to George, who put it in the front of the boat. He pulled the rope down and attached the end around the ring that was in the stem-head of the boat.

"That will hold her up for sure. You got no worries about that rope. That can swing her out over a cliff," said Az.

The grapnel was rigged so that there was a rope tied to the claws, with a small buoy tied to the end of the rope, long enough to allow the buoy to float to the surface of the water. This was what they called a "haul-up line," just in case the grapnel got hooked in a rock or some other object. The main line was tied into the ring of the grapnel. That line went to the boat and was secured to it. Every owner had his mark painted on his buoy, usually with some water-resistant paint or tar. In this case there were the letters AFR stamped on it in black. This was how Az had all of his equipment marked.

"I was looking out my kitchen window this morning. There's not a wag of sea. I figure that the northern slob isn't far away. Perhaps I'll go up on the head later on and have a look," said Az. "You should have a good trip. Make sure you don't get the boat aground."

"We'll make sure of that," said George.

"It looks like we'll have a good trip," Happy remarked.

"We should be back long before lunch," George added.

"If you have any trouble, send one of the boys back. The walking is pretty good," said Az.

"We'll have a good trip," said George as they pushed off.

With that, Sod started the 8-h.p. Acadia engine and off they went.

Az started waving and calling for them to stop. He jumped and waved again, but no one in the boat saw him.

"What's wrong, Skipper?" asked Truman, surprised.

"They forgot the punt. Where are their minds this morning, I wonder?"

Truman laughed. "Do you see what happens when I'm not there?"

Az continued to wave. "They may need that punt before they get back. Suppose they get the boat aground, or they can't get into the wood. They'll have to float the wood out."

"Don't worry about that, Skipper. Uncle George will get the wood on board."


Earlier that December, Az had received a telegram from Dr. Curtis of the International Grenfell Association at St. Anthony, saying that a vessel from Catalina was coming north with a load of provisions for the mission. The doctor advised that if Az had any freight at Little Bay Islands, the vessel would call in there, pick it up and bring it as far as St. Anthony. The name of the vessel was the *Lone Flier,* with Captain Peter Troake as her skipper.

Az knew what could happen to anyone associated with a person who could be charged with murder. In this case, it would be looked upon as if he were providing a haven for someone who had committed a serious crime, and it couldn't get any more serious than what Sod Mugford had done.

Although he had tried to have this crime brought to the attention of the authorities, there was always someone advising him to wait. He knew that eventually the axe would fall on Sod, and whoever was near or around him would get caught up in the mess. Wherever he went, the talk about the murder of the schoolteacher was the main subject. It was on everyone's lips, and Az realized that as long as Sod was in the Pigeon, fingers would be pointed at him. Even his friends were asking why Az had him in the Pigeon. "Could he be hiding him?" they would whisper. He decided that things had to change.

After the motorboat had gone out through the harbour on its way to the Clue, Az went to the kitchen table. He sat down to read the telegram announcing the arrival of the *Lone Flier.* The conversation he had with Happy the previous night was on his mind all morning. He said to himself, "This would be a great chance to get a passage down south for Sod and Wes."

He made plans to meet the *Lone Flier* at St. Anthony to deliver the two lads to the boat and pick up his freight at the same time. He sent a wireless back to Dr. Curtis and told him that he would meet the vessel at 10:00 a.m., and that he had two passengers to go south.

Only Winnie was told about this arrangement. "Sod and Wes have their passage out on Boxing Day," Az told her. "I'll give them ten dollars each, plus their passage. Winnie, you and I'll give it to them when they get on board the boat. I don't care where they go, as long as they're gone from here."

Mary Tucker was not a nervous woman. She was also not the type of woman to go around the house crying, but on this morning she was sobbing.

Her stepdaughter Susie asked her, "Mary, what's wrong? Why are you crying?"

Mary didn't know what to say. She felt out of control. "I don't know, my dear," she said honestly. "I can't help it. I'm not sick or anything. It's just that I feel like crying. I wish that your father was back from the Clue."

She smiled through her tears. "For sure, if he was here, he would say, 'You want to get saved.'"

Susie knew what she meant. "Maybe you do, Mary. What a Christmas present Dad would receive! It would be the best one you could give him—to join the Salvation Army."

"Now, you listen here. You'd better not tell your father that I was crying."

Susie looked at her stepmother. "This is Christmas Eve, Mary. I know that you've worked really hard in the last week, getting everything ready, decorating the tree, making the youngsters' clothes and working on the church. It's been too much for you. You should take it easy today."

Mary wiped her eyes and said, "No, Susie, it's not that. You have helped me, and everyone has done his part. I don't know, maybe something just came over me. You never know, your father could be right. Maybe I do want to be saved. I just wish he was here."

Susie could hardly believe what she was hearing. Her stepmother only started to go to church lately, and that was just to help with the construction of the interior.

"I should go out and tell Aunt Emily Jane that you want to get saved. I should get her to come out and pray with you," Susie said jokingly.

Mary was outraged. "Enough! Now, get this out of your mind, Susie." Susie laughed.

*It's Christmas Eve,* Az thought.

He said to Winnie, who was standing in the kitchen, "I want you to get me a cup of tea, Winnie, my dear. I see the glass is starting to go down a bit. I said we were going to have weather. I was right—it looks like wind."

She brought him his cup of tea and said, "Pop, the boat's coming back. I hear it."

Az went to the window. His house was only fifty feet from the salt water. "Yes, and I know what they're coming back for. It's the punt. They went and left her tied to the wharf. I didn't think that George would go over there without it; anything can happen."

The boat came into the little harbour and steamed all around. They saw four men standing up in the boat. The fifth person couldn't be seen.

"Sod must be in the engine house somewhere," Az said to Winnie.

They watched as the boat went on out the harbour again without slowing down.

"Pop, they never picked up the punt," said Winnie.

"No," he said. "That's strange for George to do that."

He looked at Winnie. "I wonder why they did that?"

Az looked out through the window and stared at the wake of the boat. "Only God knows where this will all end," he said. "I don't."

Winnie guessed he was referring to Sod Mugford and what was going on.

Az looked at the glass again, then told Winnie to ask Norman to go with her instead of Gladys. After Winnie left the room, he sat for a few minutes and stared at the glass. With a heavy sigh, he got up and prepared for the day's chores.

It was a busy morning for Az, Uncle Gus Bridger and Truman. They had the pig killed and cleaned. It was hanging in the forge long before eleven. The three men were sitting down near the stove, and Az was filling his pipe.

"It's too bad that the *Lone Flier* didn't get down a few days earlier," said Az, "because we would have had fresh vegetables for Christmas Day. I also ordered four quarters of fresh meat. That would be something to have hanging in the shed. That's better than all the fresh pork that's going."

Truman and Uncle Gus were excited to hear that a vessel was coming, especially this late in the season. It would be a welcome sight.

"Great," Uncle Gus said.

"Imagine, seeing a sack of onions or a barrel of apples, and above all a crate of oranges this time of the year," said Truman.

"If all goes well, we'll have our freight on Boxing Day," said Az.

"How did you know that the boat was coming, Az?" asked Uncle Gus.

"I have ways of finding out stuff," said Az.

Truman started laughing. "Skipper, you're smart. I know what you have in mind, and it's not the fresh meat or the oranges either."

"You better not open your mouth about the *Lone Flier*, Trum, and that goes for you too, Uncle Gus."

When Az had his back turned, Uncle Gus asked Trum, "What has Az got in mind?"

Truman whispered, "I think he's going to send the two lads, Sod and Wes, out of here."

"I didn't think Az was going to put up with them too much longer. Leave it to Az," Uncle Gus said with a grin. "The Pigeon might survive yet."

When not fishing, Az Roberts was always on time when lunch was served. Today was Christmas Eve, and it was Tuesday. This meant that there would be macaroni and cheese, baked to a golden brown. Az could smell the aroma coming from the oven as he walked in the house. The table was set and ready for whoever might drop in.

Az went directly to the weather glass hanging on the wall in the dining room. It was an instrument that he looked at religiously, morning, noon and night. He would say that whatever the glass says, it will happen.

He took one look at it and exclaimed, "Good God!"

Emily Jane looked up. "What's the matter, Fred?"

"The glass has gone bottom-up."

"Fred, it's too nice a day for weather," she replied.

He walked to the window and looked out. The ocean was very calm and the air was still.

"It could be the calm before the storm. One hour from now—you'll see, Emily Jane."

He was troubled. "The boys should have been back an hour ago. I hope they haven't got the boat grounded over in the Clue."

Gideon Hancock arrived right on the button, rubbing his stomach. He knew that the skipper was ready to sit at the table at twelve sharp. Gideon was in a very good mood today. His church-construction project was way ahead of schedule. There was a Christmas tree party going ahead, and a concert. He was singing to himself.

Winnie arrived with Norman Pilgrim. As Norman sat at the table, he said to Az, "Did you see the skyline, Skipper? It's got a funny look to me, like the sky is getting wild." Norman had fished with Az now for three years, and he was experienced enough to tell when a storm was brewing.

"Yes," said Az. "I was just telling Emily Jane about that. Just look at the glass. It's gone bottom-up."

In less than ten minutes, the dining room had filled with hungry people.

Winnie noticed that her father wasn't eating his dinner. Instead, he was staring out the window. "Is there anything wrong, Pop?" she asked.

"The boys aren't home yet from the Clue, and I'm nervous from looking at that glass. It's bottom-up."

Winnie knew that when her father was worried, there was reason for concern.

Gideon, who was twenty-one years old, was a carefree type of man, but as an officer with the Salvation Army, there were serious duties that he had to perform.

"Skipper," Gideon said, "I don't know if you heard, but I'm going to have a service in the barracks on New Year's Eve night." He laughed with joy and added, "I was telling Happy last night that I wanted him to be the first one to give his testimony in the new barracks before the year's end, and he agreed."

Az turned white. His mouth fell open. He put his hands to his face and got up from the table.

"Dear God," he said to himself.

Everyone grew silent as he slowly turned and stood before the window, his back to the table. He stood in silence, looking out at the ocean, and saw the first squalls of wind as they brushed the surface of the water in the harbour. For a moment, he had a vision of Happy. He could see him kneeling down in the barracks, the same as he was back in November when he told him about his dream—how there would be a memorial service held for him in the new barracks before the end of the year. Until now, Az believed that it couldn't happen because the barracks wouldn't be completed enough before then. But now Gid had the plans all made, and there would indeed be a meeting held there on New Year's Eve, and above all, Gideon had Happy scheduled for the guest of honour, as it were.

Az's mind raced. *Could this be true? Would Happy attend the first meeting and give the first testimony? Or would it be the memorial service, as predicted by Happy himself?*

No one spoke, but they suspected something was wrong. Az turned and looked at the crowd sitting at the table, watching him.

Az cried, "Where are the boys? They're not back yet. Only God knows what this day will bring forth."

He walked briskly out of the dining room. When he got to the kitchen, he called back to Norman. "Norm, when you get your dinner eaten, I want you to come down to the forge. I want to talk to you privately."

"Okay, Skipper," he said.

Az walked out and quietly closed the door behind him.

After he left, Aunt Emily Jane said, "I don't like it when Fred is worried like that. It's for a reason."

"Well, Mom," said Winnie, "ever since yesterday, Pop hasn't been himself. Whatever went on between him and Sod must have been very serious, because all last night he hardly spoke a dozen words after the crowd left."

"Sod spoke more than a dozen words last night, according to what they said," said Norman. "I was talking to Eric. He was telling us that Sod was so drunk last night that he told the boys what he helped do to the schoolteacher up at Beaumont. He also said that his time here at the Pigeon was getting short. Eric heard that someone said to Sod, 'What are you going to do, drown yourself like Edwin?' Sod just laughed and told them that when he drowns himself, he'll be taking a crowd with him."

Winnie nodded. "You see, that's the trouble. Pop heard all of that, and it's got him upset. And everyone here has to admit that there hasn't been one bit of peace here, day or night, since Sod and Wes came to the Pigeon. To tell you the truth, I'll be glad when the two of them are gone from here."

No one else spoke, but they all felt the same way. They were silent as they continued their lunch.

It was one o'clock when Norman went into the forge. The slaughtered pig was hanging from a beam. It was beginning to stiffen up.

"That's a fine-looking hog, Skipper," he said.

"Yes, I figure he's about three hundred pounds, or close to it."

"There's a lot of eating there," said Norman.

Az got down to business right away. "Listen, Norman. I'm worried sick. Maybe there's no reason to be, and I hope there isn't, but the boys should have been home three hours ago. Ever since they left this morning, I've been worried. I should never have let Sod go with them, because, as you know, he's capable of doing anything."

"Dear Lord, Skipper. The man wouldn't be crazy enough to harm the others, would he?"

"I don't know. He made away with the schoolteacher at Beaumont, and that I know for a fact. For that reason I should never have let him go in the boat with the boys."

Norman looked through the window. "Looks like the wind is picking up, Skipper, and from the northwest." To Norm, it seemed that the skipper's heart was down in his boots.

Az had a request. "Listen, Norm, it's quarter after one now. If they're not here by two, I want you and Eric to take a run over to the Clue and have a look around. Harness my dogs."

"Good enough. I'll do it," he said.

Emily Jane and her younger daughter Grace were doing the cooking. Grace was fourteen years old, the youngest daughter and what they called the "pet" of the family. George Roberts, Az's brother, wasn't married, and he lived with Az and Aunt Emily Jane for years, ever since their mother died. He was part of the family. He was there when the two girls were born, and Grace was his favourite.

George rocked Grace for hours on end when she was just a baby, and whenever George came into the house, Grace was up in his arms. He was her babysitter, brother and protector. She loved him almost as much as she loved her father. Az teased her by calling her a spoiled brat and accused George of being the one who spoiled her.

It was a known fact that the men were going in boat to the Clue to get the firewood for Uncle Happy. Even the children knew, and Grace was no exception. She heard her Uncle George say that he was going with Uncle Happy and would be back at noon. Happy had told her, "It's Christmas, Grace, so don't spoil anything. Uncle George has something special for you, he told me."

Grace was helping her mother with the cooking today, because Winnie had gone to Quirpon to get the chairs for the concert that evening. She came out of the bathroom and heard a knock on the door. Her mother was in the kitchen.

Grace said, "Mom, there's someone at the door."

"Go and see who it is," said Emily Jane.

Grace went to the door, but there was no one there. She didn't think anything of it. She went back to the dining room where she was working, when she heard it again.

"I hear the knock again—the same knock," Grace repeated.

"See who it is, Grace. There must be someone there."

Grace went a second time. She tried to sneak a look to see if it was some of the young children. She opened the door, but saw no one.

She came back into the kitchen. "There's no one there, but I swear I heard someone," she said.

Her mother chuckled. "You're hearing things, Grace."

Grace went back at her work, taking the dishes off the table, while Emily Jane continued mixing bread. Grace heard the knock again. It was a familiar knock.

"Listen, Mom. I hear that knock again, and I know who it is. It's Susie, trying to get me going this morning. But I'll catch her."

With that, Grace dashed to the door, but there was no one there.

"Susie must be knocking and hiding, trying to get me to come out of the house."

"You're not going anywhere this morning, Grace. We've got too much work to do," said Emily Jane.

It was a beautiful morning. Everything was so quiet and still outside. Grace was looking out through the curtains toward the water, when she saw someone outside, close to the window. She looked again. It was Uncle George, waving and smiling at her. She waved back at him. She remembered the knocking—it was him after all—that was why the knock was so familiar. He was having fun with her.

Just as she was going to call out to him, her mother called her to put a couple of junks of wood in the stove.

She looked again to see Uncle George, but he was gone.

Grace went out into the kitchen, where her mother was mixing the bread.

"Put some wood in the stove, Grace. I'm chilly."

"Yes, all right," Grace said. "I just saw Uncle George out there by the window. That's funny. I thought he was over to the Clue with Uncle Happy for his wood."

Emily Jane looked at her and said, "No, Grace, you didn't see Uncle George, because he went with the men in the boat early this morning. I heard your father saying something about George leaving the punt at the wharf. Your father was upset."

"Mom," she insisted, "I just saw Uncle George out there, standing by the window, waving at me and laughing."

She pointed toward the window.

Emily Jane knew there was no use in arguing with her daughter.

Grace continued. "He rapped on the door three times, Mom. It was his rap—I know it was."

Emily Jane wiped her hands on her apron."Listen, Grace," she said. "Don't you dare speak about this to your father or anyone else. He has enough on his mind now. Keep this between you and me."

Az left the forge and walked down on the wharf. He could see the wind on the water, and the clouds were beginning to form. For them to move that fast, it was obvious that the wind was building up, and soon it would hit the land and sea with full force.

"Something is dreadfully wrong," he said as he looked down at the punt tied to the wharf.

*Why didn't they take you this morning? Was it for a reason?*

Snow was blowing around now, and he could hear the wind whistling around the stage.

"I must go over and talk to Trum," he said out loud.

He called out to Norman, "Norm, get a couple of men and haul up that punt."

"Okay, Skipper."

When he was coming in off the wharf, Winnie called, "Hey, Pop! Come in and get your heavy clothes before you freeze to death. The storm's coming on."

"All right, my dear," he said as he walked toward her. "I'm going over to ask Trum to go over to Degrat and have a look around."

Degrat is a cove near L'Anse au Pigeon. It is one of the oldest place names in North America, and it is thought by some historians that this is where the great discoverer John Cabot landed in 1497.

Az stepped into the porch and started to put on his heavy clothing. He was sick with worry.

"I'm going with you, Skipper," said Gideon, as he got ready. They could hear the wind whistling around the house. The two men stepped outside. The storm had started.

Aunt Liddy and Truman greeted their two visitors.

"It looks like your house might blow away before this is all over," Gideon said to Truman.

"Boy, how quick did the weather change and the wind pick up!" Truman remarked.

"The glass has gone bottom-up. I've never seen anything like it," said Az.

"Listen. I would say there's a lot that we haven't seen the end of yet, according to what Sod went on with last night over at George Oake's house," said Truman.

"Don't tell me anything else about what Sod went on with last night. I've heard enough," said Az.

The three men were silent for a few moments as they looked at each other.

"I wonder if the youngsters are all in?" asked Lydia.

The three men didn't even hear her.

"They might be over in Degrat," said Truman.

"If they were over in Degrat, they would be home by now. If they had trouble this morning, anywhere around the islands in Degrat, you would hear them calling out," said Az.

"They may not be able to get ashore because they haven't got the punt," said Truman.

"Look, Trum, they got the sculling oar that can put them ashore anywhere, but what puzzles me, and I've been thinking about it all day, is why did George go over there this morning without the punt? Everything they did this morning was backward. I don't understand it. George won't even go to the outhouse without the punt this time of the year. I want you to go over and get Tom Hillier. Both of you go over to Degrat and make sure they're not there, just in case. Make sure you get a good look around the islands, Trum. Get on the move as soon as possible."

Truman agreed and began to put on his heavy clothes.

Az informed Truman of his other search plans. "Gid and I are going over to see Norm and a few others off to the Clue to take a good look around. They'll see if the wood is gone or not. I told them to take the dogs, but now I think it's better if they walked, with this storm on. The dogs would only get tangled up, anyway."

"You're right," said Truman. "I suppose Dad and them had enough gasoline in the tank to make the trip all right. Did he, Skipper?"

"Oh, yes," said Az. "I saw George when he filled the tank last evening. It holds nine gallons, and they can't use any more than one gallon to go and one to return."

Lydia overheard this part of the conversation.

"They never ran out of gasoline, that's for sure. When I was out at the clothesline this morning I was talking to Sod, and he was just going over to the boat. He had a five-gallon can of gasoline with him, so they never ran out of gasoline."

Az looked at Truman, then at Lydia, in shock.

"You must be kidding, Liddy. Sod didn't need to carry any gasoline with him. It must have been an empty can."

Lydia felt uneasy at Az's look. "Oh, it was full, Skipper. When he was talking to me, he had to put it down. It was heavy, and I could smell it."

Az was about to say something, but no sound came out. His mouth had gone dry.

Truman was speechless. On board the boat were his father Happy, his stepbrother Roland, Uncle George, and Allan, who was about to become his brother-in-law. And of course Sod, who was Truman's brother-in-law. His mind raced. He tried to banish all thoughts of evil out of his mind.

*No, Sod would never harm the old man. He wouldn't have the nerve. Maybe they're still at the Clue with engine trouble or something.*

"I wonder if they went in towards Quirpon due to the wind coming on, or because of some trouble they may have had?"

said Gideon, trying to be helpful. His eyes were worried as he looked back and forth from Truman to Az.

Az was trembling. He said, "I know that if there was any delay, George and Happy would have sent someone to let me know, if they could. Let's go over to see Norm. He should be getting ready to leave now."

It was two o'clock. They stepped outside into the howling storm.

Az wished Norman and his companions good luck in their search and cautioned them against the weather.

Norman, with his brother Eric and their father Leonard, walked over to the Clue using snowshoes. The wind was so strong they could hardly stand upright. It took them over an hour to get there, even with the wind at their backs.

They were expecting to see the men and boat at the Clue, but they weren't there, and the wood was missing. They looked everywhere around the cove, and went as far out as the cliffs would allow them, but saw nothing. It was obvious that they had taken the firewood and left, and it didn't appear that they had had any trouble. Their tracks were left in the snow where the wood was stacked. They concluded that the men had left the Clue early, probably before 10:00 a.m.

"Dad, they should have been back in the Pigeon around eleven, or close to it," said Norman.

"You're right about that," said his father.

"I wonder where they went? It sure looks funny to me," said Norman.

"It's not funny to me," said Leonard.

"What do you mean, Dad?"

"Look, Norm. I wouldn't send Sod to the outhouse without an escort after what he's been going on with lately, saying that he was going to kill himself and take a crowd with him.

"And, my son, let me tell you something. He's done it. You'll never see the boys again."

The three men looked out toward the White Islands. This was a group of three islands, approximately three and a half miles offshore. When the heavy seas roll in, they break and roll completely over them.

"I wonder if they've gone adrift and are out on the islands?" said Eric.

"I wouldn't say so," said Leonard. "According to what Uncle Az said about that five gallons of gasoline that Sod took aboard the boat, he never had it for anything else, only to start a fire. And that's what he did."

Leonard continued. "I'd say that when he got offshore, he turned over the gas can, dropped a match, and up she went. The gas would have gone all through her in the bottom and spread right through the boat. There would be nothing they could do about it, especially if he shut the engine off first. They had no container to throw water over the fire. For sure the bucket they had for bailing out water was in the engine house.

"And another thing, you take the tar that Uncle Az put on the inside of that skiff to make her tight. What do you think happened when that caught fire? I know what happened. In no time, there was a hole burned through her, and down she went to the bottom, like a rock. Especially with all that cement in her. Sod got his wish, and that was to take a crowd with him. Does that sound right, Norm?"

Norman knew that what his father said could be true. Would it be possible that Sod could do such a cold-blooded thing to a group of innocent people? It was his wife's family. In fact, the only one Sod ever liked in his life was Uncle Happy. Norman had heard Sod say, many times, that Uncle Happy was a saint.

*Knowing Sod,* Norman thought, *he could do anything, especially with the trouble he was facing.*

"Maybe they went into Quirpon, Dad," Eric said.

"No, they never went in there. If they did, Norman and Winnie would have seen them. Isn't that right, Norm?"

"You're right, Dad. They're not in there. If they were, Uncle Happy or Allan would have walked out to the Pigeon before noon."

Eric agreed. "You're right. Do you think they could be at Degrat?"

"Not a chance," Leonard replied, "because the same thing applies out there. They would have walked home for help. Uncle Happy could have sculled that skiff back to the Pigeon in an hour himself if he had to, and there were five of them. On top of that, the sea wasn't rough earlier, which meant that they could land on the rocks anywhere."

The three men took one last look around.

"Let's head back. There's nothing to be seen out here," said Norman. "In another hour it will start getting dark. Let's go."

As they turned to head back, Norman stated, "What an uproar there will be in the Pigeon tonight if they're not found!"

As his father bent over to tighten the sling on his snowshoe he spoke. "I don't think that Wes will go into shock from mourning over his beloved brother Sod if he doesn't return. He's just like his mother, Old Hazel. He's the devil."

# Part 3

# The Red Cross Ring

# Chapter 28

As darkness settled in around the little town of L'Anse au Pigeon that evening, everyone realized that the five men would not be home tonight. At three-thirty that afternoon, Az had sent word to Quirpon that his men were missing. At seven o'clock, ten men arrived to assist in the search. Az opened the cookhouse and put his two summer cooks, Emma Bridger and Winnie, there to cook for the men.

At eight o'clock, the storm was in full force. Az then sent a group of men over to Rangalley Head, a high mountain to the southeast of the Pigeon. Official maps record it as Ron Galets Head, but the local name is Rangalley Head. The men got partway up the mountain, but had to turn back due to hurricane winds and blinding snow with zero visibility. By nine o'clock, all the searchers had returned to the Pigeon, forced back by the storm.

An hour later, the sea started to heave. During one of those hurricane storms, even in summer, it wasn't fit to be in the Pigeon. On this night, in late December, it was outright dangerous to be there.

Az's house was built only fifty feet from the shoreline, and every time the huge waves smashed against the shore, a salty spray was carried by the wind and coated the house. It was a terrible night.

Az called a meeting at the cookhouse. He wanted every man who was in the Pigeon and all the men from nearby places who came to help with the search to be present. He wanted to look at all the possibilities and get everyone's opinion.

He began the meeting by saying, "We haven't given up hope, men, and don't let anyone get discouraged. I know there's an awful storm on, but men have been rescued from worse storms than this. I'm not discouraged or giving up hope. There are many places yet to look."

Az looked around for comments, but no one spoke. He continued. "If they were off Rangalley Head and the engine gave out this morning, they might have gotten into a tide rip and been carried up the shore toward Fortune or somewhere else, such as St. Lunaire. Due to the storm, it might be too bad for someone to come home to tell us where they are." Fortune was the northern arm of Griquet Harbour.

The men started talking. They all had suggestions and ideas, but no one held out a shred of hope of ever seeing Happy and the others again.

Az was broken-hearted. He could hardly stand up. Four of these men were his family, and of course Sod was his employee. Although he was suspicious that Sod had done something to the boat or the engine, he still felt bad about him. Worst of all, he was blaming himself for sending Sod with the boys that morning. He should have had better sense.

The thing that made him sick to his stomach was the fact that he had made Truman get out of the boat and ordered young Roland to take Truman's place. Every time he thought about it, he almost went crazy. *Why?* he cried in his mind. *Why did I do it? It's not right that Truman or Roland should die. I was the one who made the choice.*

It appeared that things for him were getting worse. What could he do? He told all the assembled men from the Pigeon to go to their homes and come back to the cookhouse at seven in the morning for breakfast. He was hopeful that the wind would die down by then. "We'll make plans then," he told them. They all agreed and Az went to his house.

Mary and her children, including Susie, were all at the home of Az and Aunt Emily Jane, and Bessie was also there with her girls. The younger children were in bed.

The house was full of people. Gladys Hillier was sitting at the table. She loved the skipper, and he thought there was no one like her. She was the kindest and the most loving person that anyone could ever know.

Emotionally exhausted, Az staggered in through the door. Everyone just stared at him as he came in. They could tell by the look on his face that he feared the worst. He went directly to Gladys and put his arms around her. She knew why. It was because of Allan, to whom she was once engaged. The rest of the older women knew the reason too. Gladys started to cry, but held herself in check, because of Az. There would be time for her to cry later, when she was by herself.

"Have you heard or seen anything, Fred?" asked Emily Jane in a voice filled with anxiety.

Without answering, he walked over to the stove and took off his gloves and cap. He took off his coat and put it on the back of the chair. Finally, he answered. "No, my dear. I haven't heard or seen a thing. It's too stormy to send men out anywhere, for fear of losing them or having them blown away."

Mary's eyes were red. It was obvious that she had been crying. "Az," she said, "what do you think?" She was desperate for answers.

He sat down at the table and put his hands to his head, his elbows on the table. "Sit down, Mary. I don't know what to say or think. It looks like they vanished into thin air. This was what we talked about down at the cookhouse."

He stalled for time as his mind raced to find the right words. He knew he would have to find a way to get the women and children through the night. "There is a possibility that they could have had engine trouble. If so, they went with the strong tide that is running up today. This could carry them up the coast as far as Fortune, or maybe even farther. Maybe as far as St. Lunaire.

"With this storm on, they might not have been able to get home this evening, and for sure they won't be able to get home tonight. In the morning, I'm going to send some men up that way on a dog team to check around, so don't be too worried. I have a feeling that they might be up around St. Leonard's Bay somewhere. There's an old cabin up there, and George knows where it is. They might be in it."

Mary couldn't take the pressure any longer. She burst into tears. "Oh my, what am I going to do? Happy and Roland are gone. I'll never see them again."

"Listen, Mary," said Az, "please stop crying. You're the one who we'll have to depend upon to be strong and try to help the rest."

She put her hands to her face and started sobbing. Everyone was crying now.

Gideon came out of the living room. This was one time that Az was glad the young Salvation Army officer was under his roof.

"Listen, everyone," Gideon said, "you may be jumping to conclusions. It may be like the skipper says. So please, wait until morning and see what happens when the storm is over."

"I have to check on the children," Mary said. She wiped her eyes and went upstairs.

On Christmas Eve night of 1929, all the Christmas trees were standing alone and quiet in the homes at L'Anse au Pigeon. Most of the women and children were at Az's house, where they would normally gather that night of the year, but instead of celebrating, they sat in silence, hearing frightful things they never thought they would ever hear. This was supposed to be the concert night. Instead, the barracks was silent. The Christmas trees at their houses were loaded down, but untouched. The gifts lay stacked, but no one noticed. Santa Claus was the last thing on everyone's mind.

"The house is shaking," said Aunt Emily Jane. "I don't think I ever saw the likes of this. Just look at the windows. There must be an inch of ice on them."

She was in her rocking chair. She had her elbow on the arm of the chair, and her hand was at the side of her jaw, as if she were holding her head up. She slowly but quietly rocked as tears ran down her face. "Poor Happy. I wonder where he is right now with this storm on?" She made sure that Az didn't hear her.

Gladys, who was near her, whispered, "I wonder what could have happened to them, Aunt Emily Jane?"

Emily Jane leaned over and whispered back. "I can tell you what happened to them, Gladys. It's that Sod Mugford. He made away with them. That's what happened to them."

All the children had gone to bed except Susie. She was now a young woman. She had more to cry about than anyone. Her true love, the man she was planning to marry, Allan, was gone.

Susie was a very beautiful girl, tall with black hair, full of life and energy. She had worked with Az during the summers, salting fish. She was a wonderful singer, in great demand at the times and in the church choir. She was a very lovable person. In fact, she was Happy Tucker's favourite daughter, always ready to help her stepmother Mary with the younger children, Susie's stepsisters. She thought back to last Christmas, the first time Allan showed interest in her.

Allan had been in a very good mood, glad to be at L'Anse au Pigeon on Boxing Day the previous year. He was sitting at the table in the cookhouse while the time was taking place. He was listening to Susie singing *Don't go into the kitchen, Dad, Nancy's in there with a fella.* He was in love with Susie, but had never asked her for a date. He had talked to her many times, but it was only about things around them—work, fishing and the future of the Pigeon. That night, his conversation with her would be different. He would be asking her for a date.

At ten o'clock the time was over and everyone had gone, except for half a dozen people who were cleaning up. Among them was Winnie, Az's daughter, who knew what Allan had in mind. She had talked to him earlier in the day. She had told him, "Allan, you've got to start dating Susie. She wants to go out with you, so tonight you've got to walk her home."

Allan laughed. If Winnie only knew how much he wanted to date Susie! As they swept the cookhouse floor, Winnie called the two of them over. "Okay, now, you two. I've talked to the two of you and you're both crazy about each other, so tonight is the night to start your romance. Allan, put your arms around Susie."

Allan laughed nervously. "Come here, Susie," he said.

Susie came close to him and started blushing.

"It's too late to blush now, Susie," Allan said as he put his arms around her and drew her close.

Winnie and her boyfriend Norman Pilgrim had laughed at the two awkward lovers; it made them happy to see the beginning of a love affair that everyone in the Pigeon would admire and envy.

So much had happened since that magical night. Young Willie Cuff had been murdered, and Edwin Burton had drowned himself shortly after. And Sod, whose presence was like a curse, had gotten his ultimate revenge.

Allan and the others were gone.

Susie Tucker watched the spray from the ocean beating on the window, and her heart broke.

Az sat at the big table. He tried to drink a cup of tea, but could hardly get the cup to his mouth. He was shaking.

Mary came over and sat at the table, across from him. Her red hair was still neatly set. She said, "Uncle Az, there are no children here now. We're all grown-ups. Let me tell you how we feel about the missing men. We talked about it before you came."

Mary's fists were clenched with tension, and there was no smile on her face. "Trum was in here awhile ago and told us about the five gallons of gas that Sod carried on board the boat this morning. He said that there was no reason why he should have had that can of gasoline.

"Now, Skipper, let me ask you this. Do you think that Sod had the gasoline to deliberately catch the boat on fire?"

Az didn't know what to say. He could offer no reasonable explanation for the gasoline that Sod took on the boat that morning. In fact, it was as puzzling as if he had taken a bag of dynamite. It would have been no different. Az knew he had to answer.

"Mary, my dear, I don't know. You see, we could be jumping to conclusions. Let's wait first and see what happens tomorrow morning. It's better, you see, that these questions aren't answered yet."

Mary persisted. "Maybe I put the question to you wrong. Let me ask it this way. Does it appear funny that Sod would take five gallons of gasoline with him on the boat with a full tank of nine gallons already on board? Don't you think that it looks a little strange?"

Az was cornered. He knew he had to answer. "Yes, it does look strange," he said.

Mary added, "Yes, Uncle Az, and we all know that he's capable of blasting that boat and everyone in it to kingdom come to avoid what might happen to him for murdering the schoolteacher."

"Mary, all I can say is that in the morning we'll continue to search for the boys, and we'll hope to find them safe."

Lydia Tucker lay on her bed. Her pillow was wet from her tears. She had been crying ever since she heard the men were missing. The house was warm from the wood stove, which was red-hot from the fire that was roaring in it. It was too dangerous to leave the fire untended, so she stayed awake all night. Truman lay on the couch smoking his pipe. Lydia smelled the tobacco smoke and thought about how close Truman had come to being one of the men who were missing, had Uncle Az not made him get out of the boat. She also thought about her brother-in-law who went instead—poor Roland, only sixteen.

She lay on the bed, very quiet and still.

Then she heard it. The great foghorn on Cape Bauld was blowing as if it were going crazy.

She thought about what had happened that morning at the clothesline. As she lay there in the semi-darkness, Sod's last words rang in her ears. She couldn't get them out of her mind. It had echoed and re-echoed all day. She had told no one.

As the great horn sounded, it reminded her that someday the great Archangel Gabriel will sound the mighty trumpet and wake up all the dead. As she listened, she was reminded that someone out there was alive, blowing the foghorn. She picked up the words of the hymn that Sod had talked about. She sang along in rhythm with the great horn. Very slowly she sang *The night is dark and I am far from home. Lead thou me on.*

She realized what she was doing. "Oh my, that's it! That's the hymn Sod mentioned. Truman, come here."

He got up from the couch and came into the bedroom. "What's wrong, Liddy?" he asked anxiously.

"Listen to the foggle horn," she said.

He listened attentively, and she started to sing. She sang very quietly, just loud enough for Truman to hear her and the great horn together.

"The hymn has been on my mind all day," Lydia said.

*Yes,* he thought, *it's the right beat.*

When she finished singing, she told him about Sod, and how he had cried when he told her about it this morning.

As Truman lay there with his wife and listened to the wind whistling around the corner of his house, he could hear the foghorn calling out to Sod, warning him that the night was dark and stormy, that death was on the trail of his family. He burst into tears.

"Why all this? Why has this happened to Father? He never did anything bad to anyone in his life. He only worked to help people. He doesn't deserve to be out on a night like this."

He cried, and the tears ran down his face. "Something tells me that I'll never see my father again, Liddy. Too much time has passed. They're gone."

# Chapter 29

Uncle Joe "Jowl" Bartlett lived on the western end of Quirpon Island. Az Roberts always said that he was a noble man. Everyone called him Uncle Jowl, due to his long beard. When he sat, his beard would touch his knees. His place was about two miles from the Pigeon. He fished around the Clue and near the White Islands, and was known by everyone as a man who was very knowledgeable.

Uncle Jowl always had large vegetable gardens and kept cows, sheep, goats and pigs. Every fall he had a large crop of potatoes, approximately one hundred barrels. He also grew huge heads of cabbage. Whenever Gladys Hillier walked into the town of L'Anse au Pigeon, she would be carrying a head of Uncle Jowl's cabbage. He gave away more than he kept. Dr. Grenfell once told Az Roberts that Uncle Jowl Bartlett was one of the seven wonders of the world, referring to the success he had in raising vegetables and cattle on rock and bog.

Uncle Jowl was also a staunch member of the Salvation Army. When he attended a meeting at the cookhouse on Sunday mornings with Uncle Happy Tucker and Uncle Gus Bridger, with Gladys singing and Gideon on the concertina, the building shook on its foundation. Az said it seemed like sparks were coming from the windows!

Uncle Jowl sat at the table of the cookhouse in the Pigeon. He was wet and cold, and had just returned from Cape Bauld. He had met with Ned Fontaine the lightkeeper, to inform Ned of what was going on and ask him if he had seen anything.

Ned told him that around eight-thirty that morning he saw Az's trap skiff go around Rangalley Head, heading west. He said his attention was drawn to that area because he saw a large flock of shore ducks fly out of Degrat. He watched them for a few minutes, and then he saw the boat. He knew right away it was Az's. First he figured that Az might be sending her up to St. Anthony to pick up the freight that was coming in from Little Bay Islands on the *Lone Flier*. Then he remembered hearing Happy say that they were going to get his firewood at the Clue first. In fact, when he saw them he gave three loud blasts on the horn. After that, Ned kept an eye on the area, but didn't see any sign of them returning.

"They never came back around Rangalley Head," he told Uncle Jowl. "If they had, I would have seen them." And knowing Ned Fontaine, he would have. He never let anything get out of his sight; he did his job well.

With these words, Uncle Jowl finished his update to the men gathered at the cookhouse. "Whatever happened to the boys happened at the Clue," he said.

All the men around him agreed. He was about to have his supper when Gideon came in.

"The skipper wants to see you, Uncle Jowl. He wants you to take your clothes and bring them up to the house and stay there overnight. The skipper's in bad shape. He's heartbroken."

"All right," he said, as he got up from the table.

"Have your supper first, Uncle Jowl," said the women. They wanted more news from him.

"No," said Gideon. "There's plenty of supper cooked up at the house."

He got his wet clothes and went on up to the house.

Uncle Jowl was a welcome sight on this sad occasion. When he walked in, all the women put their arms around him and kissed him. They were glad to see him. Just having him with them was a comfort, even if he didn't say a word. His presence helped them in their hour of grief.

The women were trying to restrain their own feelings, because they didn't want to get the teenagers upset. Everyone was quite aware that something had gone wrong with the boat and the men, and it was obvious that no one had any idea what had happened. Although Mary had questioned Az about the gasoline, she still couldn't stop thinking about how it might have been used. She wanted someone to come up with a suggestion that would give them a shred of hope.

Az greeted his new guest. "Uncle Jowl, sit at the table and have supper. Gladys, my dear, hang up Uncle Jowl's clothes behind the stove to dry."

"What a terrible storm we're having, Az, and it's still getting worse," said Uncle Jowl.

Az was so involved in his thoughts that he hardly heard him. "Yes, Uncle Jowl, and by tomorrow morning there will be a big sea heaving."

"There's a big sea heaving now."

Az agreed. "After you get your supper eaten, I want to see you privately in one of the rooms."

Az was referring to one of the bedrooms; the rest of the house was occupied. He got up and went into the bedroom off the kitchen. In a few minutes, Uncle Jowl finished his meal and went straight to the room. Az then shut the door. The light in the ceiling was blinking, powered from a windmill Az had installed in the Pigeon.

"Don't mind that light, Uncle Jowl, he said. "Whenever the winds are high we always get that, but they never go out. I want your opinion on what you think happened to the boys. It's beyond me."

Uncle Jowl didn't know what to say. "I guess, Az, you know more about it than anyone. It's a mystery to me. We know that they're not at the Clue. Norm, Len, and Eric were over there, and from what they're saying, the wood is gone. They must have left early, long before dinner—there wasn't a sign of them anywhere. What about Degrat, Az?" he asked.

"Tom Hillier and Trum searched Degrat from one end to the other, but there was not a sign of anything."

"So that part of the island has been searched; are you satisfied with what they covered—that is, the Clue and Degrat?" asked Uncle Jowl.

"If any of the men had gotten ashore, they would have been home in less than half an hour, especially if they needed help."

The two men sat and looked at each other. Uncle Jowl spoke up. "There's only one thing that I know could have happened. If the boat capsized due to the way she was loaded, someone should have gotten ashore, but even if they did, it might have been too cold for them to get home."

"That never happened," said Az. "For one thing, they didn't have a full load of wood, and even if they loaded all the wood on one side of the boat, it wouldn't cause that big motorboat to tip over. Besides that, George would never let them stack it wrong, not on your life."

"Well, we can rule out overloading, according to that," said Jowl. "What about the White Islands? Don't you think that if something went wrong they could have gotten ashore there? But with this storm on, they wouldn't stand much of a chance."

"Norm and the others were down to the Clue around three this afternoon," Az replied, "and although there was a lot of wind on, they could still see the islands pretty good, but they saw nothing. If they were out there they would have a flag up, or a fire going—they had plenty of wood."

Uncle Jowl was frustrated. "What can we do? Where can we look?" he asked.

"I don't know what to say, Uncle Jowl. If they're not in on the land somewhere, and in some kind of a shelter, there's only one thing I can say—goodbye to them all."

Uncle Jowl could hardly believe his ears, but he had to admit it. "You could be right about that."

"But we can't lose hope," Az said. "In the morning we've got to get on the move somewhere and see what we can find."

"What do you want me to do?" asked Uncle Jowl.

"I want you to take four men with you and go to Griquet for me, and spread the word. Tell everyone. I also want you to send a message to Dr. Curtis at St. Anthony, and ask the captain of the *Lone Flier*, Peter Troake, to come down and search along the coast, including the White Islands. Winnie will write out the message for you in the morning, and I'll give you money for the wireless. Send a word to Fortune and ask them to look out along the headlands, between Fortune and Quirpon. Also, send word to St. Lunaire and tell them there what's going on and ask them to have a look around."

Uncle Jowl agreed to go first thing in the morning. "I'll get on the move as soon as there's enough light to see how to get around."

"There's one thing that you're going to have to be careful with, Uncle Jowl, and that is the ice in Quirpon Harbour. With this heavy sea, the ice might be broken up by tomorrow morning, so be careful."

"You could be right, but if that's the case, I'll launch my big punt and row across the tickle."

"In the meantime, we'll continue to search Degrat and the Clue again, along with everywhere else around here," said Az. "We'll also light the tar barrels. If by chance they are on the White Islands, they might see the smoke and raise a flag or signal."

"You're right," said Uncle Jowl. With these words the two men left the room.

Az walked the floor all night. A couple of times he lay down on the couch, but he couldn't rest for a second. He looked like a man who had gone crazy. Most of the women were up, sitting around the table in the kitchen; others were sitting up with the children in their bedrooms. There were eight bedrooms in the house, and tonight they were all full.

Uncle Jowl went to bed to see if he could get a few hours rest; he knew that tomorrow would be a rough day.

In the oven was a large roaster full of baked beans that Stewart was looking after, making sure that they didn't burn. The aroma filled the house. The storm didn't let up, and Stewart and the others who were awake could hear the sea roaring outside. They watched the spray as it covered the windows.

"I suppose the wharves and stages won't get washed away tonight in this storm," said Stewart.

"Don't remind me of anything else, Stew," said Az. "A long time ago, I was told that a curse would fall on me, and I suppose it finally has." He stopped pacing and sat at the table.

"It's five o'clock. Gid, you and Stew go and lie down now; you've been up all night. You've done your part, so go and get some rest. I don't think there will be much more that you'll be able to do until the morning." The two of them agreed and left the kitchen.

Az went over to check the weather glass. "It's still bottom-up," he said. "If the glass doesn't show an improvement with the dawn, then the storm could be on for another twelve hours, at least."

At six o'clock, Az called Uncle Jowl. In less than a minute, he came out into the kitchen. "The storm is still raging, Uncle Jowl. It hasn't let up at all."

"I'd say that it's going to be on all day."

Mary came downstairs. Her eyes were red and swollen. "I haven't closed an eye all night. What with the roar of the sea and wind, and Old Man Fontaine out there on Cape Bauld blowing that foggle horn all night, I don't know what was worse. Combining that with our misery, to tell you the truth, it's a wonder I'm alive this morning." Her red hair was tied with a scarf.

"We all feel the same way as you do this morning, my dear," said Uncle Jowl.

Mary went over to him, put her arms around him, and started sobbing. "I'm glad you're here with us this morning, Uncle Jowl. What am I going to do? Oh my, oh my, I'm finished. Happy and Roland are gone. I don't think I'll ever live through it." When she finished talking, she put her head on his shoulder and held him tight.

He tried to comfort her. "There's not much that we can do, only pray that everything will turn out all right."

"Everything won't turn out all right, Uncle Jowl, because we'll never see the men again. Happy and Roland are gone; they'll never be coming home again." She started crying again, holding onto this dear old man.

After the worst had passed, she let him go and dried her tears. "Excuse me for crying like this, Uncle Jowl. I suppose in life we never know what we'll have to go through, and I suppose it's good that we don't. If we did, we'd be gone crazy long before this."

Uncle Jowl and Az nodded solemnly.

"I'll get your breakfast now," Mary said to them.

Az sat at the table. Tears were running freely down his face. He knew he would have to get a grip on himself, but what could he do? He began to stand. "I'm going down to the cookhouse," he said.

"Oh, no you're not," Mary said. She knew he was trying to hide his tears. He needed company. "You're staying here and having breakfast with me."

"All right." He sat down again at the table. While the three of them sat there with breakfast in front of them, the house shook with the wind. Mary started the conversation again.

"Az, tell me the truth. What do you think happened to the men? For sure you've done a lot of thinking about everything since yesterday, so what do you think?"

"Mary, I don't want to hide anything from you, and I don't want to avoid a question either, but for me to go guessing wouldn't be right. Maybe today we might find them somewhere. Then we would say how foolish we were to make certain statements."

He knew that she realized he didn't want to commit to a specific answer. "The only thing that I'll say this morning, Mary, is that if I had my time back, I would never have let Old Sod go in that boat." He had to be careful not to say something that would start a rumour going.

"Why? Is there something that we don't know?"

"Mary, you know about Sod's trouble, and the problems he's caused here for close to a year now. Everything comes to mind. No doubt, last night there were things that came into your mind, as they did to me. You've heard what Sod's been saying all fall; you and I have talked about it and wondered what he was going to do next. Mary, let me ask you what you think happened to the boat."

She closed her eyes. Her red hair now hung limply down around her shoulders. "I'm sure that Sod has done something with the men and the boat. There's one thing that I want to ask you—did they have a gun on board? If he did, maybe he shot them or something." She was wringing her hands tightly, squeezing them until they hurt.

"No," said Az, "he didn't shoot anyone. He wouldn't have been able to shoot all four men without someone attacking him."

"Well then, what do you think happened?"

"Mary, it's too early yet for you to know what I think, but if we don't find anything after we do more searching, I'll tell you."

She put her hands to her head with her elbows on the table and started crying again. Az put his arms around her to comfort her.

"There's no use crying, Mary. Try and bear the weight of it. I feel the same as you, but I have to go on—we all have to go on."

# Chapter 30

The men staying at the cookhouse were up and had eaten their breakfast before Az and Uncle Jowl arrived. This was Christmas morning, and Az gave a silent thanks that Mary hadn't mentioned it during their discussion.

The lights were blazing when the two men walked in. Deadly silence surrounded them. Winnie broke the spell—she asked her father if he had heard anything.

"Nothing," he replied. "There is a possibility that this storm could go on all day, or at least until the sun goes down, according to the glass. We were just looking at the sea that's rolling in. It's mountainous. There probably has been a lot of damage done. We'll know how much when it gets light."

This statement was made to indicate to the men present that nothing could live anywhere along the shoreline. They understood Az's meaning.

Those men who lived in their homes nearby soon started arriving at the cookhouse. They knew there was nothing new; if there had been news, the word would already have gone around to their houses.

As they tramped in, Winnie announced to all, "There's plenty of breakfast for everyone."

As they ate, Az had a talk with them. "Listen, men, there is a lot of talk about Sod Mugford. Some are saying that he caught the boat on fire; more are saying that he had a gun and could have shot the men. No one actually knows anything for sure, so don't say anything about it. The more you say about this matter, the harder it is on the families. It only makes them more upset. Uncle Jowl Bartlett's going to Griquet with some men to sound the alarm all along the coast, especially the people at Fortune. The boys may have gotten ashore somewhere up there. He's also going to send a wireless from me to Captain Peter Troake in the *Lone Flier* at St. Anthony, asking him to come down and take a look around the White Islands and along the coast. That depends on if she can get down in the rough sea. The rest of the men will organize themselves into groups and search between Degrat and along the outside part of the islands, right up to the western end."

Az was aware of the hazards of going too close to the edge of the cliffs, especially with snow on the ground. Everything became as slippery as glass, and with the wind gusting they could get blown away like pieces of paper. "Don't anyone go out without taking a lot of rope with you, and watch what you're doing. Don't take any chances. All we can do is have a look around, as best we can in these conditions."

Az began detailing the search. "Trum, I want you and Uncle Gus to take a dozen men and go to Degrat again for another search. Look for the firewood alongshore—anything. You might not be able to see much because of the sea." Truman and Uncle Gus agreed.

He continued with his instructions. "Len, I want you and Eric to take some men and go to the Clue again and see what you can find. Take your spyglasses and see if you can spot anything out around the White Islands."

After the men were briefed, he told them to make sure to be extra careful not to get separated. "Stay together, boys, and make sure no one gets lost. In this weather, a man wouldn't last long. We don't want to have another search on our hands."

Az cautioned the searchers about their own safety. "Now, it might turn out that it's too bad for searching. You'll know when you get out into it. If it's too bad, then come back here to the cookhouse. The cooks will be here all the time."

Everyone promised they would be cautious. Az then added, "It's Christmas Day, and I know that all of you are thinking about your families. There's no doubt that we all had different plans for today, but we'll do our best, and may God help us."

Az hung his head in despair.

He said to Norm, "There's no doubt that the wireless office is closed today, Christmas Day, so I want you and Tom Hillier, along with Stew, to come with me to Cape Bauld. We're going to get Ned to contact the lighthouse on Fishing Point and get a message through that way. Uncle Jowl Bartlett might be able to get his message through too, but I'd rather not chance it." It was almost light outside when Az finished talking to the men.

"We'll be moving out in half an hour, so we might as well start to get ready," said Uncle Jowl. Everyone then started putting on their winter clothes.

The weather that day was terrible. The storm didn't let up. Az got to the lighthouse at Cape Bauld at noon, but how, he didn't know; visibility was zero. Stewart Brenton said that it was the worst day that he'd ever been out in his life.

Az gave Ned Fontaine an update on what was going on. Then he got to work on sending the wireless to Captain Troake, and found that the *Lone Flier* was indeed at St. Anthony and that Uncle Jowl Bartlett had already gotten the message through. Captain Troake wired back to Ned and told him that he would be coming when the wind slackened. After Az and his crew had a lunch and partially dried out their clothes, they decided to head back.

Ned told them that if there was anything he could do for them, to let him know. Az replied, "For now, we'll send messages to the next of kin, telling them that we are still searching. However, as soon as we call off the search, I'll need messages sent to let the authorities know what's going on, and to let the next of kin know. I can get the messages written up tomorrow to be sent out if needed."

"I'll send those for you and it won't cost you anything," said Ned.

"Thanks," said Az.

"Listen, Az," said Ned. "My boat *Little Flower* is there in the Pigeon. You can push her off for a search as soon as the sea goes down; whenever you want her, just take her."

"I know that, Ned. Thanks very much."

Anastasia Fontaine said that the thought of Uncle Happy Tucker being out in this storm all night had her driven crazy. As the men were about to leave, she spoke to Az. "Listen Az, we're coming as soon as this storm is over. Oh my, Aunt Emily Jane and Mary must be gone out of their minds by now. Poor Happy. Tell Aunt Emily Jane that I'm praying for all of you."

Az and the others arrived back in the Pigeon at three-thirty and went directly to the cookhouse to inquire about any news, and they were told that there wasn't a trace of anything found. In fact, no one could see anywhere for drifting snow and vapour. Az went to the house to face the women and children. He knew this would be a hard task; they would be waiting for news—any news—but he had none to offer them.

When he entered the house, everyone gathered around. Mary came directly to him and pleaded, "Have you heard anything, or has anyone seen anything?"

Az couldn't give her any new information. "No, my dear, not a word of anything and nobody has seen anything, either. I went to Cape Bauld and sent the messages to the *Lone Flier* and got a reply right away. She's coming as soon as the wind drops. Uncle Jowl hasn't come back from the Fortune area yet, so we don't know if they saw anything up there."

Mary wasn't surprised. During the day, the women had been talking among themselves. They talked about all the things that might have happened to the men, and Sod Mugford was at the centre of their conversations. It was agreed by all the women, including Bessie, Sod's wife, that he had burned the boat and killed the men, every one of them. Az told them that they shouldn't jump to conclusions because the report wasn't yet back from the Fortune area.

"Listen, Uncle Az," said Bessie. "It's a funny thing. No one believed any of the stories about Sod. Here he was, in the Pigeon for almost a year, the murderer hiding under our roofs and no one wrote the police to come and arrest him. In this past year while he was here, he did and said everything he wanted. I didn't know whether or not I was going to be murdered in bed half of the time. When he got drunk he would come beating on the door, and if I didn't let him in he would smash it in. I lived in fear all the time."

She was crying. "Only God knows what I went through, and now look what he's done. He said that he was going to do it; he told people he was going to make away with himself and take others with him. And now he's done it!

"He's murdered my father and brother, Uncle George and Allan. Everyone here in the Pigeon knows it, including you, Uncle Az. We know that you're under a lot of pressure about everything, and we love you, but we have to face the facts. Sod has murdered the men."

At four-thirty, Az looked at the barometer.

"The glass is showing an improvement in the weather; the wind will drop out at sunset," he said. At least this was some encouragement for everyone. When it cleared, they could get on the move to search, especially around the White Islands.

Az took off his wet, freezing clothes. It was getting dark as he sat down and had a little supper. He was getting up from the table when Truman came in.

"It's starting to clear up, Skipper. The wind is dropping fast."

"This is what we wanted," Az replied.

To Gideon, who was sitting in a chair by the stove, Az said, "I'm going to the cookhouse right away." He put on his clothes and went out the door.

"It's clearing up, men," Az said as he entered the cookhouse. Some of the men had gone to their homes and hadn't yet returned. "We have to get on the move. We'll need to get the dogs harnessed to carry some old cod oil barrels made ready to go upon Rangalley Head, to light a fire in them for a signal. If the boys are out there anywhere, especially out on the White Islands, they'll know that we're looking for them. In fact, a group should go up there now to see if there's a flag or other signal out on those islands.

"Stew, you go around to the houses and tell the men to come to the cookhouse right away, and tell them to bring their lanterns."

Other men in the Pigeon arrived and made ready to move out. Dogs were barking, men and sleighs were in motion and the cod oil barrels were on their way to Rangalley Head. In one barrel was five gallons of cod oil. They also carried a can of gasoline to help them get the fire going quickly.

By now the moon was up and shining so brightly that Az could see that part of his wharf had gone in the storm. Everything else looked to be in pretty good shape. The shoreline was covered in ice, caused by the spray from the ocean. Ned Fontaine's boat, the *Little Flower,* was completely covered in ice also—it was a miracle that it didn't get swept away in the storm. The sea was still rolling in from the North Atlantic.

Around seven o'clock, Uncle Jowl returned from Fortune and Griquet. He had been searching all day with a crowd of men and found nothing, and no one he talked to had seen or heard anything on Christmas Eve or today. He was told that there were men out hunting shore ducks on Christmas Eve, just before the storm came on, but they saw and heard nothing.

He had no other news to offer, except that he had gotten a message sent to the *Lone Flier* and one to Dr. Curtis.

"Uncle Jowl, it seems like they've just disappeared," said Az.

"They must have. That's all I can say," agreed Uncle Jowl.

At eight o'clock, a group of twenty men arrived. As soon as the weather improved, more would be coming to help in searching.

An hour later, Az could see a fire upon Rangalley Head. All the women and children were out watching. Standing speechless in the frosty moonlit night, they could only stare and hope that their loved ones would be found alive and well, but hope was fading fast.

Susie was the one who was in the worst state of mind—she had lost her father, stepbrother, Uncle George, and Allan, the man she was about to marry.

"Imagine, Allan gone forever," Susie sobbed. It was unbearable for her—she was in despair. There were no medical personnel in or near the town, and there were no sedatives or pain killers to help. The only shoulder to lean on in the Pigeon was the one everyone leaned on, Az Roberts. Without him in this hour, they would all be lost. The nearest medical help was at St. Anthony, twenty-five miles away. There was no doubt that if Susie were near the hospital, she would have been admitted; she was about to collapse. Aunt Emily Jane had to keep cold cloths on her forehead most of the time.

By midnight all the men were back in the Pigeon. Their hopes were very low. They hadn't seen or heard anything, only the roar of the angry, savage sea as it smashed against the land.

"There is nothing out on the White Islands, or at least we didn't see anything. But of course it's a job to see anything, due to the vapour rising from the sea," said Uncle Gus Bridger. He had headed the party that was up on Rangalley Head.

"There is no other place to look here on Quirpon Island," he continued. "The only thing to do now is to get a boat and go out to the White Islands. They may have gotten on the lun side and anchored the boat to the cliffs out there. You never know what men will do when they're in a jam."

Az knew there was no need to comment on that statement, and he knew that Uncle Gus was only saying it to keep hope alive for the women's and children's sake. "You never know," Az offered.

He sent for Norman, and when he arrived, Az asked him to take on the task of getting a place to stay for the twenty new men who arrived to assist in the search. "I think we can put them in the houses belonging to Mary and Bessie. There's no one in them. They're all at our place. But I want you to go up and let them know first, and then go and get a fire lit in them. By now the houses are very cold.

"They can all eat here in the cookhouse. There's plenty of grub. Winnie, you'll know the right amount to cook, especially for breakfast. Whoever you can't get into those two houses, make sure you get them in somewhere. We might be able to get some more in up at our house. You can check with Emily Jane."

"Don't worry, Skipper," Norman said, "I'll get them in somewhere. What do you think the weather's going to be like in the morning?"

"According to Uncle Gus, it's going to blow again. He said that the wind is going to drop with the sun. He could be right, but I'll know when I get home and see the glass."

Az lay down on the couch in the dining room. Grace came over and put her arms around him and started to cry. He knew that she was broken-hearted. She was a big girl, built with a strong frame, but now she was shaking. She had been so close to George. Within the last two days, Az didn't have time to comfort her in her sorrow. He had been too busy with the search. He would try to bear his own sorrow alone.

271

"Grace, my dear, you're going to have to face it. Uncle George is gone, and he is gone forever. Please, don't cry. Your tears will never bring him back. He wouldn't want you to cry. Remember when you were just a little girl, how he used to tell you not to cry, that crying was for only if you were afraid? Grace, don't be afraid. I'm still here with you."

Grace wanted to tell him how she had seen Uncle George on the morning that he left, standing near the window, waving at her. But she knew that he had enough to think about already. Anything else that he heard would only hurt him. She knew that she, likewise, would have to carry on, no matter what.

As he lay on the couch in the dining room with a heavy blanket over him, memories flooded him. His mind went back to when he was a boy, living with his father at Lushes Bight. He had watched his father, John Roberts, die as a young man, from a blood-poisoned arm. From that time on, he had to start going to Labrador as part of a fishing crew to support his mother and family. When he was seventeen, his mother Sally had died suddenly one day while carrying a lunch to a group of men who were building a schooner. She delivered their lunch, sat down and died.

This was a devastating loss to Az. He had been very close to her, supporting her from the time he was nine years old. But since then he had struck out on his own and had lived a very prosperous life. He had worked long and hard, and it had paid off. He was successful because he had good men around him and he showed them respect.

Now he was fifty years old with a lump in his throat from the loss of his men and dear friends, and it was Christmas Day, when everyone should be celebrating. All year he had lived in great misery, haunted day and night with this Sod Mugford racket. Then there was Happy having that dream.

Lying on the couch, all these things loomed like some monster reaching out to him and saying *The curse, the curse, the curse, Az.*

What could he do? He had never hurt anyone or anything in his life. He knew that he was too old to learn, and maybe he was a little too young to die. He lay in the darkness, surrounded by the faces of the men who were lost. They were his crew, his friends, and in some ways they were his children. He could see them one at a time, passing by, calling for help, but he knew they could never be reached—they were gone forever.

"The die has been cast and only eternity will reveal what their end was," he whispered.

Az started to drift off to sleep as the wind outside blanketed the houses with drifting snow.

# Chapter 31

The following day was Boxing Day, Thursday, December 26, 1929. Daylight brought high winds and drifting snow. Az got up from the couch at 5:00 a.m. The room was warm; the fire had been going all night. By the roar of the sea, he could tell that the wind was blowing hard outside. He looked at the weather glass. "The glass is starting to look better; the wind will drop with the rising of the sun, just as Uncle Gus said."

Gideon sat at the table. He had been up all night keeping the fire going. Az said later that he wouldn't have known what to do if Gideon hadn't been at the Pigeon during their time of trial. He was the one they all looked to for spiritual help, especially the women and children. Wherever he was, he was doing something to help them.

"Gid, I'm glad you're here with us. Without your help I don't think we could pull through," Az said.

Gideon replied, "I'm only doing my duty, Skipper. This is as hard on me as it is on you. I suppose we're all suffering."

"You're right."

Grace was up and busy cooking breakfast. "I'd like to have a little breakfast, Grace," Az said to her. "I'd like to have it right away because I have to go to the cookhouse to get the men moving."

"All right," she replied, already slicing bread.

By six-thirty, all the men were ready to be filled in on what they had to do. By then the wind was dropping fast, but the sea was still mountainous. "I don't know if the *Lone Flier* will be able to get here this morning or not. Nothing can live out there on that ocean. We'll have the same crowd go up on Rangalley Head to light the tar barrel, like last evening. Keep an eye out for the *Lone Flier,* and be sure you take the spyglasses and watch her signals, to see what her message is. The *Lone Flier* has a barrel with a man in it, up in the mast. Captain Troake always goes to the seal hunt in that vessel. If there's anyone who can get here, he can."

Az knew that there were several men among the group of searchers who knew the captain personally. They were expecting him this morning. "It's like I said before, spread out the same as yesterday, but be careful not to have an accident or get astray from your group."

All were clear on their instructions, and they left.

"Norm," said Az, "take the Union Jack with you. If the *Lone Flier* signals that she has seen anything, you wave the flag twice; if she signals that she hasn't seen anything, wave the flag three times."

Norman agreed and went to get the Union Jack, the national flag of Newfoundland.

Az told Winnie what was going on and asked her to make sure and keep the frost off the windows of the cookhouse, and to keep looking with the spyglasses. She agreed.

That morning, after the men left the Pigeon to start searching, Az went back to the house to get a pair of heavy woollen gloves. As he entered the door he noticed that all the women were up and dressed. He also sensed that there was something wrong. Tension was high. He looked at them and asked, "What's wrong?"

For a moment, no one spoke. Then Gladys broke the silence. "Skipper Az, there's a lot of talk about young Wes Mugford."

Az wasn't surprised. He knew it would come sooner or later. He had been thinking about it himself. "What is it?" he asked.

Bessie spoke up. "We have just been saying that Wes hasn't shown his nose outside George Oake's door since the men left to go for the wood on Tuesday. Don't you think that's funny? Sod is his brother, so why isn't he searching?"

Mary then spoke up. "I know what should be done. He should be sent right out of the Pigeon, bag and baggage, because as far as I'm concerned he's been the root of all our trouble from the very beginning."

Az knew that there could be trouble if some of the men got mad with Wes, and it was sure to happen, especially if the women egged them on. "Listen," said Az in a stern voice, "I don't want to hear anything else about that. You leave it to me."

They were all silent. Az took his gloves and left.

He walked directly to the cookhouse and asked Winnie if she would write out a wireless telegram for him. She got the pencil and paper and wrote it up.

Winnie looked at her father and asked, "Who is going south, Pop?"

He answered without looking at her. "Wes Mugford, Winnie."

She wasn't surprised to hear that, because they had been talking among themselves about the same thing.

"Where's Stew?" he asked.

"He was here a minute ago. He's gone to the well for a turn of water and will be back in ten minutes," replied Emma Bridger.

"Tell him that I want him the minute he gets back."

"Okay, Skipper," Emma said.

In ten minutes, Stewart arrived with the water. Az had a request. "Stew, I want you to go to Cape Bauld and brief Ned on what's going on here. Then I want you to ask him to contact the *Lone Flier* and try to find out if Captain Troake has seen anything of the men. Stay there until you get a reply. Ask Ned if he'll send this wireless to Peter Troake for me, and make sure you get a reply. In fact, don't come back without one." Stewart agreed.

"I have another job for you before you go." He looked from the women to Stewart and said, "Go over to George Oake's and tell Wes that I said for him to pack his bags. He's going to St. Anthony to join the *Lone Flier* going south. That is, if Peter Troake agrees to take him, but I'm sure he will. Don't tell Wes why he has to pack his bags, but tell him to get ready anyway.

"If the passage is confirmed, get back from Cape Bauld as soon as possible. Take another man with you, and ten dogs, and leave with Wes right away. You should make the trip in five hours. Don't waste any time at Cape Bauld. The minute you get a reply about the search, head back right away."

"Okay, Skipper," said Stewart.

"Winnie, I want you to get ten dollars ready to give Stew when he gets back, and also get another five dollars for the passage on the vessel."

Az turned back to Stewart and said, "When you see Captain Troake, thank him for me, for helping to search for the men. Tell him that I will write him. Also, give him the five dollars for Wes's passage. When the boat is pushing off from the wharf, give Wes the ten dollars. Tell him that he doesn't have to pay it back—say it's cod oil money. I don't want him to think that I'm paying him to leave the Pigeon."

It was agreed that Wes Mugford would be moving out of the Pigeon that day.

Az said, "Oh yes, Stew, there's one thing that I forgot. You have him out of here before I get back!"

"Yes, Uncle Az. He'll be gone."

It was 10:00 a.m. when the searchers first caught sight of the vessel *Lone Flier.* She was a long way off from the shoreline, steaming with great difficulty toward the White Islands in the heavy seas. As the vessel came nearer, the men on Rangalley Head saw the struggle between the vessel and the huge seas. The waves were so high that there were times they thought she had gone to the bottom. One moment they saw her high on the waves, and in the next she disappeared, as if swallowed in the depths of the sea.

The searchers on land watched as the steamer came close to the outside of the White Islands. She slowed down but didn't stop. Those who were sitting on the frozen snow were following her with their spyglasses; they could see men in the rigging. The men on the top of Rangalley Head had the smoke towering out of the oil barrel—this was easily seen by Captain Troake and his sailors. It was clear to everyone that he saw nothing on the first pass.

The captain watched his chance and turned his vessel around to check the islands a second time. He came in toward the Clue and steamed as close to the shoreline as possible, but again saw nothing. He later reported that not even a seal could have stayed on or near these islands. He then signalled to the men on shore that he had seen nothing. To be sure, he had men with spyglasses look all along the shoreline, but again seeing nothing, he turned around and headed for St. Anthony.

Norman saw the vessel's signal that the crew hadn't spotted anything. The men with him weren't surprised. After studying the sea out there, they knew that nothing could live on those islands in such a blizzard. He then took the Union Jack and waved it three times to the people in the Pigeon.

Captain Peter Troake had his wireless operator send a message. "To the lighthouse on Cape Bauld: Attention Edward Fontaine. Please notify Az Roberts, L'Anse au Pigeon, it is with regret that we have searched and saw no trace of your men. We are returning to St. Anthony. Please notify me if further assistance is needed. Signed Peter Troake, *Lone Flier.*"

Ned Fontaine replied. "To the *Lone Flier*: Received message okay. Thank you for your kind assistance. Stop. Have message for you. Would like you to give passage to one passenger going south. Stop. Give reply. Signed Az Roberts."

Captain Troake replied. "Leaving St. Anthony tomorrow noon, passage confirmed."

It was still Thursday, Boxing Day, and all the men of the Pigeon were at the cookhouse. The cooks had a big scoff prepared, consisting of all the regular vegetables and fresh pork, with bread pudding and gravy. Most of the men from the surrounding towns had gone home. Every inch of Quirpon Island had been searched, but nothing, not a trace of anything, had been found.

After the men had finished their supper, Gideon came over and had a short church service with them. He read from the Bible and prayed.

With the men gathered there, Az did a review of what had taken place that day. He asked every man about what he thought of the search that was done, and he asked them for suggestions about what they should be doing. No one had anything to offer.

Tom Hillier said he thought everything they had done should have turned up something, that is, if the men had ever gotten near the shore. He said, "There hasn't been a trace found of anyone or anything, not even a piece of wood. I can say they're nowhere on this island."

Az asked, "Does anyone here think it's worthwhile looking any further around this island?"

There was silence.

Uncle Gus Bridger spoke. "I'm prepared to spend the rest of the winter out there along the shoreline if it would do any good, but I know it would be in vain. Therefore, we might as well face it, men. They're all gone. The storm came on too quick. They all went down to a watery grave, and to look any further would only be labour in vain."

Everyone knew Uncle Gus was right. The search for the five men was over. There was nothing else that could be done.

Az hung his head. Tears fell from his eyes. "Tomorrow morning we'll notify the next of kin. It's all we can do. I'm glad poor Mom died years ago. Imagine if I had to tell her that George drifted off to sea in a storm and was never heard tell of again. It would break her heart."

Gideon said, "I think the women have already come to realize that the men will never return. Mary has already told me that she's accepted the fact that Happy and Roland are gone."

After Az dried his eyes he said, "We might as well call off the search. There isn't very much that we can do. Who knows? Maybe something will turn up somewhere that will explain what happened to the boat."

No one said anything, but they all knew that he was right. The search was over.

"What do we do next, Skipper?" asked Tom Hillier.

"Tomorrow morning we'll have to send out pink messages to all the next of kin." A pink message was one that carried bad news, usually a death. "I'll have to send one to Lushes Bight and Beaumont. Also, I'll send one to my sister Sarah. She will have to notify the rest of the people up around there. The news about George will break her heart."

He sat down. "Gid, you and I will have to go to the house and tell the women, I suppose. How can we do it? How can we go up there and tell them that their fathers are gone, or their husbands are gone, or that their brother is gone? How can I tell Grace that we won't be looking for George anymore—that the search has been called off? That all hope of finding them is over? I can tell you it won't be easy."

Az felt sick to his stomach. "I can't see how I can bring myself to tell them, but it has to be done, and we'll find a way to do it. Uncle Gus, you'll have to come with us, and Norm, you'll have to come with us too. All of us together might be able to do it."

Az continued. "We'll tell them that the search has been scaled back. We can't come right out and say that we won't be looking for them anymore, that they're gone."

It was agreed. The five men left for the house, to tell the sad news. The rest of the men went to their homes, to tell their families that the search for the men had been called off.

They walked into the kitchen where the women and children were. Az looked around the house, and for the first time he realized that it was Christmas. He saw the Christmas tree. Everything was as it was on Christmas Eve. Now it was Boxing day, and the stockings were still hanging on the wall. The gifts for the children were still stacked under the tree. He groaned inwardly, not for the men that had been lost, but for those left behind, both young and old alike. The small children just stood around and stared, while the women and teenagers sat around, as if waiting to receive the fatal blow.

"The skipper has something to tell you," Gideon said in a very calm voice. Although he was only twenty-one years of age, he was already a professional. He had received exceptional training at the Salvation Army College in St. John's. He knew how to deliver good news and bad. "It may not be pleasant, but we have to face it." He turned to Az.

With trembling lips Az said, "We have searched every inch of Quirpon Island, and we haven't found a trace of our men. I'm afraid that in spite of doing everything we possibly could, we have found nothing.

"I know I'll continue to look for them every day of my life, 'til the day that I die, but as for the searching we've been doing for the last days, we have decided to scale it back."

He sat down at the table. He put his hands up to his face. "God knows we've gone through enough in the last two days. I'll never be the same again. It would have been better if I'd never been born, or if I'd never come here to L'Anse au Pigeon. You would never have known this tragedy."

Bessie stepped out from among the crowd. She wiped her eyes. "No, Uncle Az. Don't blame yourself. It's not you. I'm the one who brought this trouble on everyone. I should have stayed at Beaumont instead of running down here with you.

And how nice it was before that monster arrived! Since then there's been no peace, and it all led to this."

She was almost hysterical. "When I disobeyed Dad and went against his pleadings for me not to marry Sod Mugford, that's where it all started. He said that I would spend a lifetime of sorrow for as long as Sod lived, and so far Dad's been right. Don't blame it on yourself, Uncle Az. It's not your fault. It's because of me that Sod destroyed those men."

She ran for the bedroom. Gladys followed her.

Az was silent. He didn't know what to do or say. Most of the children were crying.

"In other words, Skipper, you have called off the search," Mary said calmly.

Az looked at her. "Like I said, Mary my dear, we're here in the Pigeon, and we will be searching yet for days. But I don't see any use of having a crowd of men from the other towns searching any longer. There isn't a shred of hope left of even finding anyone or anything. I guess we'll have to accept the fact that the men are gone."

Mary knew he was right. Az and the other searchers had done everything they could to try and find their family members, under the worst of conditions. She knew, when her husband and son didn't show up the first night, that they were gone, and she would never see them again.

Mary said, "Skipper, how will I ever be able to live through it? I know the struggle will be greater from now on without Happy. What will I do?"

"You won't have to struggle, Mary, as long as I have food under my roof. And the same goes for Bessie. Nothing will change."

Mary knew he meant what he said. He had always been good to them.

When the children finally went to bed that night, all the women and the men sat around the table. Each was waiting for one another's comments. Winnie had closed the cookhouse and brought the large coffee pot up to the house. She had the pot on the stove, brewing, and the aroma was strong throughout the room.

Bessie had come back into the dining room after Gladys had consoled her. She held up her hand to get everyone's attention. She spoke in a clear voice, trying to be brave. "I think that tomorrow morning we should open the gifts for the children. We might as well begin our new life. And let me tell you something—I won't be shedding any tears for Old Sod."

No one spoke as she continued. "There will be tears for my father and brother, and for Allan and Uncle George, but none for Sod. In fact, with Sod gone, I'm rid of my troubles."

Bessie steeled herself for the future. "Dad and Roland are gone, and I'm broken-hearted, but as for Sod, I'm glad. I pity his poor soul—if he had one."

Gladys said, "I think we should do as Bessie said. I think that tomorrow we should open the gifts for the children. Something has to be done to help get the thoughts of this tragedy out of their minds."

Everyone agreed. Life would have to go on.

# Chapter 32

When Friday morning dawned upon the little town of L'Anse au Pigeon, most people had recovered enough to carry on with their usual duties. Those who were lost had now been gone for four days. Four days wasn't very long, but the fact that they were never coming back was starting to sink in.

Az left early in the morning. He went over to the Clue to have a last look around. When he got there, he could visualize what had happened that fateful morning, although he didn't have a shred of evidence to back a conclusion of foul play. The only thing that he was sure of was the fact that Aunt Liddy had seen Sod carrying the five gallons of gasoline. There was no reason for him to take it, other than to start a fire. To prove that he started one was a different matter. He knew that this would never be proven unless someone found the boat or some other piece of evidence, and he was sure that the boat would never be found. There was so much cement in it that it probably had sunk like a rock. He also knew that there was so much tar coating the inside, that it wouldn't take long for a hole to burn through the side when it caught on fire.

It could have happened close to the shore, or not far from it. It was strange that no one had seen anything that morning, especially smoke. He also figured that the fire must have been in the rear section of the boat.

If Sod had shut the engine down and then set it on fire, Happy would have put the sculling oar out and put her ashore in a few minutes. It was a mystery. If the boat had been burning for any length of time, someone in Quirpon would have seen the smoke for sure.

If only they had taken the punt. They would only have had to get on board it and row ashore. But it wasn't meant to be. Az thought about all this as he viewed the cove called the Clue. He thought about the five men, and wondered what they were thinking as they spent their last few minutes alive.

"I wonder what they were talking about as they were loading the wood, especially so close to Christmas?" he asked out loud. He knew that his question would never be answered.

*Or, would it?* he mused.

Az turned around and walked back home.

Gideon Hancock lay down on his bed. His mind was moving in all directions. He hadn't held the Christmas concert, or the Christmas tree party that he had planned, and the appropriate time to have them had passed.

A thought came to him. He should be holding a memorial service for the men.

*Yes, I think that's what I'm going to do. I'll hold it for them on New Year's Eve. Happy would be proud of that. The service that I was planning to hold on New Year's Eve, I think I'll turn that into a memorial service for Uncle Happy and the others. Happy was the driving force behind the building of the new barracks.*

Gideon felt relieved to know that there would be something done to remember the men. It would help their families to cope.

"I'll talk to the skipper about that as soon as he gets back," he said out loud. He then went down to the kitchen and told Aunt Emily Jane about what he had in mind.

She was delighted. "Wait until Fred hears about that, Gid. He'll be pleased with you."

Winnie and Grace thought it was a great idea. "We'll have Gladys sing Uncle Happy's favourite hymn."

When Gideon announced his plan, the families brightened up with anticipation.

Az returned from the Clue. The weather was clear but cold. He came inside and went directly to the stove. He removed his woollen gloves and took off his heavy coat and hung it up.

"Did you see anything, Fred?" asked Emily Jane.

"No, not a trace of anything," he answered.

"My, they've just vanished."

Az said nothing. Grace brought him a cup of coffee. "Thanks, Grace, my dear," he said.

He sat at the table and sipped the hot coffee. It seemed to burn down through him, after he had been out in the bitter cold. It was delicious.

Gideon poured himself a cup and joined him. "There's still no trace of anything, Skipper?" he asked, hoping to start a conversation.

"Not a trace," said Az.

"It's a puzzle to me," said Gideon.

"Yes," said Az, "but life has to go on. That's the only thing I can say."

Winnie came over to the table and sat down near him.

Az was out of sorts. "I don't know what to say this morning. It seems like everywhere I look I can see the face of Happy or George staring at me. For some time, we had been planning to put out a couple of seal nets this morning, and go on to St. Anthony for the freight. Can you imagine? Now they're gone, boat and all. When I think about it, I feel like I'm losing my mind."

"Pop!" said Grace, "Gid's planning to have a memorial service for the men on New Year's Eve."

Az froze. "What did you say, Grace?"

"I said that Gid is planning to have a memorial service for the men at the barracks on New Year's Eve."

Az got up from the table and started pacing the floor. He felt like a caged animal that was unable to break loose. He knew that he would have to be careful about how he acted and what he said. A memorial service would send a signal to everyone that all hope was lost.

He stopped pacing the floor for a moment. "You do what you have to do, Gid. You're the Army officer here, and we can't do without you. I'm not going to object to this. I guess it should be done."

He was about to say something more, but stopped. He almost told them about Happy's dream, the one involving his memorial service, but decided against it. He knew that it would only create another round of upsetting talk around the Pigeon.

Around noon, Edward Fontaine Jr. arrived at the Pigeon. He was a young man whom everyone liked. His father, Ned, had received a telegram for Az, and this was the reason for his visit.

The wireless was from Dr. Charles Curtis at St. Anthony. He was advising Az that he would be arriving at the Pigeon late in the afternoon and would be holding a medical clinic at night.

"I'm glad that there are still wonderful people left in the world," Az said when he opened the wireless message. "Thank God, Dr. Curtis is coming."

It would be welcome news for everyone in the little town. "Go down to the cookhouse, Winnie, and get everything ready. For sure, there will be at least three dog teams coming with the doctor and two nurses. Sound the news around town."

"Yes, Pop," she said. "Everything will be ready."

It was four o'clock when the doctor arrived. It was like Az said; he had three dog teams with him and two nurses assisting him. Az welcomed the doctor and his wife to his home.

The doctor expressed his sadness at hearing the details about the loss of the men. He then requested to be taken around to the homes of those who had lost loved ones. Az accompanied him to all the houses and introduced him to everyone. It was an uplifting experience for them to have this well-respected man come into their homes at such a dark hour as this. The doctor had a great spirit.

When the medical clinic was over, Az and Dr. Curtis talked privately. They had a long talk about what had happened to the men. Az told the doctor everything, about what the people were saying about Sod Mugford, the gasoline he carried aboard the boat and how they suspected there had been a fire. Dr. Curtis was shocked to hear it. He was aware of the Cuff fiasco at Beaumont, having learned about it from previous conversations with Az, but he found it hard to believe that a man would murder his own relatives and then commit suicide.

"Do you think that we should call for an investigation into the matter?" the doctor asked.

"I don't know if it will do any good. For one thing, who would we investigate? Sod is somewhere on the bottom, and there's no one else that we could talk to. It's not as if someone stole something, or that there's a murderer on the loose and there's a possibility the killer will show. That isn't the case. You can't ask a dead man why he killed himself."

"Yes, you're right," said the doctor. "I suppose it's a lot better to leave some things alone."

The next morning, Dr. Curtis and his group left the Pigeon. The next few days went by, with everyone distraught in their sorrows. They all drew their strength from Az—he was their only comfort. Every day he made the rounds to all the houses.

When Stewart came back from St. Anthony, he had a load of freight, including a thirty-pound box of candy, a fifty-pound barrel of apples and other items. When Az visited the houses, he carried some of these items with him for the children. The impact of the losses began to ease somewhat.

Gideon was getting everything ready for the memorial service. He sent letters to the surrounding towns, inviting the residents to come. Emma Bridger and Winnie were preparing a large evening meal at the cookhouse for all who showed up, and everyone was willing to take visitors into their homes in case of a storm. There were many people who would have to stay anyway, because it was too far for them to return home in the darkness.

There were six lamps burning brightly along the walls of the little church. The place was filled with people, and almost everyone was crying. The night was dark and stormy, and the winds were howling. Ned Fontaine and his family had arrived from Cape Bauld. Their son Francis stayed back to man the lighthouse.

Gideon started the meeting. "We welcome everyone to this memorial service for the late Absalom Tucker, his young son Roland, Allan Hillier, Sod Mugford and George Roberts, who were lost at sea December 24, 1929. May God rest their souls."

Gideon opened the service by singing "Amazing Grace." He played the concertina as the drummers accompanied him, and he led the congregation in singing. He talked about Happy Tucker, what kind of a man he was, and how he was the driving force behind building the new church. Gladys Hillier sang a song requested by Happy's family.

Every time Az thought about what Happy had told him about this evening, he shuddered. Could it be, that what people say about their dreams could come true?

*I want you to listen to me, Az. A few nights ago I had a dream, and in my dream someone came to me and gave me a message. He told me to tell you to make sure that the barracks is completed by New Year's, because the first service to be held in it is going to be a memorial service for me.*

Sweat ran down his back. He would be glad when the service was over.

Nine o'clock arrived and it finally ended. Everyone went outside, and as the stars shone brightly, the great foghorn on Cape Bauld blew five times as promised, once for each man. Gideon played the concertina and started singing, accompanied by Gladys Hillier. *Brightly beams our Father's mercy from the lighthouse evermore, but to us he gives the keeping of the light along the shore. Let the lower lights be burning...*

# Chapter 33

The year was 1930. It was the last week of February, and there were a couple of men hunting shore ducks. They were at the Clue, watching a large flock of eiders feeding near the spot called Salmon Rock.

The hunters were on a small cliff about thirty feet above the water, where they could have a good view of everything across the cove. They were dressed in white canvas clothes, camouflaged to blend in with the snowy surroundings. They also had their guns painted white. They took turns watching the eiders through the binoculars.

"I think I see something off there. It looks like a bobber," one of them said. A bobber was the local name given to a small buoy.

The other man looked. "Where?"

His partner handed him the binoculars and said, "Just off the Salmon Rock, about three hundred feet. It's right in Uncle Life Taylor's trap berth."

"Yes, I see it. It's one of Uncle Az's bobbers. Here, have another look." He handed back the binoculars.

The man then took a closer look. "You're right," he said, "it's Uncle Az's bobber all right."

The two men looked at each other. "After we get a shot at those ducks, let's row out and pick it up."

"You know something? I bet that's the bobber that the skipper put aboard for Uncle Happy."

The other man took the binoculars and looked more closely. "Forget about the ducks—let's row out and see."

"Okay."

The two men went down to their small rowboat, a gun rodney, built especially for use in the winter for picking up ducks that were shot off the shoreline. It was approximately twelve feet long and three and a half feet wide, equipped with two sets of oars. Right away, they put the boat in the water and rowed out to the bobber.

"It's Uncle Az's bobber all right—the one he put on board the boat," one of them said. They took it on board and started pulling on the rope attached to it. They pulled until the rope became tight. "There's something attached to it. If we had a bigger boat we could haul all of it up."

Now they had good reason to think about the men who were lost. On the bobber were the initials AFR, for Azariah Frederick Roberts. One of them spoke to the bobber. "If only you could talk."

His partner added, "Yes, it could tell the whole story. There's no doubt that this is the one that the men had. Uncle Az never had reason to throw out a grapnel over here in the Clue."

"You're right. Let's go and get Uncle Az to come over for a look."

"Yes, that's what we have to do," the other man agreed. They let go of the rope and tossed the bobber back into the water.

Az Roberts and Norman Pilgrim were bent over, fixing a crank-up ice cream maker. Two men walked up to them and said, "Uncle Az, we would like to talk to you alone."

Az looked at Norm, then at the two men. "Alone, in private?"

"Yes," one of them said.

"Okay, Norm, you go outside."

The hunter said, "Just a moment, Norm, you can stay."

Norm stayed to hear what they had to say.

"Uncle Az, we were down to the Clue, hunting ducks."

"Just a moment," Az interrupted. "Shut the door, Norm."

Az stood up straight and walked over to the work bench and put down the wrench he had in his hand as Norm shut the door. "What is it?" he asked.

"We were over at the Clue looking at a flock of ducks when we saw something about three hundred feet off the Salmon Rock. We looked closer and noticed it was a bobber, so we launched the punt and went out to it. It was one of your bobbers, Skipper, the same one you put on board the skiff that morning for Uncle Happy and the boys. We pulled up the rope until it brought up tight. Then we threw it back and came straight here."

Az was speechless.

Norm spoke. "Are you sure it was one of the skipper's bobbers?"

"Yes," said the hunter. "There is AFR written on it, and the bobber is painted white."

"It's ours. It's just like your father, Leonard, predicted, Norm," Az said. "The boat went down in the middle of the cove."

Az thought for a moment. "Maybe it's only the grapnel that's there; they may have cut the ropes on something. We won't know that until we haul it up. Listen, boys. Don't mention this to anyone. I'll handle this. Everything has pretty well cooled down now. We don't want to get everybody riled up again. Here's what we'll do."

He turned to Norman. "I want you to go and get some men and push off the small trap skiff. Take Stew with you and check out the engine. If anyone questions you, tell them we're going to haul the seal nets. I want only you and Stew, and these two men with me. That's enough."

He looked at the two hunters and asked them, "Can the two of you go?"

"Yes, we can," they said.

"Good. The same goes for you two; if anyone asks where you're going, tell them you're helping me with the seal nets."

In an hour, the small trap skiff was in the water and the engine was idling. Az and Norman went into the shed and got two capstans and put them on board. In a few minutes they headed out the harbour. It took them only twenty minutes to reach the Clue, and as soon as they arrived, the two hunters pointed out the bobber to the skipper.

"Look, there it is."

"Keep the boat over a bit, Skipper—there," said Norman. "Slow the engine down, Stew."

Stew cut the engine, and Norman hooked the rope with a gaff to haul the bobber aboard.

"There's no doubt it's one of our bobbers," said Az, "and it's the one that I put on board that morning. I can hardly believe that I'm looking at something that came from the boat the men were lost in two months ago."

Norman started hauling in the rope until it became tight. He then started to pull harder.

"The tide is running in the Clue pretty hard," said Stewart.

"Yes, I can see that," said Norman as he pulled up the sixty-pound grapnel. It struck the edge of the boat as lightly as if it were a cod jigger.

Norman Pilgrim was a giant of a man who was well known for lifting heavy objects. It was said that he once lifted the main shaft from a large vessel. The shaft weighed eighteen hundred pounds. Compared to the shaft, the grapnel felt like a cork float. The main line was still tied to the ring in the grapnel, and Norman started pulling it in.

"If the rope brings up, there'll be no surprise what's on the other end. It would have to be the boat," said Norman. Az said nothing as Norman continued to pull in the rope. It stopped.

"The rope's tight, Skipper," he said. "What will we do?"

"Just a minute," said Az as he tried to make sense of the thoughts that were flashing through his head. What would he see if the monster that was just a hundred feet below them came to the surface? He thought about the many times that he had said, "I wonder, I wonder, did Sod catch the boat on fire? I wonder if he was really that bad?"

Just below him was the answer. Someday it would leak out, and what would it mean to everyone, especially to Bessie and her children? *What will we see if the boat comes to the surface? Will it be worth it? Suppose the men are tied to the boat. What will we solve by lifting her up?*

The more he thought about it, the angrier he became: angry at himself; angry at Sod, and angry at Happy for predicting his own death.

"Yes," he yelled, "we'll pull to the surface whatever is attached to the rope—supposing it's the Devil himself!"

Stewart looked at Az and was frightened.

Az looked possessed as he carried on. "Boys, keep your eyes open for any sign of a body. If you see one, try and retrieve it."

They began hauling up the object. It turned out to be the boat, but it wasn't heavy because it wasn't yet sodden with the salt water. "When we get it up so far, we'll start our engine and tow it in toward the bottom of the Clue, near the land."

When the boat was up far enough, Az said, "Take a couple of turns around one of the capstans, and Stew, start the engine."

Stewart started the engine as everyone watched; they saw the boat come to the surface. It was bottom-up, but as they towed it, it rolled upright, only fifty feet behind them.

"Slow the engine, Stew, slow the engine," Az ordered.

Stewart slowed the engine. They looked and saw the blackened inside of the boat, where it had been burned. They also saw a hole near the engine house that had burned through the side.

"Everyone, get a good look at her. You can all see that there was a fire on board her. Keep your eyes open."

Norman shouted, "Turn back and have a look in her." Stewart slowed the engine to turn, but as soon as he slowed, the boat behind them sank below the surface.

Az was hysterical, crying in despair, and swearing on Sod Mugford. He whipped out his pocketknife and cut the rope; the boat sank to the bottom.

When Az recovered from the shock of seeing the boat and the evidence of the fate of his brother George and Happy and the others, he had a talk with the men.

"Men, listen, I don't want any of you to mention this to one soul. We can say that we only found the grapnel. Just that will stir up enough painful memories. We'll tell them that there was nothing else on it. They'll suspect that we didn't go to any seal nets, so we will say that a bobber was spotted with my name on it, and we hauled it up, and it was just the grapnel.

"You need to remember what will happen to poor Bessie and her children if it was ever learned that we pulled up the boat and saw that it had been burned. The poor girl would never live with the memory. Another thing. The women and youngsters will be having nightmares and crying for another month, so the less they know, the better."

They all agreed not to speak about it.

As the winter wore on, the wounds of the survivors of the tragedy began to heal. On the fifth of March, shortly after the blackened boat was found, Az started to build a new trap skiff. He finished it by spring and had a new engine come for it when the first coastal boat arrived in late May. Things were getting back to normal as the cold weather subsided.

The cod trapping season started in early June, and there was a lot of codfish. Az had several new men come down to the Pigeon to fish with him. They replaced the men who had been lost.

However, Az was still plagued with the thought of how Happy and the men died. *Did they drown in trying to get ashore, or did they hold onto the boat and get burned?*

He tried not to think about it, but every night he lay awake, thinking of Christmas Eve of 1929.

# Chapter 34

In mid-June, 1930, the codfish was as plentiful as Az had ever seen. He was up every day at 4:00 a.m. and had the trap boat moving at 5:00 a.m. It was "load and go."

The Pigeon was in full swing. Az had a lot of light-salted fish to be made by drying it in the sun, creating a lot of work for Mary and Bessie, who needed to keep busy. With so much fish, they could also make some extra money by working in the salting shed. Susie went to work in the cookhouse with Emma Bridger and Winnie.

One night, Az went to bed early, as usual. He had been up at 4:00 a.m and was very tired. Emily Jane came to bed at 11:00 p.m., and two hours later Az still wasn't asleep. He lay there thinking, in a semi-conscious state. This is Azariah Roberts's account of that morning, in his own words.

"I was as wide awake as I've ever been. As I lay there with Emily Jane sleeping soundly, I was thinking about Happy, when all of a sudden the room started to lighten up. I looked at the timepiece near me on the chair, and it said two-thirty. I didn't know what to think of it. Everything was so bright, and suddenly I saw the door to the bedroom come open. Who should walk in, but Happy! He was just as plain as I had ever seen him. He stood in the middle of the room and motioned for me to be quiet. He then came closer. I wasn't afraid. It seemed like he was still around, like he had never left.

"I don't know why he didn't wake Emily Jane. 'Listen Az,' he said, 'I have something to tell you about your Red Cross ring.'

"I said, 'Yes.'

"'In the morning you have to go over to Mary's house and ask her for your Red Cross ring. Don't go before nine o'clock; just tell her you want your ring.'

"'How can she have my ring, Happy? I lost it at the Cape in a trap full of codfish. She hasn't got my ring.'

"'You do what I want you to do, Az. She also has a story to tell you. Promise me.'

"'Yes, I promise.'"

There was no doubt that it was his dear old friend Happy Tucker, and Az would keep his promise.

Happy looked at Az and smiled, saying, "Someday this story will be told on the housetops and around the countryside, Az, but to complete the story you have to go and ask Mary for your ring."

"Yes, I will," said Az.

Happy turned around and started to walk away. Az noticed that part of his coat was missing, and its edges looked funny. It was the same coat that he had worn the morning he got on board the boat. It was a brown Mackinaw coat with a zipper in it, and a hood made of white canvas duck had been sewn onto it. The hood had a drawstring to close it in around the face. Az remembered that as Happy got on board the boat that morning he had the hood up, and he pulled the string tight, because it was severely cold. Only part of his face could be seen.

As he neared the bedroom door, Happy turned around again to face Az, who was now sitting up. "Az, listen," he said. "I have another message for you."

Az was now speechless. He couldn't have said a word if his life depended on it.

"Az, I'm coming back, and I'm coming back *soon,* and you will know what to do. The curse has to be broken, so don't forget to get the ring and wear it. It's the only way."

With these words he went out the door.

Az fell back in the bed and the room went dark. He felt weak and his body broke out in a heavy sweat.

He called Emily Jane, who awoke and sat up in the bed. She felt the sweat all over his body.

"Fred, what's wrong? Oh my. Are you sick?"

Az got up and sat on the edge of the bed. He looked at his wife who was also sitting up by now, wide awake. "I have something to tell you, Emily Jane." He was shivering. "I saw something."

Emily Jane looked at him. She had never seen her husband in such a state as this; he looked like an old man.

He stammered. "I swear I was wide awake, just as much as I am now."

Az tried to stand, but couldn't. "I saw Happy. He came into the room and stood close to the bed, right there," he said, motioning to the spot. "He said, 'Az, I want you to go over to Mary's at nine tomorrow morning, and ask her for your Red Cross ring. She has it. She will give it to you, and she has a story to tell you, so go over. Make sure you do.'

"Emily Jane, I know that Mary hasn't got my Red Cross ring. It's impossible. I lost it in twenty-two fathoms of water in the Atlantic Ocean, but Happy made me promise to go and get it from her. He also said that he was coming back again, and soon, and said that if I want the curse to be broken, to make sure to ask Mary for my ring and wear it, that I would know what to do. I think I'm going out of my mind. There's no hope for me. What can I do?"

Emily Jane didn't know what to say. Az continued. "If I go over and tell Mary I want my Red Cross ring, she'll say, 'Az, you've gone out of your mind,' and she'll drive me out. On the other hand, if I don't go over and ask her for it, and she actually does have it, then I'll feel like a condemned man again."

He was pacing the floor now. He was at his wit's end. "I don't know what to do, Emily Jane," he said.

"Fred—now, Fred—just listen to me. I know you've had a bad dream or something, but anyway, I'll tell you what you should do. Don't go out in the boat this morning; make up your mind as to what you're going to do. If you think you should go to see Mary, then go. If not, you and I will go somewhere for a few days."

Az knew she was right. "Listen, Emily Jane, I think I'll stay ashore and see Mary in the morning and tell her what happened. I won't ask her for the ring, because she hasn't got it—it's impossible—but whatever you do, don't tell a soul. Imagine if the men find out that I'm having dreams about Happy, and going over to Mary's and asking for my Red Cross ring! They'll know for sure that I've gone out of my mind. What kind of gossip that would make."

"There won't be any talk, Fred. No one will know, only you and me, and I suppose Mary, but she'll never say anything if you don't want her to."

"Maybe you're right," he said as he lay back on the bed.

It seemed like only five minutes had passed when the clock alarmed at four o'clock. "Can you ask Stew to come here? I want him. Please," Az said to Emily Jane.

"Okay," she said, and she went to Stewart's room.

In a few minutes Stewart came in. "What's wrong, Uncle Az?" he asked, a little excitedly, not knowing what to expect.

"I have a severe toothache and can't go out in the boat this morning. I might have to go to St. Anthony and get it out."

Az was lying and Stewart knew it, but he said nothing.

"Tell Art to watch the tide and make sure the boys don't overload the skiff."

"Don't worry, Uncle Az. Everything will be okay."

With that, Stewart left the bedroom, wondering what was wrong with the skipper. His uncle had never missed a day's work in his life.

It was hard to explain to the men that Az Roberts was out of the boat because he had a toothache. It was only a short while ago that Az had a bad tooth which he pulled out himself, using a set of pliers. A toothache couldn't be the reason.

"There's something happening to the skipper," they said, although in the last couple of weeks it had seemed like he was getting back to his old form. He was starting to laugh and joke with the men, especially when they were hauling the cod trap.

But now something serious was going on.

Az got up after the men left to haul the trap. He went to the kitchen and got himself a mug of coffee and lit his pipe. It was a weird feeling, to be watching his trap boat going out of the harbour. It reminded him of Christmas Eve, when George and Happy had gone out. The thought frightened him. "This whole thing isn't over yet," he said. "What's it all about?"

It was a clear day. The sun was coming up. It would be a wonderful morning if he didn't have this foolishness to deal with. "There's no harm to say that a man's mind is what drives him insane," he said. "Make no wonder that people go off their rocker," he said to Emily Jane who was at the table.

When Winnie came downstairs, she was very surprised to see him.

"Pop," she said, "what's wrong?"

"I have a toothache."

"No, you don't," she said.

He knew he couldn't lie to her. "I have a problem, Winnie, and I don't want you to ask me about it yet. I'm not sure how I can handle it."

Winnie came over and stood behind him. She put her arms around his neck and said, "Pop, I thought you were getting over the loss of Uncle George and Happy. Has something else come up?"

Az was both surprised and touched at his daughter's affection. Tears welled up in his eyes. "Yes, Winnie, it has. But I can't tell you."

Az knew he could tell his family anything, and that if he told them not to speak of it to anyone, they wouldn't. However, this was too personal. It affected him in such a way that it seemed like it was supernatural. He couldn't take a chance on telling his daughter. But what if Mary did have his ring? He was ordered by Happy to wear it. Then everyone would see it and ask questions. What would he do then? He was dumbfounded, at a loss for words.

"Winnie, listen. I have something to do this morning that I can't tell you about, but after it's over I will tell you all about it. So, please don't ask me any more questions."

"Okay, Pop," she said. "But I'll be watching, and listening with both ears."

"Okay," he said. "You'd better get going. The men will be in from the boat at around nine-thirty for breakfast."

"I know," she said. "Everything will be ready."

"I know it will," he said.

The morning dragged on like years for Az. He rehearsed a hundred times what he was going to say to Mary about the ring. How could he say that he saw the ghost or spirit of Uncle Happy? She would laugh at him. How could he ever have the face to ask her for his ring when he knew it was impossible for her to have it? Not in a thousand lifetimes could she have it.

"No," he said out loud. "I might as well go to her house and declare myself to be insane as fast as I can, in no other words, only plain English."

He looked around to see if anyone had heard him talking to himself. He thought, *This is a sure sign I'm going crazy.*

Gideon came downstairs. He was more surprised to see the skipper in the dining room than Winnie was. "Good morning, Skipper," he said in a cheerful voice, not showing any surprise, as if this were an every-morning occasion.

Az didn't speak. He pretended not to hear him.

Gideon knew that Az wanted to get out of the house. He suspected that he had something on his mind, but wouldn't dare ask him. "Skipper, let's you and I have breakfast together at the cookhouse."

"Yes, I think we will, Gid, but before we go down to the cookhouse, I want you to read from the Bible."

"I sure will," said Gideon.

Gideon read aloud from the Bible. When he finished, the two of them went to the cookhouse and had breakfast, with few words spoken.

After the children had all gone to school, Az went out the back door of his home and walked the short distance to Mary's house. He had walked there hundreds of times before, but today the trip made him feel sick. It was one that he didn't want to make. He knew Susie would be home, because she didn't go to school.

He opened the door at Mary's house and stepped inside.

Mary was quite surprised to see Az this morning, due to the fact that he was always gone in the boat six days a week, except when the weather was bad. However, she was glad to see him. "Az, what in the world are you doing here this morning? Sit down."

Mary was neatly dressed and already had her house tidied away. The children had all gone to school. "Az, my son, what's on your mind this morning? Has Aunt Emily Jane driven you out, or have you got something to tell me?"

Az knew this was a woman whom he could trust with his life. She was always like that. "Mary, I suppose I'm going out of my mind. Does it look like it to you?" He thought and then asked, "Where's Susie?"

"She's at Bessie's house."

"Good." he said. "Listen Mary, I want you to brace yourself and listen to what I have to say."

"Okay," she said. "I'm ready."

"First of all, I think my mind's gone," Az said. "Last night I was in bed, wide awake. It was about two-thirty, when the room lit up."

Az fumbled with his matches and lit his pipe.

"I watched as the door opened," he continued, "and in walked Happy, as plain as day. There was no doubt."

Az's hands were shaking as he put the pipe to his mouth. He took a puff and continued. "He walked over to me and said, 'Az, I want you to go over to Mary in the morning and ask her for your Red Cross ring. She has it.' Mary, I know you don't have it—that's impossible."

Mary was going to say something, but he held up his hand to stop her. He continued. "Happy said, 'She has a story to tell you, so make sure you go over first thing in the morning.'"

Mary wasn't smiling now. She was wringing her hands. When she put her hands to her face, Az saw that she was crying. She took the lower part of her apron and wiped her eyes as the tears fell. He reached and put his arms around her and tried to console her.

She finally spoke. "Az, just a minute. Wait here. I have to get something."

He let go of her as she turned and walked into her bedroom. She came out carrying a small package. She went to the table and put the package down.

"Sit down, Az my dear. I have something to tell you."

Az sat down and listened. "Last October, while you were at St. John's, Happy was working at the roof of the shed near the water."

Mary told him the story of how Happy had found the ring and sent it away to be fixed.

Az felt sick.

Mary continued. "Last evening, Gideon was over to Quirpon and got this package in the post office. It was a C.O.D. of over eight dollars from the jewellers in St. John's. I haven't opened it yet—Happy said that he wanted to be the first one to tell you about the ring."

Az was speechless. His pipe had gone out, and his gaze was fixed on the package.

Mary said, "I'm going to open it now. It must be fixed, because they charged me over eight dollars."

Mary went and got a knife and cut the package open. Az stared, and he leaned back, as if something would jump out and grab him. She reached into the small box and took out a carefully-wrapped package. It was wrapped in a red velvet cloth. She took the cloth off to reveal the Red Cross ring.

Az stammered, "My ring—my Red Cross ring!"

Mary held it in her hands. She offered it to him, but at first he wouldn't touch it. Then she looked at it and read the engraved letters: AFR.

Az reached out and took it from her.

"My God, my God!" he cried. "What's going on?"

"Put it on your finger and see if it's the right size," Mary asked.

Az slipped it on his finger. "I can't believe it. It's perfect!"

He took it off again and laid it on the table.

"There's a letter with it in the package," Mary said. She reached into the small box and pulled out the letter that was folded up and stuffed inside.

She handed it to him. "You read it, Uncle Az," she said.

With trembling hands he unfolded the letter and began to read.

*"Dear Mr. Absalom Tucker. I am sorry that I couldn't have this ring back to you for Christmas. I know you were disappointed in not being able to have it as a surprise for your closest friend on Christmas Day. However, we hope and pray that it will serve a much better purpose now. We are astounded at the piece of material that you sent with the ring to be used in splicing. We have tried to match the material with every kind of metal available, but have been unsuccessful. Would you be kind enough to write us back and let us know where you acquired the material? Signed, Management."*

306

Az looked at Mary. "What are they talking about, Mary? I had it made big enough first with lead. What did Happy send them? What are they talking about?"

Well," she said, "Happy had an idea. He said it would be nice if he went and got a piece of that sword down at the forge—you know, the sword that they dug up with that body over on the bog. Well, he sent a piece of it away with the ring."

It was hard to believe. "A piece of that Viking sword is spliced into my ring?" Az picked it up and closely inspected it. "You can hardly tell it from the gold," he said.

"You're right," Mary said. "Maybe it's gold."

"I can never wear it," he said. "That sword might have killed dozens of poor Indians or Eskimos. If I wear that, only God knows what kind of curse may fall on me."

She looked at him. "Maybe there's a curse on you now, and this may be the very thing that Happy was trying to tell you about last night. It might break the curse. I don't know."

Az was speechless.

Mary continued. "Az, you put that ring on now and keep it on. Whatever will happen, it will happen and we can't change it."

He took the ring and put it on his finger.

She went to him and hugged him, her husband's best friend, one whom he had loved as a brother.

"I have something else to tell you, Mary," he said. "When Happy was going out of the room he turned around to me and said, 'I am coming back, Az, and I am coming back soon, so you know what to do.' He then turned and walked out and shut the door."

Mary turned white. "Well, that's one thing that will never happen this side of eternity."

The ring fit perfectly. Wearing it gave him an eerie feeling, but he didn't remove it. "There have been so many things predicted that have happened—anything's possible, Mary. Anything's possible."

With these words he walked out of Happy Tucker's home and shut the door behind him.


Az had his hand in his pocket when he walked into his home that morning. He didn't feel well.

"What's the matter, Fred?" asked Emily Jane when he walked in. "You're as white as a sheet."

He didn't answer her as he went straight for the bedroom. Emily Jane followed him.

She sat down on the bed and watched him as he stood facing the wall. He turned around and looked at her before speaking. "Emily Jane, you won't believe this."

He held up his hand.

His wife stared wide-eyed at him when she saw the ring on his finger. "Fred! Your ring! Is it your Red Cross ring?"

"Yes, it's my Red Cross ring," he said.

She caught his hand and brought it closer to her eyes. She peered through her glasses to make sure that it really was his Orangeman's ring.

"Yes, it is, Fred."

She was shocked, especially after what he had told her earlier that morning. He told her then about how Happy had found it among the fish bones at the head of the wharf, and how he had sent it away to the jewellers in St. John's.

"If Happy wasn't involved in this, I would say that it's witchcraft," she concluded.

"I'm beginning to feel scared, Emily Jane. There have been too many things happening for this to be normal."

She looked at him and said, "Are you going to wear the ring, Fred? You know what you promised me when you lost it. You said you would never get another Red Cross ring as long as you lived."

"I didn't get this one, Emily Jane. It came like a person being raised from the dead."

"Listen, Fred. Ever since you dug up that Viking, things have gone wrong, and now you're wearing part of what came out of that grave. My son, I would be frightened to death if I were you."

"You're forgetting something, Emily Jane."

"Forgetting what?" she said.

"First Happy told me where to get it; then he told me to wear it. Next he told me that he was coming back, and that I would know what to do with the ring. I'm convinced now that he'll be back, one way or another. How, I don't know."

Emily Jane couldn't take anymore. She turned and left the bedroom.

Mary sat at her table. She had bread ready to put into the oven. It was in the pans and had risen to her satisfaction. However, she wasn't paying attention to it. She put her apron to her face to wipe her tears away. Susie came into the kitchen.

"What's the matter, Mary?" she asked. "Are you still grieving over Dad and Roland?"

Mary was a little startled. She hadn't heard Susie come in.

"Susie, put the pans of bread in the oven for me, my dear. They're starting to run over."

Susie opened the oven door and placed the four pans of rising dough inside. She closed the door and put a couple of sticks of wood in the stove.

Susie saw the empty package on the table. "What's wrong, Mary ? Did you have a parcel come?" she said, picking up the box and paper. She looked at the address. "Mr. Happy Tucker, St. Barbe District, L'Anse au Pigeon, NFLD."

Mary dabbed at her eyes with the handkerchief. "Yes, we received a parcel. It was the skipper's Red Cross ring. It came in the mail yesterday evening."

It took a few seconds for Mary's words to sink in.

"What did you say it was, Mary?" she asked again, not believing what she had heard.

"It was the skipper's Red Cross ring."

"He has another ring? I thought he said he would never buy another Red Cross ring as long as he lived," said Susie.

"It's not a new ring—it's his old one. You know, the one that he lost out in the cod trap last spring."

Susie was surprised. "His old ring! Where in the world did it come from, Mary?"

"Your father picked it up among the fish bones in the harbour last fall, and it just came back, repaired, in the mail yesterday evening."

Susie looked at her stepmother with disbelief. Mary then told her the whole story of how her father had found it and about the piece of the sword that was spliced into it. Mary related how Susie's father had appeared to Az in the night and told him about the ring and how he said that he was going to come back, and soon.

"Listen, Susie. I don't know what to say about the whole mess, to tell you the truth. I think that we're all under some kind of a curse or something, especially when all this happened to people like us, and especially what's happening to Az. You know, I think it's time for us to get out of L'Anse au Pigeon."

Susie didn't know what to say at first, but finally she said, "Mary, maybe it's time that we went back home to Lushes Bight. Whenever I look around here, I see Allan and Dad and poor Roland. I can see their footsteps in every grain of sand. I can see their faces reflected in every pool of water. I can feel Allan's breath, as if he walks around near me."

She was crying now. "Mary, I can hear him singing in the wind that blows. What can I do? I'm living in a world where Allan is watching and talking to me every minute."

"I know, Susie, my dear, but you're so young. You have your life ahead of you. Maybe you could find another fine young man who would love you and marry you. As for me, it isn't likely that I'll ever marry again."

Susie suddenly laughed through her tears. "Maybe if Aunt Emily Jane died, I could marry Uncle Az."

Mary smiled and rolled her eyes.

As Mary and Susie sat in the little house at the Pigeon wondering what was going to happen next, someone called from outside. "It's time to go to work, Mary. The men are in with a load of fish, so come on."

On their way out the door, Mary said, "Yes, Susie, when the fall comes we'll go back home."

Word quickly spread that Az had his ring again; even the small children were talking about it. Az hadn't gone out to the trap and he didn't even go to the stage. He stayed at home all day, but as evening came, he started to feel a little better. Gideon had talked to him and assured him that there was nothing to worry about.

"You have never hurt anyone in your life, Skipper, so I don't think that Our Blessed Master will let anything happen to you."

Az wasn't so sure. "Gid, I don't think that we have seen the last of this yet. Happy said that he was coming back, and all the things that he said so far have come true, so you never know."

"Now, listen Skipper, rest easy. That will never happen—it can't happen."

Az said no more. He twisted the ring around and around on his finger. "I should throw this ring in the stove and get rid of it."

# Chapter 35

There was an elderly and respected man fishing out of Quirpon by the name of Lancelot "Life" Taylor, who had four of his sons fishing with him as his crew. Uncle Life, as everyone called him, had his cod trap set at a place called Salmon Rock, which was situated just offshore from the Clue. This trap berth yielded a lot of codfish and was coveted by most fishermen around the area. There was always someone around to give Life help in hauling the trap. For this he gave away many hundreds of barrels of fish.

This area was where the duck hunters had spotted Az Roberts's bobber back in February.

One morning in late June, Life Taylor went to Salmon Rock at the Clue to haul his cod trap. With him were his four sons. The sun was sending its first early morning rays around the high towering cliffs, but the men and boats were still in the shadow of the heights of Rangalley Head.

On arriving there, Life Taylor saw Uncle Jowl Bartlett waiting for him near the trap. He waved to Uncle Jowl to come and give them a hand to haul it up. There was no tide running this morning and very little sea rolling. It was the perfect time to haul the trap.

"This is the morning to take her up, boys," said Uncle Life to his crew.

"The fish is in her this morning, I'd say," said one of the boys.

"You could be right," said Life. At once, the span line was taken across the boat and the door lines placed around the capstans. In fifteen minutes the heavy chains on the doorways came to the surface of the water.

"Something's wrong, men," said Life. They all looked at him for an explanation.

"What do you mean, Father?" asked one of his sons.

"There's something wrong—there's no fish in the trap. And just look in there," he said. He pointed toward the shoreline.

"Yes, Dad, I can see what you're talking about."

"There's something tangled in the leader and has it pulled down. It's stopping the fish from going into the trap," said the old man. Everyone looked in that direction.

"There's no doubt about that," one remarked.

"I wonder what it is?" said Life.

There was some fish in the cod trap, but nowhere near the amount that they had been getting all along. "I know what we'll have to do. I'll get Uncle Jowl to help."

Uncle Jowl was already at the back of the trap with the span line across his boat and the back of the trap lifted up on the gunwales. "There's something pretty big in it, I think, because all the floats are underwater. Hey, Uncle Jowl, can you come over here and use your small boat to under-run the leader?"

Uncle Jowl heard Life's request. "I sure can," he said.

At once, he moved from under the span line and went around to position the twenty-four-foot motorboat at the front of the trap, near the doorways. With great difficulty, the young men got the foot of the leader across the boat. The leader was weighted with lead, spread two feet apart, over its full length of four hundred feet. Three of the Taylor boys got aboard the small motorboat with Uncle Jowl, who was keeping it in place. The men started pulling on the leader at the same time as they moved the boat toward the shoreline. They pulled whatever was tangled up in the leader near the surface, and let it drop back again. They did this half a dozen times.

"What do you think it is?" asked one man.

"I don't know," said another. "Whatever it is, it's not alive. I'd say that it's a dead whale."

They stopped to rest for a minute.

"When we get it up the next time we'll be ready to tie it up tight and have a look at it," said Uncle Jowl.

The Taylors started hauling again. They were halfway in to the shoreline, when suddenly the leader broke loose.

They figured it was gone for good. "I bet the leader is torn to shreds, but we'll see," someone said. They began to pull at the leader again. "There's still something heavy tangled in it, a rock, maybe. I'd say that it's a big rock or something."

One of the boys spoke up. "There's an awful tear in the linnet—the foots are ripped off." They kept pulling, and without warning, something struck the boat.

"Don't haul any more, boys, you might put a hole through our side," said Uncle Jowl.

Someone looked over the side of the boat at the object that was now only a couple of feet under water. "Hold everything, boys," he said as he looked closer. "You won't believe this."

"We won't believe what?" someone asked.

"Just a minute now," he said as he took a closer look. "It's an engine!"

Everyone looked at each other. "An engine?" they repeated.

"Yes, an engine," said the man. "Pull in some more linnet."

They pulled again and the engine came to the top of the water. They stared at it for a moment.

"That's Az's engine," said Uncle Jowl. "It's the one that was in the boat when the men were lost. It's his new 8-h.p. Acadia engine."

The four men looked at each other. Each knew what the others were thinking.

"Take her aboard," said Uncle Jowl.

Two men reached over and grabbed the engine. They lifted it over the gunwales as the others pulled in the linnet. Uncle Jowl could hardly believe it. "It's Az's engine all right," he said as he looked closer, "and do you know something else boys? That was the boat that we had hauled up just now. The engine broke loose from the bedding and the boat just sank to the bottom. It must have been just like they said—the boat was set on fire. Burned right here in the Clue."

"What have you got there, boys?" shouted Life from the trap skiff.

"We just hauled up an 8-h.p. Acadia engine, and Uncle Jowl says it's the one that was in Uncle Az's trap skiff when she got lost," said one of Life's sons.

Life untied his rowboat and pushed out to where they were. He looked at the engine and said, "Do you know something, boys? This is a graveyard, right here. I feel uneasy about this—it gives me a weird feeling."

"That's all that can be done about it, Father," said one of the boys as they began to untangle the engine.

Life said, "Look, boys. There's no paint left on the engine. It should be green. Only fire could take that paint off. We'll have to carry this over to the Pigeon and give it to the skipper."

The floats on the leader were high on the water. "We're going to have to scun the foots back and check everything over to see how much damage has been done," someone said.

"Yes," said Life. "Az will go crazy for sure when he sees his engine, but the worst thing is that feelings will all be stirred up again in the Pigeon. All the women and youngsters will be thinking about the crowd who were lost. I think that the best thing that we could do is take this engine out about a mile and dump it in the deep water. No one will ever know anything about it. All we have to do is keep our mouths shut."

315

They were silent. Then one of Life's sons spoke. "Father, I think the best thing for us to do is to pull on out, in under the leader, and fix it on our way back. Then we can decide what we should do with the engine."

"Okay," he said.

The men then set to work under-running the leader, hauling in the linnet and inspecting it.

One of them spotted something. "Look there—some old clothes or something."

The work stopped. They all looked. "Oh my God," said one of the boys. "I know what that is. It's a body—a human body!"

They went to the side of the boat and stared at the object tangled in the leader, all except Uncle Jowl, who stood paralyzed and speechless. It was as if someone had spoken into his ear.

*That's Uncle Happy Tucker, Jowl.*

"Well, whatever or whoever it is, it will never get away, that's for sure, because the linnet is wrapped around it as if someone did it on purpose," said one of the boys.

"Take it on board the boat, boys. Take it in the boat, whoever it is," Life said to his sons.

Two of them very gently lifted the remains into the boat. They took their knives and cut the linnet away from the wrapper around the body. There was a piece of small rope tied around the body, proof that it had been tied on, maybe somewhere on the boat. They then looked closely at the clothing. It consisted of a heavy pair of overalls with patches on both knees, and the coat appeared to be a Mackinaw jacket with a hood that had been sewn on it. The front of the hood was pulled together by a drawstring.

Small shrimp and sea worms were crawling out of the clothing. It was obvious to everyone that there was very little flesh left on the bones. What they recovered was really a human skeleton; what the men lifted up was a bag of bones. They could see the skull plainly through the opening in the hood. They laid out the remains in the bottom of the boat.

The men took off their caps. Uncle Jowl said, "I'm going to pray, so I want you to be quiet for a moment, please."

Life Taylor, who was a religious man, motioned for his sons to be quiet while Uncle Jowl said a short prayer. When he finished, Uncle Jowl said, "It's Uncle Happy, boys."

"How do you know that, Uncle Jowl?" they asked.

"I just have a feeling, that's all."

"Maybe you're right," Life said. "He looks the right height for Uncle Happy. Do you know what kind of clothes he had on when he left home? That's the only way to tell for sure."

"No, I don't," said Uncle Jowl. "We won't know until we talk to Az."

"My, oh my," said Life.

"I wonder what all this is about?" the youngest son said. He was shaken up when he saw the remains. After he helped pull the body aboard, he just sat back, silent and staring. His father noticed him and thought he was about to throw up.

Life went to him and said, "Son, don't take this too hard. We should be glad we've found at least one of the lost men, and although it's lifeless, it was once a human being. You don't have to be afraid of it." The young man seemed a little better after that.

"What will be our next move now, Uncle Jowl?" Life asked.

Uncle Jowl thought for a moment. "We'll have to be very careful about this. We'll have to contact Az before we do anything."

"We'll have to take the body over to the Pigeon right away," said Life.

Uncle Jowl had a different idea. "We'll go and get Az and bring him here to have a look at it to identify it."

"Maybe you're right, but he can do that at the Pigeon," said Life.

Uncle Jowl didn't want the body brought into the Pigeon. "Can you imagine what kind of an uproar there would be if we pulled up to the stagehead with Uncle Happy's body on board the boat? We would upset everyone again."

Life and his sons agreed. "Well, what will we do?" they asked.

"We'll transfer the body and the engine to your boat. I'll go over to the Pigeon and get Uncle Az and Gideon, bring them over here and let them decide what's to be done."

Jowl continued. "I think we should land in the Clue and take the body out on the land right in there." He pointed to a spot in the Clue where there was a small beach.

"That is the last place where this person, whoever it is, walked on this earth. We should take it back there," said Life.

They agreed.

The four men left the leader, started the engine and steamed into the bottom of the Clue. "Dear Lord, Dear Lord," said Uncle Jowl, as if he were praying. "What a person doesn't have to do in a lifetime! Only God knows."

"You said that right," said Life. "Just because some nut goes wacky, like Sod Mugford."

One of the young men said, "Dad, look at the back of the jacket." He pointed at the jacket on the corpse. "It looks like the back's burned out of it."

Life looked closer and said, "You're right—that's burn marks for sure."

Near shore, the men stopped the boat by putting a small anchor out behind. One of the men jumped out on the rocks with the painter; there was no sea heaving in the bottom of the cove.

Uncle Jowl and Life went ashore and walked up towards a small cluster of low trees, about one hundred feet from the high-water mark. Uncle Jowl said, "We can bring the body up here and put it under those trees and cover it up. This will keep it secured 'til Az gets over here."

"You're right," said Life.

They returned to the boat and started to get the body ready to take ashore. While they lifted up what remained of the body, Uncle Life said, "It's only a skeleton, not much more. The skull is still here." The bones of the hands were visible, since the flesh had fallen off.

"There's no doubt that this is Uncle Happy," said Jowl.

The eyes of the skull looked vacantly through the hood at him.

*Yes, Uncle Jowl, it's me. Go get Az.*

They carried the remains up to the low, broad trees, and there they placed them, laying them out with the greatest of care. Uncle Jowl knelt down, and to everyone present he said, "Will you leave me alone with Uncle Happy for a few minutes? I want to talk to him."

"Yes," they said as they walked down to the boat.

Uncle Jowl's voice sounded like something supernatural. It wasn't a voice at all—it was like a trumpet. Life and the others would say later that they couldn't identify what was said, but they swore that they heard two men talking.

The trip to L'Anse au Pigeon was a quiet one. Uncle Jowl and Life knew what the other was thinking; their minds were on the lost men and their last few minutes alive. As they came around the point, they looked into the Pigeon and saw the large cod boat, partly empty, tied to the stagehead. It was a beehive of activity.

"Let's land at Gus Bridger's wharf, Life," said Uncle Jowl. "I think it would be better. There are too many people over at Az's wharf."

"You're right," said Life.

The night after Az had the dream, or whatever it was— some said it was the ghost of Happy Tucker—he was nervous, and whenever he thought about it his skin had broken out in goosebumps. About midnight he had gone to bed. He had left the light on, and pillowing himself up high he decided to read the copy of *The Family Herald* that had come in the mail the evening before. It came in the same batch of mail as the package containing the ring.

Emily Jane had come into the room, dressed in her nightgown. After saying her prayers, she had gotten into bed. She saw Az reading the *Herald* and tried to be as quiet as possible. In a few minutes he put the paper down and looked at her. "Emily Jane, are you asleep?"

"No," she said. "I'm just lying here, thinking."

"Emily Jane, I'm having a hard time. I've had a rough day. What's happened to me has been nothing but a glorified case of witchcraft, as far as I'm concerned. The most ridiculous thing about it is that I'm going along with it."

She didn't know what to say.

"Just look at this." He held up his hand with the ring on it and moved it closer to her so she could see it. "Just imagine! I'm afraid to take it off—because someone appeared to me and told me to wear it, and someone who has been dead for close to six months! I would say that I'm going totally insane." He wiped cold sweat from his forehead.

"I know you're having a rough time of it, Fred. I'm praying for you. That's all I can do. I'm lost for words." She closed her eyes and put her handkerchief to her face.

"Ever since the men were lost, I've been harassed. George came to me and put his arms around me and told me not to worry; Sod Mugford came to me in a dream and wanted to fight me, and last night, look what happened, here comes Happy with two messages, one about my ring—this ring."

He again held up his hand. "The other message was that he's coming back, and very soon."

He groaned. "You know, Emily Jane, I'm just as big a fool to believe it. You know, I do believe it; somehow Happy will be back."

Emily Jane believed what he said about his dream—but Happy coming back? She knew it was impossible. The only thing she could say now was, "Fred, are you all right?"

"I wonder when this will end, Emily Jane?" he said.

"It doesn't matter, Fred. God will protect you and bring you through."

"Suppose the Viking who owned the sword comes looking for me! Then what will I do?" he asked.

"Fred, don't say things like that," she replied.

He was the only man she had ever known, and he was the only man that she would ever know. The two of them lay in bed all night and talked; neither of them slept for a minute.

Az stood in the salting shed door and saw Uncle Jowl and Life Taylor come into the harbour and go to Gus Bridger's wharf. He turned to Gladys and said, "Jowl Bartlett is here, and look who is with him—Life Taylor. There's a problem somewhere."

Gladys, who was pushing a wheelbarrow full of split cod, didn't have time to look, and went straight to the fish pile. Az walked out on the stage and headed around the little harbour to meet them. It only took five minutes to catch up with them at the bottom of the harbour. Az was the first to speak. "Uncle Jowl, how are you? Life! What brings you here this morning?"

The two men looked at Az as if he were a stranger. They said nothing, turning away from him, not wanting to look him in the eyes.

"What's up, boys?" he repeated.

Uncle Jowl turned to Az and asked, "What kind of clothes did Uncle Happy have on when he left the Pigeon that morning?"

These words confirmed what was promised by the apparition of Happy Tucker as he left Az's bedroom. *I am coming back, Az, and soon.* Now, it was two weeks later, and Happy was back—Az knew it. He didn't need to hear anything else. Uncle Jowl's question said it all.

"Lets go up to the house."

They entered, and to their surprise Gideon was there. For some reason he couldn't explain, he had let the schoolchildren go home early.

Grace was also there, and Az asked if she would leave and go to the cookhouse for awhile. She left at once, sensing something wrong.

"Gid, I want you to stay here with us," Az said. "Uncle Jowl and Uncle Life, sit down." Az indicated for them to sit at the table.

"What have you found?" he quietly asked.

Uncle Jowl was the first to speak. "We've found a body over in the Clue, and it looks like the body of Uncle Happy."

Gideon was more shocked than Az. "What?" he exclaimed.

"Yes," said Life.

"Az, do you know what Happy was wearing that morning he left home?" asked Uncle Jowl.

"Yes I do. He was wearing a Mackinaw jacket with a white canvas duck hood that had been sewn on it. I think he also had on a pair of denim bib overalls."

"It's him, Az. It's Uncle Happy. We found him."

"He's back, then," Az said. "He said he was going to come back, and he's shown up, like he said." Az couldn't believe what Uncle Jowl was saying. He put his elbows on his knees and buried his face in his hands.

Gideon was dumbstruck.

Az looked up suddenly. "Where is he now?" The first thing that came to mind was that they had him on board their boat over at Uncle Gus Bridger's wharf.

Uncle Jowl answered him. "We carried him into the Clue and took him ashore. Life's sons are over there watching him."

"You did the right thing, men. We'll tell no one, and we'll arouse no suspicion. I don't want to refresh anyone's memories. Everything has cooled down pretty good. We'll decide what to do later, so don't mention this to anyone."

They all agreed.

Az said, "Gid, I want you to walk over to the Clue without anyone seeing you. I'll go with Uncle Jowl and Life in the boat."

Gideon agreed, and nothing else was said about the finding of the body.

"Uncle Jowl, I want you to pick me up at Degrat. I'll walk over. Pick me up on the east side of Degrat Tickle. You can go on out of here and act as if you came for something. The two of you go down to the store and get a coil of manila rope, nine thread. Tell Winnie to mark it down on your engine account, Uncle Jowl. I'll fix up with you later. Life, you say to her that you had trouble with your leader at your cod trap. If any questions come up they'll think I'm gone over to give you a hand. Make sure the people at the stage who are putting away fish see you with the rope."

After they went out the harbour, Az sneaked across the neck to Degrat without being seen. He told Winnie to tell Art Windsor that he wouldn't be going out to the cod trap anymore today, that he had something to do.

On the way to the Clue, Uncle Jowl and Life told Az all that had happened—how they had found the remains, and what kind of clothes were on the body. Az knew that it was Happy; he didn't have to look at the remains to know who it was.

The voice of Happy Tucker was calling him.

As they went into the Clue, Az looked around, wondering about the morning when the men took the boat to the Clue. *What really happened? I wonder. We know there was a fire, because Happy was on fire, according to his clothes, but what happened before that? Did Sod use the shotgun on the men before burning the boat?* They would never know that.

Life's sons were on the beach with Gideon. As they neared the shore, Uncle Jowl threw over the grapnel and Life threw the painter to the men. Immediately, Az spotted the engine and confirmed that it was his.

The group quietly walked up to the low trees near the edge of the barrens, a beautiful place with flowers all around. Az noticed the flowers as he neared the spot where the remains of

Happy lay, covered in oilskins. The plants seemed to be growing there on purpose, to lift their spirits in the midst of gloom. Az was also glad for the sunny, calm morning. He later said that if the wind and sea had been roaring that morning, he didn't think he would have had the courage to go ashore.

Everyone gathered in a circle and looked down at the covered remains. "Uncover the body, someone," said Az.

No one moved at first. Finally, Uncle Jowl slowly stepped forward. He took off his cap and gently removed the oilskins that were covering the body.

Az wasn't surprised to see the clothing. It was the same as Happy had been wearing that morning he stepped on board the boat on Christmas Eve. As he looked, he was reminded that it was the same clothing that he saw just two weeks ago when Happy came into his bedroom.

*I'm back, Az. I'm back. Don't be afraid. Don't be afraid of me.*

Happy's voice seemed to echo around the cliffs of Rangalley Head and high up on the granite mountain.

*Az, you're strong. They call you the steel man. The burdens of the Pigeon have to be carried on your shoulders. Mary or Aunt Emily Jane can't carry them—they are for you.*

Az knelt down by his friend. Life, Uncle Jowl and Gideon knelt beside him. He picked up the remains and pulled them close to his breast, crying. "Happy, Happy, I miss you. My world has been torn apart. What can I do?" He hugged the remains for a few more minutes, before gently laying them down.

Gideon cleared his throat and told everyone that he was going to pray.

"No, not yet, Gid," Az said as he wiped his eyes. "We'll bury him right here, without anyone else around. I think this is the way Happy would want it. He wouldn't want to be separated from his son Roland, and I'd want him to be buried near the place where George spent his last few moments on earth.

"If we announce that we have found his remains it will create an uproar for the families in the Pigeon. It would open up the whole affair again and start the hard feelings against Bessie and her girls. It's better if we keep this to ourselves and bury him right here in the Clue."

Everyone agreed. Az said, "Listen, Uncle Life. Can your sons keep a secret for a lifetime, to never speak about this?"

Life looked at him said, "They're like me and you, Az. They can keep a secret."

Az was glad to hear that. "This is what we'll do, Uncle Life. This evening around seven o'clock, I want you to meet us at Uncle Jowl's wharf. We'll come back here and bury Happy. Gid will conduct the funeral. It won't take long. Uncle Life, can you and your boys dig his grave?"

"Yes we can, Uncle Az," they said.

Az thanked them and said, "We'll now pick out the most suitable place to bury him."

They walked up to higher ground, to a place where they could look out over the Clue. They could see down into the boat that was tied to the cod trap at Salmon Rock. They knew that on the bottom near the cod trap lay the remains of the burned-out boat in which the men had spent their last moments, fighting for their lives.

This was also a place where the last rays of the evening sun shone as it set. There were flowers all around and a few shrub trees to break the cold wind in December. Az sized it up and decided. "We'll bury him here. Take care of his remains until we get back this evening. Life, I'll pay you for your trouble."

"Az, don't worry about a thing. We'll meet you here whenever you get back."

Az and Gid left with Uncle Jowl, who put them off at Degrat. From there they walked home.

# Chapter 36

Several people noticed Az as he left the Pigeon that morning. Seeing Life Taylor and Jowl Bartlett carrying a coil of rope around the harbour to their boat, they thought that Life's cod trap had gone adrift. They guessed that Az had gone to give Life Taylor some help over at the Clue. No one had seen Gideon leave or return, therefore no suspicion was aroused about what was going on.

Art Windsor asked Az where he had been in the morning, but Az had no trouble putting him off, mumbling something about Uncle Life's cod trap. In the afternoon, Art and the crew were in again with a full load of codfish and had put most of it away. Az was about to leave a second time, so he offered an explanation to Art and the crew.

"I'm going over to Quirpon to see Ike Newell this afternoon, Art." Isaac Newell was the social worker at St. Anthony. In those days he was the relieving officer, and was responsible for giving out the dole, or relief. Az issued food to people who were in need, and Ike would send the invoices to the appropriate government departments. He was responsible for setting up co-operatives and social committees around the district. Ike also organized a night school, which Az sponsored.

Az meeting the relieving officer in Quirpon was a regular enough occurrence, so Art thought nothing of it.

Az told him, "I'm taking Gid with me; he wants to visit some of his congregation. It will be dark before we get back, so don't worry."

"Okay," said Art.

Gideon closed the school to prepare for the journey. At 4:00 p.m., he and Az left the cookhouse and went aboard the small motorboat. Gideon had a packsack and Az carried a large envelope. There were no questions asked.

"Don't forget to check the mail, Pop," said Winnie.

"Okay, my dear," he said as he left.

They went directly to Esau Hillier's grocery store at Quirpon. Esau Hillier was the local merchant, and he was glad to see them, especially the young Salvation Army officer. They also went to the post office, but there was no mail. They talked with some old friends until it was time to cross the harbour to Jowl Bartlett's house.

They went up to the door of the plain dwelling, where Uncle Jowl, a very poor man, welcomed them in and gave them a cup of tea. Gideon had been there just a few weeks ago; he wasn't a stranger there. In those days, the Salvation Army officer travelled and visited his flock on a regular basis. At 7:00 o'clock, the three men went outside.

"Gid and I are ready to go out to the Clue, Uncle Jowl," Az said. Uncle Jowl had been ready and waiting for them for hours.

Uncle Jowl replied that Life and a couple of his boys had already gone out. "They'll meet us there at the time you said."

"All right, you take your own boat, Uncle Jowl, and we'll follow. I want to thank you for all you've done. I'm going to write off your account on that 4-h.p. Acadia engine, so you don't owe me a cent. She's yours."

Uncle Jowl didn't know what to say. "Thanks, Az," he stammered. "God will take care of you."

"I know He will," said Az.

He would have said more, but he was in a very sombre mood. The task ahead was great, and he knew it would take all that was in him to see it through.

Earlier that afternoon, as they walked from L'Anse au Pigeon to Quirpon, Az and Gideon talked about the decision to bury Happy in the Clue without letting anyone else know.

They knew that if they broke the news to the families there would be trouble again. Right after the men were lost, there had been a lot of friction between all the families and Bessie, because Sod was her husband. Mary had lost a son and a husband, and Allan, who was to become her son-in-law. Although Bessie was her stepdaughter, there were times when Mary became angry with her. Susie was broken-hearted, and for awhile was depressed, but she was coping.

Everyone had moved along well, and to bring the remains of Happy into the Pigeon now would revive all the old hurts.

"If there was a murder investigation underway and the murderer was on the loose, then by all means, I would have Happy's body brought forward. However, this is a different case," said Az.

He had made up his mind that Happy Tucker would go down into his grave on a hillside overlooking the ocean at the Clue.

"I think you're right," said Gideon. "We'll bury Happy out in the Clue. It will be the best thing for all of us."

Az was unusually quiet as they headed to the funeral of Happy Tucker. It took half an hour for Uncle Jowl's boat to reach the Clue. Az and Gideon stayed close by him on their journey. When they neared the cove they saw Life's trap skiff tied to the cod trap. There was very little sea rolling, just enough to make a little motion.

They went into the cove, and Az was reminded that just beneath him was his own boat, on the bottom, the one that had caused untold heartaches and grief for the little town of L'Anse au Pigeon. With great pain, he thought about the cement he had put in her; he was sure that was the cause of her sinking so fast.

Life and two of his boys met them at the beach and helped secure the two small motor boats.

"Everything's ready," said Life. "We made a small casket and put the remains into it."

"You did?" said Az, very pleased. "Thank you very much. I'll never forget this."

"We were glad to do it; we all knew and admired Uncle Happy," said Life.

Gideon took his packsack, and together they all reverently walked up to the high hill where the grave had been dug. Near the grave was the coffin, a box made of plain wood. Inside, Az saw the remains laid out, just as they had found it. He could see the skull.

*It's me, Az. Look at me. I am back, as I told you, but only for a short time. Now, Az—the ring—the ring, Az. You know what you have to do with the ring. The curse will be lifted, and lifted from you forever.*

Az somehow found his voice. "Close the coffin and seal it, Life. Nail the cover down. Let eternity reveal the rest."

In a few minutes, the sound of the hammer was heard as Life Taylor nailed down the cover, and closed the last chapter of Absalom "Happy" Tucker's journey. With this done, they lowered the box into the grave.

Gideon reached into his packsack and took out his concertina, and with his two hands through the straps, his fingers pressed the keys as he slowly pulled it open, making a sound that was never heard before by the cliffs of Rangalley Head.

"There's a hymn that Happy sang at the last gospel meeting that he attended," Gideon said. "It was the last public one that he ever went to. Being our Sunday School superintendent, I think he would like this sung."

As the sun was sinking, Gideon began to sing.

*Hark 'tis the Shepherd's voice I hear out in the desert, dark and drear, Bringing the lost sheep to the fold, where they'll be sheltered from the cold. Bring them in, bring them in, bring the wandering ones to Jesus.*

Gideon recounted Uncle Happy's life and gave everyone the assurance that he had gone to a better world. He picked up some sand and said, "Ashes to ashes. Dust to dust."

He started to sing again. *Let the lower lights be burning, send a gleam across the wave.*

Without warning, the great foggle horn on Cape Bauld blew a mournful sound. Ned Fontaine was making it sing once more.

*Goodbye, Happy. You're gone, and gone forever.*

In tears, Az stepped forward. He took off his Red Cross ring, the ring that was tempered by the blood of England's conquests, and spliced with the sword of a warrior Viking. The letters AFR stared up at him.

He dropped it into the grave, and it rattled along the top of the coffin as if to say *It's over, Az, it's over. The curse is no more.*

The last ray of the sun was high on Rangalley Head, and moments passed in silence as it slipped away. The light finally left Rangalley Mountain, and so did the curse of the Red Cross ring.

# Epilogue

In the early 1950s, the coastal boat *Northern Ranger* came to one of her ports of call, Roddickton. On board her was the family of the late Ned Fontaine. They were retiring and leaving Cape Bauld. As soon as Captain James Snow had the ship secured, Edward Fontaine Jr. sent for Winnie. This was Az Roberts's daughter who was living in the town. He wanted to see her for old times' sake. When she received word, she immediately came to the room on board the ship.

After the greeting was over and the tears wiped away, Edward, who was a very humorous man, said, "Winnie, there's a funny story I've got to tell you." He grinned.

"I hope Captain Snow doesn't blow the whistle yet!" she said.

Ned told her the story. "After Dad died, we buried him at Goose Cove. The priest started visiting us at Cape Bauld. Now, we knew Dad hadn't died a saint."

They laughed. "The priest told us Dad was in a place of torment, and asked us what we were going to do about it. Now, poor old Mom jumped right up and asked what could be done. Well, Father said he could intercede and have Dad brought out of this place of torment, but it would be expensive.

"Well, you know Mom—she was prepared to sell her shirt. We paid to get the old man out of one place and into another. Finally, we got him to Fiddlers Green, but Mom wasn't satisfied to leave him there. She wanted him moved into a better place, so she paid more money.

"One day the priest came to visit us again. He walked in and sat down. Before we could even offer him a lunch he started. 'Mrs. Fontaine,' he said to Mom, 'we have moved your husband out of Fiddlers Green, but where he went he's in a worse state than he ever was before.'

"'Oh, my,' said Mother. 'Poor Ned. Where is he?'

"'Well, my dear,' he said, 'something went dreadfully wrong. I have a job to explain it. However, your husband is now part of a crew that's on the Jordan River, fishing, and I know the skipper's name.'

"He then leaned over and whispered to Mom, loud enough for me to hear, 'This crew is a bunch of Orangemen!'

"Mom started crying and said, 'What an awful thing to happen to Ned!'

"'Just a minute,' I said to the priest. 'Did you say you know the name of the skipper?'

"'Yes.'

"'What is it?' I asked.

"The priest looked at Mom and then at me before answering. 'Azariah Frederick Roberts.'

"When Mom heard the name, she stopped crying. 'I have something to tell you, Father. Nothing has gone wrong. In fact, it's the first time since the old man died that anything has gone right. He has finally landed in a place where he wants to be, and that is buddied up with Az Roberts, fishing on the Jordan River. And, Father, I don't care if he even joins the Orange Lodge and goes to live with old King William himself. We're not paying you one more cent. He is now where he wants to be!'"

Ned Jr. and Winnie laughed together. It was the last time she saw any of that wonderful family.